UNDERSTANDING HEALTH
AND SOCIAL CARE

Also available in the series

Understanding disability policy
Alan Roulstone and Simon Prideaux

"Disability policy has changed dramatically over the last fifty years and especially so since the turn of 21st century. Roulstone and Prideaux have produced a comprehensive and accessible analysis of these changes that will prove to be an invaluable text for students, researchers and policy analysts across a range of disciplines: highly recommended." Colin Barnes, University of Leeds

PB £21.99 (US$36.95) **ISBN** 978 1 84742 738 0 **HB** £65.00 (US$89.95) **ISBN** 978 1 84742 739 7 256 pages January 2012 **INSPECTION COPY AVAILABLE**

Understanding housing policy (Second edition)
Brian Lund

"An excellent historical and theoretical review of housing policy: thoughtful, well informed, critical and up to date." Chris Paris, Professor of Housing Studies, University of Ulster, Northern Ireland

PB £22.99 (US$34.95) **ISBN** 978 1 84742 631 4 **HB** £65.00 (US$85.00) **ISBN** 978 1 84742 632 1 352 pages April 2011 **INSPECTION COPY AVAILABLE**

Understanding the environment and social policy
Tony Fitzpatrick

"The intersection of social policy and environmental policy is strategically and morally vital yet has remained a strangely neglected area. No longer. This comprehensive book covers real world challenges, sustainable ethics, a host of applied policy issues, and some bigger questions about the possibility of a green welfare state." Ian Gough, Emeritus Professor, University of Bath

PB £21.99 (US$36.95) **ISBN** 978 1 84742 379 5 **HB** £65.00 (US$85.00) **ISBN** 978 1 84742 380 1 384 pages February 2011 **INSPECTION COPY AVAILABLE**

Understanding community
Politics, policy and practice
Peter Somerville

"In developing his conception of beloved community, Peter Somerville brings a fresh and radical perspective to communitarian theory and practice. This book will inspire and provoke readers in equal measure." Jonathan Davies, University of Warwick

PB £19.99 (US$34.95) **ISBN** 978 1 84742 392 4 **HB** £65.00 (US$85.00) **ISBN** 978 1 84742 393 1 304 pages February 2011 **INSPECTION COPY AVAILABLE**

For a full listing of all titles in the series visit www.policypress.co.uk

www.policypress.co.uk

INSPECTION COPIES AND ORDERS AVAILABLE FROM:
Marston Book Services • PO BOX 269 • Abingdon • Oxon OX14 4YN UK
INSPECTION COPIES
Tel: +44 (0) 1235 465500 • Fax: +44 (0) 1235 465556 • Email: inspections@marston.co.uk
ORDERS
Tel: +44 (0) 1235 465500 • Fax: +44 (0) 1235 465556 • Email: direct.orders@marston.co.uk

UNDERSTANDING HEALTH AND SOCIAL CARE

Jon Glasby

Second Edition

First published in Great Britain in 2012 by
The Policy Press
University of Bristol
Fourth Floor, Beacon House
Queen's Road
Bristol BS8 1QU
UK

t: +44 (0)117 331 4054
f: +44 (0)117 331 4093
tpp-info@bristol.ac.uk
www.policypress.co.uk

North American office:
The Policy Press
c/o The University of Chicago Press
1427 East 60th Street
Chicago, IL 60637, USA
t: +1 773 702 7700
f: +1 773-702-9756
sales@press.uchicago.edu
www.press.uchicago.edu

British Library Cataloguing in Publication Data
A catalogue record for this book is available from the British Library.

Library of Congress Cataloging-in-Publication Data
A catalog record for this book has been requested.

ISBN 978 1 84742 623 9 paperback
ISBN 978 1 84742 624 6 hardcover

Cover design by Qube Design Associates, Bristol.
Front cover: photograph kindly supplied by www.alamy.com
Printed and bound in Great Britain by Hobbs, Southampton.
The Policy Press uses environmentally responsible print partners.

Contents

Detailed contents

List of tables, figures and boxes

Tables

Figures

Boxes

Acknowledgements

Many thanks to everyone who helped with ideas, references and comments for this second edition – in particular to Saul Becker (as series editor) and to The Policy Press.

Chapter Two of this book reproduces some elements of a previous unpublished article that appeared in an in-house booklet of contributions compiled by Toynbee Hall (Toynbee Hall, ed, *The settlement difference*, London: Toynbee Hall) – many thanks to Toynbee Hall for permission to reproduce this material.

Chapter Four of this book is based on an initial attempt to explore the management of health and social care partnerships published in the first edition of *Healthcare management* edited by Kieran Walshe and Judith Smith (Open University Press, 2006), and the chapter in this book reproduces a small amount of text from it (with permission), while also developing some of this initial thinking for a social policy and practitioner audience.

Thanks for permission for other reproductions go to: Pete Alcock (Figure 2.3), Jane Campbell (Box 5.1), Simon Duffy/John O'Brien and the Centre for Welfare Reform (Box 5.6), In Control (Box 5.7) and Paul Hoggett (Figure 7.2).

List of abbreviations

Health and social care are characterised by a large number of policy initiatives and new organisations, both of which lead to a large number of abbreviations and acronyms. Some of the more common health and social care abbreviations used in the book are set out below:

A&E   accident and emergency
AHP   allied health professional
BAME   Black Asian minority ethnic
CEHR   Commission for Equality and Human Rights
CIL   Centre for Independent Living
CQC   Care Quality Commission
DH   Department of Health
GMC   General Medical Council
GP   general practitioner
GSCC   General Social Care Council
HAZ   health action zone
LINks   local involvement networks
NHS   National Health Service
NICE   National Institute for Health and Clinical Excellence
NMC   Nursing and Midwifery Council
NSF   National Service Framework
OSC   overview and scrutiny committee
OT   occupational therapy
PA   personal assistant
PACE   Programme for All-inclusive Care for the Elderly
PALS   Patient Advice and Liaison Services
PBR   payment by results
PCG/PCO/PCT   primary care group/organisation/trust
PCP   person-centred planning
PHCT   primary health care team
PROMs   patient-reported outcome measures
SCIE   Social Care Institute for Excellence
SHA   strategic health authority
SIPA   System of Integrated Services for Aged Persons
WHO   World Health Organization

Introduction

More than any other area of the welfare state, UK health and social care are big business and are everybody's business. Each year, they spend billions of pounds of taxpayers' money, employ millions of staff and work with millions of patients and service users. While this is true of other services as well, health and social care touch all our lives at so many times and in so many places. Overall, the NHS in England employs 1.4 million people and has an annual budget of some £110 billion. In a typical year, people visit a GP practice 300 million times, visit A&E 19 million times and make over 6.5 million calls to NHS Direct (NHS Confederation, 2010). In adult social care, there are some 1.26 million people receiving local authority-funded social care, an annual budget of around £13 billion and a workforce of some 1.6 million people (HM Government, 2008, pp 21, 45; Skills for Care, 2010, p 9). Unlike the NHS, which has often been dominated by public sector provision, social care staff work in a wide range of public, private and voluntary sector organisations – spread across an estimated 17,300 organisations and 40,000 individual establishments (i.e. local units of employment; see Skills for Care, 2010, p 8).

And yet, health and social care touch people's lives much more than the statistics alone imply. For some people, services are provided in an emergency, and the rapid availability of high quality ambulance, hospital and surgical services can quite literally be a matter of life and death. For others, contact with services is life changing – whether through the birth of a new baby, a serious accident or illness, the death of a partner or increasing frailty in older age. For another group of people, the existence of a chronic or long-term condition means that health and social care become a fundamental part of their everyday routines, crucial to whether they are able to live chosen lifestyles or not. As a result of this, health care in particular is a key aspect of all our lives – when asked which services were most important in making somewhere a good place to live, people in 82% of local authorities ranked health services as the first or second most important factor (Lyons, 2006).

On an even deeper level, some of these services are of central importance to us as a nation and in terms of our identity. In a rapidly changing world, it is hard to find things that help to define us and to sum up who we are and what we value about our society. However, if we asked the average man or woman on the street what made them proud about their country or what makes them British, the NHS is likely to figure highly – and Nigel Lawson famously described the NHS as 'the closest thing the English have to a religion' (quoted in Appleby, 2011). Over time, moreover, the British Social Attitudes Survey suggests that public satisfaction with the NHS has been increasing to the highest levels since the Survey began in 1983 (Appleby, 2011). For reasons discussed later in this book, social care in the UK has a much more ambiguous image and history, and does not attract the same amount of loyalty or popularity.

For all these reasons, the health service in particular attracts significant media and political attention. While various governments and Secretaries of State may talk from time to time of devolving power down to local level and of granting the NHS greater day-to-day independence from ministers, the reality is that the NHS is such an important national institution that it seems almost impossible for politicians of any persuasion to leave it alone. At times this can be both a blessing and a curse – while it leads to almost constant government intervention in the detailed running of the health service, it means that all governments have a vested interest in portraying themselves as key supporters of the NHS. Over time, this has ranged from Margaret Thatcher's assertion that 'the NHS safe with us' to Tony Blair's '24 hours to save the NHS'. More recently, Prime Minister David Cameron has stressed his 'huge respect and admiration for our doctors and nurses' and his determination 'to deliver a world-class health service for all' (Conservative Party, 2011), while the 2010 Spending Review protected NHS funding relative to other areas of expenditure (HM Treasury, 2010). For social care colleagues, the power and popularity of the NHS is sometimes a source of envy, although the lower profile of adult social care arguably allows it to stay 'under the radar' more than is possible in health care. For those social care leaders wishing for more policy attention, it may be a case of 'be careful of what you wish for!'

Against this background, this book seeks to provide a comprehensive and up-to-date analysis of community health and social care. With services for children and for adults increasingly diverging (see Chapters Three and Four), the focus is on health and social care for adults (that is, for community care user groups such as older people, people with mental health problems, people with physical impairments and people with learning difficulties).

With health care often dominated by the highly visible and expensive acute sector, moreover, the book concentrates on community services that seek to support people at home or in as homely settings as possible outside hospital.

In particular, the book seeks to comply with the Social Policy Quality Assurance Agency (QAA) for Higher Education benchmark statement (www.qaa.ac.uk) through its emphasis on interdisciplinary and applied approaches; knowledge of the origins and development of UK welfare institutions (as well as of contemporary activities and organisation); knowledge of key concepts and theories; and knowledge of social needs, of funding mechanisms and of public/private and voluntary sector provision. As part of The Policy Press's *Understanding Welfare* series, moreover, the book is aimed at undergraduate social sciences students (in particular social policy, sociology, health studies); those on health and social welfare/social care/social work professional training programmes (social workers, nurses, community care workers and so on); lecturers on these programmes; professionals and policy makers working in health and social care; and those involved in the planning and delivery of welfare services and programmes. In addition it may have a broader appeal to some postgraduate students and to other sectors of service provision (for example, the voluntary and community sectors). To meet the needs of these groups, each substantive chapter (Four to Eight) adopts a similar format, with a user/patient-focused case study, an introduction and summary of the policy context, a summary of relevant concepts and research, key policy and practice dilemmas, further reading/relevant websites, and practical reflection exercises. The latter are designed to be appropriate for use either for individual readers or for students/practitioners in group settings (such as small group discussions or team meetings).

While recognising that this is an oversimplification, a key aim is to provide some practical material to populate the theoretical and conceptual knowledge of social policy students, and some conceptual material to help make sense of the practical experience of professional students and practitioners. Inevitably, this attempt to appeal to a dual audience raises a key issue about the appropriate use of theory – while some readers may feel that the book does not have enough theory to be sufficiently academically rigorous, others may feel that it has too much and is not sufficiently grounded in 'the real world'. In many ways, this is a dilemma faced by social policy academics and those involved in professional training and development, and thus reactions to this book may well reflect tensions in current education and practice. In response, an attempt is made in each of the substantive chapters to explore current policy and practice dilemmas as well as to relate these to broader theoretical and conceptual frameworks (with reflective exercises and further reading to signpost those who wish to explore particular practice or theoretical issues in more detail). In practice, if different readers really do think that the book is both insufficiently theoretical and yet too theoretical at the same time, then the balance between theory and practice might be about right!

Above all, the book is designed to be interagency in nature, appealing across the health and social care divide (see Chapter Four). As outlined in subsequent chapters, the desire to deliver more 'joined-up services' is leading to a much greater emphasis on partnership working between health and social care, with the result that traditionally separate professions and services are having to work together in a much more co-ordinated way than ever before. With the emergence of new roles and new services, *Understanding health and social care* seeks to address the issues of readers in both health *and* social care, as well as those working in interagency positions and settings. However, this comes with a caveat – a common criticism of some government policy is that it derives from an NHS perspective, and sees social care as an 'add-on' to core NHS issues. In contrast, this book tries to focus equal attention on health care and on social care *in their own right*. With social care a much more uni-professional service than the NHS (which is made up of a broad range of professions and disciplines), this can sometimes look like social work is dominating discussion. Thus, in Chapter Two, equal time and space is devoted to the history of health and of social care, yet the social care section focuses mainly on the history of the social work profession, while the health care section inevitably has to deal with a range of different professions (medicine, nursing, allied health professions etc) and each receives less individual coverage as a result.

In particular, the core chapters of the book (Four to Eight) explore a number of different policy and practice dilemmas (which are often common to both health and social care, but with some key differences in terms of the approaches adopted by different partner agencies). These include:

- How best to promote interagency collaboration.
- How best to support people with long-term conditions.
- How best to challenge discrimination.
- How best to involve service users and patients in decisions about their own care and about services more generally.
- How best to support carers.

As these chapters demonstrate, differences in approach can often be the result of diverging underlying frameworks and value bases, and each chapter seeks to expose and explore such differences.

Although the book takes a UK focus, it includes comparative material to illustrate how similar issues have arisen in other settings and the responses made (particularly in the substantive Chapters Four to Eight). Rather than have a separate chapter on international health and social care systems, the book seeks to incorporate this material into each main chapter, often via a series of short textboxes. In doing so, the intention is to provide a snapshot of the way in which similar issues have been dealt with in very different settings (both currently and in the past) and hence of potential alternative approaches. However, this is only a very brief illustration of potential common themes and alternative approaches, and each text is fully referenced to enable interested readers to explore international comparisons in more detail. Within this UK focus, many of the specific organisational structures cited are those in place in an English setting. However, an attempt is made to focus on the underlying themes and issues wherever possible, rather than on the specific national context.

As an introduction to this material, the remainder of this chapter sets out the background to the book, emphasising:

- the growth of community care and the current emphasis on rebalancing the health and social care system away from acute services towards community provision;
- the importance of community care services for individual service users and for society as a whole;
- the increasingly interagency nature of such services and the importance of effective health and social care partnerships;
- the current pace of policy change and the need to place recent developments in a wider historical and policy context;
- key features of UK health and social care, and the different types of system that exist in other relevant countries.

Nature and importance of community care

In most health care systems, acute hospital care dominates service provision, employing significant numbers of staff and consuming a large amount of health care spending. In addition to inpatient care (both planned and emergency treatment), hospitals often also provide a range of diagnostic and outpatient services, as well as services that span the divide between hospital and the community (for example, rehabilitation, specialist medical support to primary care etc). Even in a more specialist area of provision such as mental health (where there has been a strong emphasis on community-based services since the 1960s), acute care still accounts for the largest slice of the annual budget. In social care too, the bulk of the adult budget is still spent on buildings-based services such as residential and day care, reflecting the historical legacy of an institution-based past (see Chapter Two).

However, despite this, the second half of the 20th century has been characterised by an attempt to develop 'care in the community' or 'community care' (health and social services that enable people to remain living at home or in a community setting that is as homely as possible). Thus, since the late 1950s, the number of acute hospital beds per 1,000 of population has nearly halved (Black, 2006, p 6), with patients increasingly supported at home or in community-based settings and, if hospital is required, receiving more day case surgery and staying for less time in hospital. In overall terms, this represents a reduction in the total number of hospital beds from 245,000 in 1959 to 145,218 in 2004 (a reduction of 40%) (NHS Confederation, 2006). At the same time, these reductions have been accompanied by an increased (and faster) level of activity in remaining beds, with a 57% increase in inpatients (1984-2004) and a 341% increase in day cases (NHS Confederation, 2006). While there have been many delays, problems, exceptions and retreats along the way, therefore, the health and social care system is undoubtedly more community-focused than in the past, and the rhetoric (if not always the reality) of community care is generally accepted by policy makers, front-line practitioners and the public alike.

Since 1997, there have been three key additional features of health and social care policy: the investment of substantial sums of money, the increasing emphasis placed on a more preventative approach and subsequent public spending cuts:

1. *Extra funding:* despite the initial intentions of the architects of the NHS (that expenditure would decline as health improved), health spending has risen steadily over time. Far from reducing the overall level of ill health, the NHS was successful in curing people and returning them to the community, only for them to become sick again in the future and generate extra need. Thus, as Ham (2009, p 78) demonstrates, health spending rose from £447 million in 1949 to over £4,200 million by 2006 (at 1949 prices), increasing from 3.5% of gross domestic product (GDP) to over 7%. Following the Wanless Review of 2002, moreover, the NHS saw rapid and record investment (7% increases per year in real terms up to 2007/08), with a view to tackling historic under-investment and bringing the UK closer to international expenditure on health care. In return for this investment, health and social care services were asked to do more and to do things differently, and subsequent chapters of this book explore some of the key changes that have accompanied this additional funding.

2. *The importance of prevention*: at the same time, extra investment has been accompanied by a greater emphasis on prevention and well-being. This has been recognised by the Wanless Review (2002), which put forward several different scenarios for the future based around the extent to which people become more engaged in relation to their health. Since the early 2000s, there has also been a growing emphasis on public health, on the role of local government in promoting well-being, on self-care and on the importance of improving services for people with long-term conditions and chronic diseases (see Chapters Three and Five). As a result of these changes, there is more money available for health and social care, but also extra responsibilities and an imperative to rebalance the current system away from acute hospital, crisis-focused work. In many ways this culminated in 2006 with the publication of a joint health and social care White Paper, *Our health, our care, our say* (DH, 2006a), which set out a 'new direction for community services' (the subtitle of the document) in which the public have 'rapid and convenient access to high-quality, cost-effective care', but are also 'more in control of their own health and care' and receive support which enables 'health, independence and well-being' (p 13).

3. Since 2010, a rapidly changing financial context has led to a very different set of challenges for both health and social care. Following an international economic crisis and the public spending cuts introduced by the Conservative-Liberal Coalition government (2010-), delivering a more preventative approach has become an even more important policy priority (so as to reduce the cost of expensive hospital and institutional care). However, a very challenging financial context has arguably made delivering a community-based approach much harder. For health and social care leaders and practitioners used to working in an era of plenty, the sudden imperative to transform services in an era of austerity is going to be challenging – to say the least.

Interagency working and current policy

Since coming to power in May 1997, the New Labour government repeatedly emphasised the importance of multiagency working, frequently stating the need for 'joined-up solutions to joined-up problems'. Under the Coalition government of 2010-, such an imperative became even more important in a difficult financial environment (although probably even harder to achieve – see Chapter Four for further discussion). As set out in Chapter Four, the UK welfare state is based around a fundamental distinction between health and social care, with each service provided by different organisations, funded differently and organised differently (with a range of subsequent financial, legal and cultural barriers to joint working). This frequently means that someone with complex needs will potentially require support from a range of different practitioners working for a number of different organisations. As a result, co-ordinating this support and organising services in such a way as to maintain specialist skills while also providing care in an effective and cost-efficient manner has long been a key concern. In terms of an everyday example, the parallel is often drawn with fitting a new kitchen, where different workers will bring different skills (the builder, the carpenter, the plumber, the gas-fitter and the electrician), but where some degree of crossover is possible and where a high degree of co-ordination is essential. Put simply, the builder may also be able to do some aspects of the carpenter's role, but needs to know enough to recognise when it is essential to call in a qualified gas-fitter for this part of the process. Similarly, the project needs careful management to make sure that each of the component parts happen in a timely and well-sequenced way. Ultimately, the hope is that the whole will be greater than the sum of its parts. If this is the case with something as apparently routine as a kitchen, it is even more important for something as potentially life and death as health and social care.

Arising out of the desire to promote more 'joined-up' (and hopefully more cost-effective) services has been a sustained attempt to promote more effective interagency collaboration. As Chapters Three and Four suggest, this has taken a number of different forms, with different approaches (some apparently contradictory) at different times. However, the net result has been that the overall ethos of the system has started to change, with partnership and interagency collaboration increasingly seen as an automatic policy response. With any new central initiative or new source of funding, there was usually a corresponding need to form a new partnership, and research suggests that there may be as many as 5,500 individual partnership bodies at a local or regional level stimulated or directly created by government. These cluster into around 60 types of different partnerships, spending some £15-20 billion per year. There are also some 75,000 places on partnership boards (compared, for example, to 23,000 local councillors) (see Sullivan and Skelcher, 2002).

Although interagency working has long been a policy goal, the pace of change undoubtedly increased after 1997 and has remained frenetic since the general election of 2010. Thus, as a crude but insightful example, the word 'partnership' was recorded 6,197 times in 1999 in official parliamentary records, compared to just 38 times in 1989 (Jupp, 2000, p 7), and a similar exercise now would probably show even greater usage of the term. Rather than being seen as an 'optional extra', interagency collaboration is increasingly seen as a default position, and working in partnership between health and social care is now a statutory duty. While this is explored in more detail in Chapter Four, the result of these changes is that health and social care practitioners and managers will increasingly be working with colleagues from different organisational and professional backgrounds. This can take a number of different forms, but the underlying message is that single-agency ways of working are no longer desirable or feasible (if they ever were). Anyone learning about social policy or wanting to work in health or social care therefore needs to understand this new policy context and be familiar with a range of themes and issues across the health and social care divide. Working with others also requires a particular range of skills, knowledge and experience, and professional training may need to look very different in the future as a result. Although trying to appeal to a health *and* a social care market (as this book tries to do) is difficult, front-line services are now so 'joined up' that a multiagency perspective is essential. Moreover, while the focus here is primarily on the NHS and social services, links are made wherever possible to broader services such as housing or social security in recognition of a much broader partnership agenda beyond merely health and social care.

The UK system in context

Although this book focuses primarily on the UK and (when it comes to the detail of policy and structures) on England, regular international comparisons are made via textboxes in each of the substantive chapters. However, a helpful insight is provided by Esping-Andersen's (1990) well-established framework, which divides welfare systems into three different 'regimes', each with different types of welfare arising out of different political contexts. The three regimes are:

- social democratic (state commitment to full employment and generous universal welfare provision, illustrated by the example of Sweden);
- corporatist (conservative-dominated governments with well-developed services, often funded via a mix of private contributions and social insurance, for example, Germany);
- liberal (limited public welfare services, with the state providing residual services for the poor and with a key role for the family, charities and religious organisations, for example, the US).

Interestingly, the position of the UK within this framework is often unclear, and debate continues as to whether the UK is genuinely different from other countries and/or whether the initial framework is unhelpful. While inevitably an oversimplification, the Esping-Andersen classification does seem to suggest that the UK may have an unusual mix of principles and approaches, with a combination of social democratic commitments and a more recent emphasis on liberal approaches to social policy (see Chapter Three). In many ways, this uncertainty feeds into debates about the 2010 NHS White Paper (DH, 2010a), with some commentators seeing this as building on previous market-based reforms to continue to modernise services and others seeing these changes as a fundamental undermining of the principles of the NHS (see, for example, Millar et al, 2011; see also Chapter Three for further discussion).

Whatever the approach to comparing systems, placing the UK in an international context can sometimes provide a helpful insight and challenge. For example, debates about NHS spending and outcomes have often been influenced by international comparisons, and there is scope to understand recent policies around support for people with long-term conditions, approaches to tackling delayed hospital discharges and the move towards direct payments and individualised funding in a broader international context. Different countries also have very different approaches to financing long-term care for older people, to the involvement of patients and the public in decisions about service provision (Chapter Seven), and to the needs of carers (Chapter Eight).

With increasing globalisation, moreover, national policy and practice is increasingly under pressure from international economic forces. Certainly current health and social care policy seems to be heavily influenced by a series of public spending cuts following an international banking crisis and worldwide recession. As a result, international developments become of interest not just for comparative purposes, but as an insight into wider global changes that could directly affect the UK too. Thus, there are periodically reports of NHS staff being recruited in large numbers from developing countries (BBC, 2003), of multinational companies keen to establish themselves in the UK market, of growing medical tourism (Lunt et al, 2010) and of UK citizens who have emigrated to France and Spain becoming increasingly frail and requiring support from formal services (Hardill et al, 2005; *Community Care*, 2006a). With an ever-greater role played by institutions such as the European Union (EU), the United Nations (UN), the Organisation for Economic Co-operation and Development (OECD) and the World Health Organisation (WHO), moreover, it may well be that future health and social care is influenced much more by international trends and changes than in the past.

Remainder of this book

Having set out the background to and rationale for this book, subsequent chapters seek to provide a broad but critical overview of UK community care services. This begins in Chapter Two with a summary of the development of UK services, highlighting key moments in the history of health and social care and seeking to explain why some aspects of the current system are the way they are. Next, Chapter Three summarises the current state of affairs in services for each of the main community care user groups (older people, people with mental health problems, people with physical impairments and people with learning difficulties), as well as highlighting the needs of people who cross traditional service boundaries (for example, disabled parents). After this, Chapters Four to Eight explore the central topics of the book – partnership working between health and social care, the principles of independent living, anti–discriminatory practice, service user involvement and support for carers. Finally, a brief postscript summarises key themes and issues and poses some key challenges for the future development of community health and social care in an increasingly difficult financial context.

two

Origins of community health and social care

Overview

This chapter discusses:

- the importance of the voluntary sector in pioneering new approaches to social needs, some of which have subsequently become part of mainstream welfare services;
- the origins of the current welfare state in the 1942 Beveridge Report, and the subsequent tendency to focus on hierarchical and relatively well demarcated central government departments;
- the origins of social care in the Poor Law and in Victorian philanthropy, with services often associated with means testing, with stigma and with the workhouse;
- the long-standing evolution of current NHS services, with a system often dominated by the medical profession and by the maintenance of medical power and independence;
- a postwar desire for a national health system, but considerable disagreement about the form this should take and a significant power struggle during subsequent negotiations;
- the importance of primary care as an arena for developing more community-based responses to need, for acting as a gateway into more specialist services and, potentially, for controlling costs;
- the political importance of the NHS (which has tended to lead to ongoing attempts to be seen to be 'doing something' decisive about health services and hence to repeated large-scale reorganisations).

In a new century and a 24-hour news cycle, it is tempting to see every issue as new and every solution posed as a radical departure from the past. Thus, both Labour and the Conservatives have portrayed their reforms as being about *modernisation* and *transformation* – and all governments have a tendency to emphasise the distinctive nature of their own policies. The Labour governments of 1997 to 2010 are a good example of this, with the re-badging of the party as *New* Labour and therefore as being fundamentally different to what went before. In practice, Hegel and George Bernard Shaw are often quoted as concluding that 'we learn from history that we never learn from history,' while the Bible is clear that 'there is nothing new under the sun' (Ecclesiastes, 1, 9-14). Against this background, this chapter reviews the origins of health and social care services, charting the development of different professions and the way in which this historical legacy continues to influence current provision. While summarising some of the chronology, this discussion does not provide a full overview but instead highlights the key implications of specific aspects of this history (while also signposting to further reading for those who wish to explore these issues further). Essentially, this account does not explain how things have developed over time, but represents a more selective attempt to explore why some things today are the way they are (and perhaps to lay the foundations for readers to reflect on where things might be headed in the future).

Although health and social care in the UK are often portrayed as key public services, it is more accurate to see them as predominantly publicly funded rather than necessarily provided by the public sector. To some extent this has always between true, although the mixed nature of service provision has increased since the community care reforms of the 1990s and the more recent emphasis on NHS services delivered by 'any willing provider'. In Britain, as in other welfare capitalist countries, moreover, voluntary action in particular preceded the development of statutory welfare provision, pioneering many of the services and concepts that now form part of the 'welfare state' (Alcock, 2008). Thus, affordable housing, income maintenance initiatives, health care, free legal advice and a variety of educational and leisure opportunities were provided by a range of charitable organisations, individual philanthropists and mutual aid bodies long before the state began to work in these areas. In many cases, these services were unevenly distributed, poorly co-ordinated and often inaccessible to those groups that needed them most, but, nevertheless, they did provide some sort of safety net for people in need in the absence of a significant statutory contribution.

Contrary to popular opinion, many such voluntary agencies were able to survive and adapt to the advent of a comprehensive welfare state, supplementing public services, receiving government subsidies, working with user groups traditionally regarded as low priority, pioneering new responses to previously unmet needs and providing a range of specialist services (Davis Smith et al, 1995; Kendall and Knapp, 1996). Under New Labour, there was significant interest (and investment) in the 'third sector' (as it became known), with the creation of an Office for the Third Sector within the Cabinet Office and a new national Third Sector Research Centre (www.tsrc.ac.uk). By 2007-08, there were thought to be some 171,074 voluntary organisations in the UK with income of £35 billion and a paid workforce of some 668,000. Twenty-six per cent of people were volunteering at least once a month and 41% at least once a year (see Clark et al, 2010 for all third sector statistics). Under the Coalition government, a series of policies have been badged in terms of the desire to create a 'Big Society' – although there is debate as to whether this will usher in a 'golden age' of civic responsibility and voluntary action or whether it may simply mask more ideologically motivated cuts in public services (see, for example, Alcock, 2010; Coote, 2010). In addition to the role of formal voluntary organisations, considerable support is also provided informally by family and friends (see Chapter Eight), and a wide range of services are provided by private, for-profit organisations (see 'Key concepts' for further discussion).

Origins of the welfare state

Often credited as the founding document of the postwar welfare state, William Beveridge's 1942 report on *Social insurance and allied services* identified five 'giants' or social problems that welfare services were designed to tackle: Want, Disease, Ignorance, Squalor and Idleness. Although much has changed (including the language we use to describe these issues), much of this diagnosis and approach can still be mapped across onto current services (*Table 2.1*). While this is inevitably a simplistic portrayal of a more complex reality, these social problems still remain and have often been synonymous with particular government departments. Since the 1940s, this structure has often focused on the role of the public sector (without always recognising the role played by informal carers, and by voluntary and private organisations) and has tended to be organised via large, top-down, bureaucratic central government departments (*Figure 2.1*). Arguably this is a way of organising based on a *hierarchical* approach to service delivery, which has since given way to more *market*-based approaches in the 1980s and 1990s, and to more *network* or partnership-based models from the late 1990s onwards. As discussed in 'Key concepts', this is an inevitable simplification, but does provide a useful shorthand for understanding the

Table 2.1: UK welfare services

Beveridge's giants/social problems	Government response/service
Want	Social security
Disease	NHS
Ignorance	Education
Squalor	Housing and regeneration
Idleness	Employment and leisure

evolution of some services. Since 1997, therefore, the emphasis of New Labour on 'joined-up solutions to joined-up problems' has led to a greater focus on services organised around the needs of the individual (*Figure 2.2*). Since these are often complex and cross-cutting (see Chapter Four), this has tended to lead to much greater interagency collaboration and a blurring of some professional and organisational boundaries. At the time of writing, there is now a Conservative-Liberal Coalition which has emphasised the creation of a 'Big Society' (see Chapter Three for further discussion), but which in practice has continued to emphasise the importance of partnership working while also introducing additional market-based reforms.

In addition to this, Beveridge's legacy has two more implications. First, the focus on 'giants' has led to an emphasis on serious social problems and crises, rather than on lower-level preventative services. When the NHS is criticised for being an 'illness' rather than a 'health' service, for example, it is helpful to remember the origins of the service in a postwar desire to combat the 'giant' of disease. In some respects, the Coalition's policies to integrate public health into local government might be seen as recognition of the need to promote health and well-being in a broader context (see Chapter Three for further discussion). Second, it is by no means clear where social care fits in the structures set out in *Table 2.1*. Is social care responding to a sixth giant that Beveridge did not identify? Is social care the glue that holds the other five together? Is social care a crisis service that works with people who have fallen through the holes in the safety net that

Figure 2.1: Top-down, hierarchical services

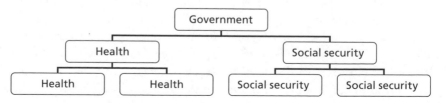

the other five services are meant to provide? These issues become significant in subsequent chapters, where it is suggested that current social care is finding it difficult to articulate its role and contribution. With Beveridge's 'five giants' in mind, some of this tension and confusion becomes more readily understandable.

Origins of social care and social work

In social work, like other areas of welfare provision, voluntary action was crucial in shaping the origins and development of the profession. While a more detailed account is provided by Payne (2005a) and by Means and Smith (1998a), social support for those in need has often been religious in nature – provided by the monasteries in pre–Tudor times and often continuing to have a religious ethos and motivation through Christian philanthropy in the 19th and early 20th centuries. However, for many people, social care is perhaps most associated with the now notorious Poor Law and the equally infamous workhouse (see, for example, Rose, 1988; Englander, 1998). While 'support' for the destitute had been available since Tudor times, the principal response to such social need soon became the workhouse. From the beginning, there was a strong emphasis on punitive approaches and on deterrents, with Tudor legislation establishing a range of responses (compulsory labour, branding, even slavery) to prevent vagrancy and to tackle a perceived link between poverty and crime and disorder. Although this system developed from the reign of Elizabeth I onwards, it became increasingly significant in the 18th and 19th centuries

Figure 2.2: Services organised around the person

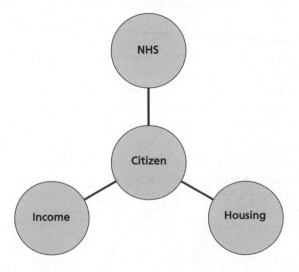

as industrialisation and urbanisation made social need more visible and concentrated it in Britain's rapidly expanding towns and cities. Over time, concerns that 'generous' support would encourage 'fecklessness' and 'thriftlessness' led to doctrines such as 'less eligibility' and the 'workhouse test' (essentially limiting support to institutional forms of care and making these deliberately harsh, so as to deter all but the most needy of people).

While outdoor relief (financial payments to those in need) continued in practice long after it was formally abolished in 1834, workhouses had to become increasingly sophisticated and demarcated in order to meet demand, with a range of different approaches emerging. Over time, this included traditional workhouses for the able-bodied poor, workhouse infirmaries for the sick and frail, a growing network of mental health hospitals and 'colonies for sane epileptics and feeble-minded persons' (learning disability hospitals; see Hutchings, 1998, for a case study example). Indeed, this may well mark the starting point of the health and social care divide, with the sick considered blameless for their plight and hence eligible for support, and those without a recognised limiting disability being viewed as paupers undeserving of assistance (and hence dealt with more punitively). In addition to these services, local authorities began to develop increasing responsibility for public health functions such as sanitation, controlling infectious diseases and measures with regard to housing standards, employment practices and workplace safety.

Such was the stigma associated with the workhouse, that the postwar welfare reforms sought to distance social care from its Poor Law origins in order to ensure that those in need could receive support free from such negative historical associations. While this was very much seen as a positive step, it has resulted in a longer-term tendency to view social care and social security as separate activities, failing to recognise the financial problems that many social care service users face (see, for example, Becker and MacPherson, 1988; Burgess, 1994; Becker, 1997; see also Chapter Six). This is unusual in other developed countries, where financial issues and social care are much more linked and where social workers have much more of a role in determining access to social security payments (see *Box 2.1*). This separation of 'cash' and 'caring' has also had implications for recent policies such as direct payments and individual budgets (see Chapter Five), which to some extent ask workers to re-establish this link (see also Glendinning and Kemp, 2006, for a more recent discussion of changes in the relationship between cash and care).

As McKay and Rowlingson (1999, p 59) explain:

Box 2.1: Historical/international splits between 'cash' and 'care'

Typically, many EU countries have historically had a less rigid distinction between (non-cash) social care and cash benefits, with the two often combined and/or the responsibility of one local government agency:

- In Belgium, services for older people have traditionally been based around locality based service centres, providing material, health and social help.
- In Germany, the social insurance system has included three sub-areas: social insurance, public assistance and compensation, and welfare. 'Welfare' includes both social services and social assistance, with public welfare providing means-tested financial support and 'help in particular conditions of life' (for example, for disabled people, homeless people, older people, ex-prisoners etc).
- In Greece there has been a single central Ministry of Health, Welfare and Social Security.
- In Italy, locally based communes are responsible for the delivery of social welfare services and all cash benefits (except those that are insurance-based).
- In Portugal, a unified social security and social action system was created in 1971, including both social care and social security. This was subsequently separated in 1991, and it is felt that this has given social care an enhanced status (beyond complementing social security payments).

Source: Munday and Ely (1996); see also Glendinning and Kemp (2006)

[The National Assistance Act 1948] repealed the old Poor Law and replaced it with assistance provided by the National Assistance Board and local authorities. Whereas the Poor Law had dealt with the financial and non-financial welfare of those in need, this Act now divided these up: financial welfare was to be dealt with by the National Assistance Board, whereas it was now the responsibility of local authorities to deal with the non-financial welfare of disabled people, older people and others. Thus, the system developed a sharp separation between cash and in-kind assistance. Social security was to be about the provision of cash, subject to national rules. The social services were to operate locally and apply a much greater degree of discretion in their day-to-day work. This split is not typically found in continental Europe, where local social workers are often involved in the payment of cash benefits.

In terms of *social work* itself, the origins of the profession (for the purposes of this discussion) can usefully be seen as having its roots in two 19th-century movements, both of which emerged at a similar time in response to similar social needs, but whose methods increasingly diverged as time went on. The first such movement, the Charity Organisation Society (COS), was founded in 1869 by a group of individuals that included Octavia Hill, the renowned housing reformer and a founder member of the National Trust (Bosanquet, 1914; Rooff, 1972; Lewis, 1995). This was a reaction against a recent proliferation of philanthropic activity following the depression of the late 1860s and 'indiscriminate almsgiving' became the avowed enemy of the COS. By offering charity to the poor, the rich were encouraging them to become dependent on alms and exacerbating rather than resolving the problem. For leading COS figures such as Charles Loch or Helen Bosanquet, poverty was caused by individual and moral failings – by fecklessness and thriftlessness. As a result, the solution lay in individual casework, with a COS worker assessing whether an individual was worthy or not of assistance. For those deemed deserving, access to charitable resources may be permitted, although the emphasis was still very much on the need for moral reformation and for the individual to change and improve their ways. For the undeserving, charity would be denied and the applicant left to rely on the harsh mechanism of the Poor Law and the workhouse. This 'scientific charity' was an attempt to co-ordinate existing provision and to promote independence, but failed to acknowledge that poverty could often be the result not only of individual failings, but also of wider social forces and inequality.

The second voluntary initiative that was later to influence the advent of modern social work was the Settlement movement (Reason, 1898; Picht, 1914; Gilchrist and Jeffs, 2001). Established in 1884, with the foundation of Toynbee Hall in London, Settlements were colonies of educated people, living in a large, communal house in poor areas of large cities. These settlers would come to know the poor as neighbours and as friends, educating them, socialising with them, learning from them and using their knowledge of local conditions to promote effective social reform. Although founded several years after the COS, Settlements were essentially a response to the same concerns about the limitations of philanthropy and the need to find an alternative method of encouraging social reform. Unlike the COS, settlers quickly came to realise that poverty was more than an individual failing on the part of the poor, focusing not only on changing behaviour, but also on the root causes of poverty: those social, economic and environmental factors beyond the control of any individual. Settlement provision was also typically multipurpose in nature, providing a holistic response to complex social needs. In the course of their work, Settlements developed many of the services that have since become mainstream features of statutory welfare provision: old age pensions, legal advice, free health care and so on.

Although the origins of social work have been described in more detail elsewhere (Smith, 1956; Young and Ashton, 1956; Woodroofe, 1962), key COS and Settlement contributions include:

- the pioneering of a casework approach to social problems;
- the provision of training and practical experience for volunteers, residents and students;
- some local branches worked closely with nearby universities (for example, Birmingham, Liverpool and the London School of Economics and Political Science) to develop social work training.

Nor was the Settlement/COS contribution merely a historical one – today Settlements continue to provide a range of social care services (Banks, 2001) and offer a range of educational opportunities for students and trainee social workers (Manthorpe, 2002).

These, then, are the two founding bodies of modern social work: a highly individualised casework approach that focuses on individual characteristics on the one hand, and a more community-based movement, seeking to work in partnership with local people to provide multipurpose services and to tackle some of the underlying causes of poverty on the other. Of course, the distinction between the COS and Settlements should not be overemphasised, and there were many similarities between the two movements. However, the two approaches were ultimately incompatible and do provide two very different models for understanding and responding to the problem of poverty. At different stages in its history, the social work profession has tended to move closer to or further away from each model as ideas of social inclusion and the core values of the discipline have changed (see, for example, Adams, 1996; Hill, 2000). In the 1970s, for example, many practitioners adopted a Settlement-like approach with the advent of radical and patch-based social work, which sought to challenge the structural causes of disadvantage and focus on small geographical areas where workers could get to know the local community. Social services departments (SSDs) at this time were also generic in nature, working with a range of child and adult user groups. By the 1990s, however, social work had returned primarily to a COS-like approach, working with individual cases and focusing on the individual rather than on wider society. SSDs, too, are no longer generic and workers are increasingly specialising in work with particular user groups (see Chapter Three). Now, in the early 21st century, these debates are very much to the fore following the advent of the personalisation agenda and ongoing discussions about the future role of social workers (see Chapters Three and Five).

Following the emergence of modern social work from its voluntary sector roots and from the welfare reforms of the 1940s, a number of additional events have helped to shape the subsequent development of the profession. These include:

- The 1968 Seebohm report, with its emphasis on community development and prevention. This review rejected calls for separate children and adult services, instead calling for the creation of local authority SSDs, which brought together a range of rather disparate social care services under a single department. Also significant was a series of additional changes to social work training and education designed to develop the skills of workers and enhance the professional status of social work (Younghusband, 1947, 1951, 1959, 1978). Mirroring Seebohm, these brought together a series of specialist approaches to social care under a generic and nationally recognised system of social work education and qualification. These reforms also led to the creation of the National Institute of Social Work Training (subsequently the National Institute of Social Work or NISW, which was later merged into the current Social Care Institute for Excellence or SCIE). In 1982, the Barclay Report emphasised a similar vision of community-based social services to the Seebohm report, acknowledging failure to deliver the Seebohm vision, but re-stating the importance of such an approach.
- In 1988, a review of social services by Sir Roy Griffiths led to a fundamental overhaul of the social care system via the NHS and Community Care Act 1990. This was in part a response to the very institutional nature of social care (and the rapidly escalating costs associated with such provision), and further discussion is provided in Chapter Three.
- In the early 21st century, many commentators would argue that the role of social work is increasingly unclear. While there have been a number of new national social care organisations established to promote and develop the profession, the abolition of generic SSDs and the increasing split between (multiagency) children's and adults' services risks increased fragmentation and professional isolation (see Chapters Three and Four for further discussion). Crucially, there has been no official comment as to why the generic SSDs created by Seebohm are no longer the right way of meeting social care needs (or why Seebohm's rejection of the notion of separate children's and adults' services has now been overturned). Equally, there has been no suggestion as to how the current vision of preventative, community-based services is to be achieved, given that very similar visions were put forward in 1968 by Seebohm and in 1982

by Barclay. Above all, different commentators disagree as to whether the current personalisation agenda (see Chapter Five) will reunite social work with its underlying professional values or represents a major threat to the identity and contribution of the profession.

Origins of the NHS

The NHS – described by government as 'the public service most valued by the British people' (DH, 2000a, p 2) – came into existence on 5 July 1948, yet owes much of its structure and culture to a much more gradual process of evolution (for a more detailed overview, see, for example, Abel-Smith, 1964; Porter, 1997; Baggott, 2004; Ham, 2009). Even older than the Tudor Poor Law, hospitals date back to medieval times with the foundation of famous institutions such as St Bartholomew's and St Thomas's in the 12th and 13th centuries. From an early stage, medicine was divided into three different strands, with physicians (university trained and the most powerful), barber-surgeons (serving apprenticeships via guilds) and apothecaries (shopkeepers providing drugs and basic care). Over time, this distinction evolved, with the 1518 formation of the College of Physicians of London to license physicians, the foundation of the 1745 London Company of Surgeons (later the College of Surgeons) and the Society of Apothecaries (to regulate general practitioners or GPs). Under 19th-century legislation (such as the Medical Act 1858), a system of regulation was developed with a register of qualified medical practitioners. As is often the case, this was both to ensure standards, but also to limit the number of people admitted to the profession and thus protect medical incomes.

By the end of the 19th century, the system was based on an increasing separation between community-based GPs and hospital-based specialists, with a series of public, private and voluntary hospitals. GPs at this time were private practitioners charging a fee for their services. In the early 20th century, the Liberal reforms of 1908-11 saw the use of National Insurance to enable free access to GP services for certain groups of workers (usually men and usually not the worst-off workers). Despite considerable medical opposition, the reforms were passed by ensuring that GPs were to retain their independence by being paid per patient (a capitation system) rather than via a direct salary.

Similar concerns were also to dominate discussions around the creation of the NHS. During the Second World War, existing hospital provision was brought together under a regional and national system (the Emergency Medical Service) to cope with the casualties of war, later paving the way for a fully national system. In particular, this seems to have raised awareness about the patchy nature of hospital provision across the country – inappropriate in many ways for the needs of wartime and for a population temporarily used to more central co-ordination and planning during air raids and rationing. With increasing calls for a national system (including, for example, the 1942 Beveridge Report), there was nevertheless substantial disagreement about whether this should be funded by insurance or via general taxation, whether the system should be controlled by local government or not and about the independence of medical practitioners. Perhaps unsurprisingly given this background, the eventual system that was negotiated effectively nationalised existing hospital provision and made GP services available free of charge to all, but retained a number of distinctive features of the old system as well as some new incentives (for example, GPs remaining as independent contractors, the ability for hospital consultants to engage in private practice, lucrative distinction awards for doctors, a system outside local government control, and medical representation at all levels of the new organisation). Never a man to keep his opinions to himself, Bevan (the minister in charge of negotiations) admitted that he had 'stuffed their [doctors'] mouths with gold' (quoted in Abel-Smith, 1964, p 480).

Away from medicine, other health professions and disciplines developed piecemeal over time. With increasing concerns about the health of army recruits in the Boer War, for example, a series of policies sought to improve the health of children. Thus, the early 20th century saw the introduction of free school meals, school medical services and the increasing regulation of emerging midwifery and health visiting services. It was also during a period of war – in this case via the work of Florence Nightingale during the Crimean War – that nursing received growing attention. Prior to this, nursing had developed out of domestic service and charring, with women bringing experience of caring for their own families into 'nursing' work in the voluntary hospitals and workhouses. Severely condemned by later reformers as 'too old, too weak, too drunken, too dirty, too stolid, or too bad to do anything else' (Nightingale, quoted in Abel-Smith, 1960, p 5), nursing was initially an unskilled role, with doctors more involved than today in patients' personal care and with more educated women working as sisters and matrons (whose roles were more administrative). However, this was to change through the efforts of reformers such as Nightingale, with a new emphasis on training, on hospital cleanliness and on the role of the nurse as a skilled helper, attending and closely monitoring patients. Other reformers such as Mrs Bedford Fenwick were also instrumental in campaigning for a system of registration in order to raise skills and standards, to keep out undesirable recruits and increase the status of nursing.

More recently, new roles have emerged, including community psychiatric nursing (which developed from the 1950s to reduce pressure on hospital beds; see Lester and Glasby, 2010) and community learning disability nursing (with ongoing questions about the extent to which this is a legitimate part of general nursing or not; see Mitchell, 2002). Away from nursing, the so-called 'professions allied to medicine' (now known as 'allied health professionals' or AHPs) have also developed, with occupational therapy (OT) emerging from the demand for rehabilitation following the First World War (Douglas and Evans, 2005) and with four nurses founding the 1894 Society of Trained Masseuses (now the Chartered Society of Physiotherapy) to 'give credibility to their profession which was under threat from individuals offering other services under the guise of massage' (Hawes and Rees, 2005, p 109). By 2010, the DH website listed 14 AHP disciplines, including OT and physiotherapy, as well as art, music and drama therapy, chiropody, paramedics, radiography and speech and language therapy.

More recently still, many of these community-based roles have been consolidated via the growth and development of primary care. Despite the relatively low status of general practice (compared to hospital-based medicine), primary care and the primary health care team (PHCT) have become more central features of the UK system since the late 1980s. This is both a feature of UK policy and a growing international trend (see *Box 2.2*). In spite of recognition of the importance of primary care services by the WHO International Conference on Primary Care held in Alma Ata in 1978, primary care in the UK (and elsewhere) has often been neglected in policy and practice. However, this began to change from the 1980s onwards, with recognition that primary care is the first point of contact with (and hence an entry point into) the health care system (WHO, 1978), and that strong primary care services can both improve health outcomes and reduce costs (Starfield, 1998). Within the NHS, the growing focus on developing primary care services and infrastructure has been explained in terms of policy makers' desire to:

- improve health outcomes
- manage demand and control costs
- engage primary care practitioners in commissioning
- enable greater integration of services
- develop services in community and primary care settings
- enable greater scrutiny of primary care services (Smith and Goodwin, 2006, p 3).

> ## Box 2.2: International trends in primary care
>
> In other areas of Britain, Scottish community health partnerships and Welsh local health boards are the equivalent of English PCTs, yet potentially have a broader and more community-based remit.
>
> In the US, a system of managed care is used to control costs, with insurers competing for clients and managing providers on the basis of disease management protocols. A particular US organisation – Kaiser Permanente – is of particular interest in a UK context (see Chapter Five).
>
> In Sweden, county councils provide both health and social care (see Chapter Four for a discussion of health and social care partnerships), with primary care provided mainly by salaried public doctors. Since the introduction of a purchaser–provider split in 1989, there has been a growing internal market.
>
> In New Zealand, patients contribute towards the costs of primary care on a fee-for-service basis. Since the 1990s there has been growing emphasis on primary health organisations as a means of developing a more corporate structure.
>
> In Australia, health care has traditionally been universally available and provided predominantly by independent GPs on a fee-for-service basis. Following a series of reforms, there is a move away from a small business model towards larger, multiprofessional practices and towards some aspects of managed care.
>
> *Source:* All examples are drawn from more detailed summaries in Smith and Goodwin (2006, pp 12-24)
>
> For additional international examples around integrated care and around US medical groups, see Curry and Ham (2010) and Thorlby et al (2011).

Arising out of these (very ambitious) aspirations, the NHS has witnessed a series of policy initiatives to develop a more managed approach to primary care and a series of new primary care organisations (PCOs). In particular, this desire to create a 'primary care-led NHS' (NHS Executive, 1994) has involved the creation of a 'purchaser–provider split', with GPs seen as natural gatekeepers to the rest of the health care system and given various financial incentives and autonomy to manage costs and deliver care closer to home. The strategy of giving GPs a vested interest in the finances, it is argued, reduces the tendency to refer on to potentially expensive hospital services and gives an incentive for ambitious and entrepreneurial GPs to think more broadly, to redesign local services and to develop alternatives. Since this inevitably requires a degree of support, a management infrastructure and some form of accountability, individual practitioners and practices have increasingly been brought under the remit of a series of evolving PCOs (with clinical commissioning consortia the latest English incarnation). At the same time, GP contracts have changed, both to incentivise the meeting of particular policy priorities and to focus more on the quality of services provided and the outcomes achieved rather than simply on the amount of activity carried out. In addition, this process has witnessed an expansion of the PHCT and the development of new roles for other professions, with groups such as practice nurses and nurse practitioners taking on a broader role and with new services emerging such as primary care-based counselling, rapid response nursing teams (to prevent hospital admission) and links to wider services (for example, GP-attached social workers, Citizens Advice Bureau sessions in GP surgeries, exercise on prescription etc).

Reviewing these developments, Smith and Goodwin (2006) describe in detail the complex changes that have taken place, but also the frequency with which certain key messages and lessons recur in the recent history of UK primary care. In particular, the evidence suggests that it takes at least two years to establish a new PCO, that management and organisational support is crucial but patchy, that GP engagement is fundamental but problematic, that other professions can struggle to challenge traditional medical hierarchies and that involving the public and working with local authorities both remain challenging. In terms of outcomes, PCOs are able to deliver positive service changes in primary and community care, but changing secondary care services is much more difficult (see also Mannion, 2011). Internationally, US experience suggests that clinical ownership, strong and well-established leadership, the active involvement of other doctors, the ability to handle risk, a commitment to improving quality and efficiency, the integration of primary and secondary care, performance management of doctors and high quality management and IT are all potential success factors – a number of which appear problematic in a UK context (see, for example, Thorlby et al, 2011).

Throughout the postwar history of the NHS, there has often been a preoccupation with structural reform, and the NHS has been reorganised on multiple occasions (see Walshe and Smith, 2001a, 2001b, for a critique of this process). Often, this seems to involve a move along the spectrum from local responsiveness to larger economies of scale, with each change moving backwards and forwards between these two extremes over time. Returning to the kitchen analogy in Chapter One, some commentators have likened this to getting two thirds of the way through installing a new kitchen, then deciding there is a design back in the showroom that you prefer, ripping the new kitchen out and starting again. Over time, however, the providers of health care (hospital and mental health trusts) have remained relatively stable, and it is the commissioners of health care (the PCOs) that have experienced rapid and ongoing reorganisation (with a stated aim of strengthening commissioning). Of course, the evidence suggests the complete opposite, with such reorganisation only serving to create organisational upheaval and staff turnover that hinders positive service change and increases the power of providers relative to commissioners (see, for example, SSI/Audit Commission, 2004; Peck and Freeman, 2005; Dickinson et al, 2006; Edwards, 2010).

Such an approach also presupposes that the 'perfect' organisational structure is just one more reorganisation away and that 'we just haven't found it yet'. Once again, both the evidence and common sense suggest that this is unlikely (and that if we have not found the perfect structure since 1948 this might be because the perfect structure does not exist). Instead, the commissioning of health care might best be seen as a continuum, with different services needing to be commissioned at different levels (for example, the individual level, practice level, locality, community, region and nation) (Smith et al, 2004). However, such is the public and political importance of health care that being seen to do something bold and decisive can often be more important than doing what the evidence suggests may work best, and the 'permanent evolution' of the NHS seems unlikely to slow down in the immediate future.

Key concepts

In seeking to make sense of this brief overview, there are a number of concepts, frameworks and theoretical approaches that help to illuminate some of the key underlying issues. Of these, perhaps the most important is the notion of *professional power*. While there are various definitions of a profession, a common and central feature is the autonomy of members to determine the content of their work (Ham, 2009, p 223). In the NHS, this relates particularly to the medical profession, which, despite a range of reforms aimed at curtailing and harnessing the power of doctors, continues to enjoy considerable autonomy and discretion. As an excellent summary of the situation, Ham (2009, pp 222-3) quotes an explanation from the former Department of Health and Social Security (1978, pp 424-5) that is as true now as it was then:

> At the inception of the NHS, the Government made it clear that its intention was to provide a framework within which the

health professions could provide treatment and care for patients according to their own independent professional judgement of the patient's needs. This independence has continued to be a central feature of the organisation and management of health services. Thus hospital consultants have clinical autonomy and are fully responsible for the treatment they prescribe for their patients. They are required to act within broad limits of acceptable medical practice and within policy for the use of resources, but they are not held accountable to NHS authorities for their clinical judgements.

Because of this, NHS policy makers and managers can shape the context in which doctors practise and can influence health service priorities. However, they cannot use managerial authority to 'make' practitioners change aspects of their behaviour. As a result, persuading doctors to adopt particular policies typically involves 'incentivising' new behaviour, and this is different to social care and to other areas of the public sector where there is much more managerial control. As a crude but insightful example, a teacher who refused to teach a new aspect of the national curriculum might ultimately be sacked; a GP asked to implement new health action plans for people with learning difficulties (see Chapter Three) might well need to be paid to do this specific task, otherwise they might not do it. With the recent advent of clinical commissioning, this remains an intriguing tension in current policy.

Closely linked to the notion of professional practice is that of *accountability* (which is a complex and multifaceted, if revealing, issue). To whom do medical practitioners feel accountable: their Royal College, their medical peers, their chief executive or their patients? Traditionally, the value base and organisation of the profession has tended to emphasise the first two in this list, and recent manifestations of this might include medical opposition to publishing the death rates of surgeons and to proposed reforms of the General Medical Council. In a fascinating case study, one acute hospital proposed linking doctors' pay progression to patient satisfaction, although encountering what the hospital chief executive described as 'the kind of objections you would imagine' from hospital consultants (*Health Service Journal*, 2006, p 5). While there might be many reasons for this hostility, the hospital's trust's approach can arguably be seen as an attempt to change the accountability of medical practitioners so that they are more directly accountable to their patients. A similar example may also be found in Chapter Five, where direct payments can also be seen as a social care attempt to change behaviour by changing accountabilities.

Also in this chapter (and in Chapter Three), the chronology provided has hinted at an underlying move from *hierarchy* to *markets* and then to *networks* (Thompson et al, 1991). Often, the tendency is to portray this as a linear process, with welfare services moving from a top-down hierarchy in the 1940s, to a market-based system under the governments of Margaret Thatcher and on to a notion of networks and partnership working since 1997. At face value, this certainly helps to understand the ideological and policy shifts that took place during these periods. Following the Second World War, there was something of a postwar consensus with strong commitment to publicly provided services and full employment. While the notion of consensus has been critiqued more recently, this was still a time of relative stability and continuity in social policy, with some aspects of state welfare fundamentally unquestioned by all major political parties. Following the economic crises of the 1970s and the 1979 election of Margaret Thatcher as Prime Minister, however, there was a strong emphasis on the importance of markets, consumerism and general management as a way of improving the responsiveness of welfare services and driving down their costs (see above and Chapter Three). From 1997, the commitment of New Labour to so-called 'third way' politics led to an approach that is sometimes portrayed as being somewhere in between the public sector ethos of the postwar Labour governments and the market ideology of Thatcher. Here, a defining feature was an emphasis on interagency working as a way of responding to so-called 'wicked issues' (see Chapter Four).

Helpful though these concepts are, they inevitably overstate the extent to which this is a linear and chronological progression. To begin with, notions of hierarchy, market and network are never quite as clear as they first seem – an example here is the growing number of 'public–private partnerships', which are essentially contract-based market relationships, but which do imply a long-term relationship between what could also be seen as 'partners'. More fundamentally, the NHS (and perhaps to a lesser extent social care) seem to have a cultural preference for hierarchy and have a tendency to enable voluntary networks to develop, but to turn these quickly back into hierarchies when the issue at stake is seen as politically important (see **Box 2.3** for examples). These hierarchies can then seem quite bureaucratic and inflexible, quickly leading to calls for the hierarchy to be opened up to competition and to the market. Thus, notions of hierarchy, market and network – while a helpful shorthand – may be more cyclical than purely chronological, and are certainly more complex than often suggested.

Of course, throughout the second half of the 20th century and beyond, health and social care services have always been provided via a mixed economy of care (that is, from the informal, voluntary, public and private

Box 2.3: Markets, hierarchies and networks

In mental health services, community mental health teams often began life as local and autonomous groups of professionals coming together, sometimes under the influence of some sort of charismatic co-ordinating figure (often a psychiatrist). These were initially very loose and informal network-based relationships, but have since become increasingly hierarchical and prescriptive as a result of reforms in the 1990s and 2000s. Thus, there is now a National Service Framework (NSF) specifying the types of community teams that should exist, as well as policy guidance that specifies how many workers such teams should have, how they should function and how they should be managed (for an overview see Chapter Three and Lester and Glasby, 2010).

Health action zones (HAZs) were initially locally based and innovative collaborations, specifically funded to bring together local practitioners in new ways and to develop new relationships (Barnes et al, 2006). Over time, this policy became much more centrally controlled, with many HAZs appointing directors in place of initial facilitators. Later, some HAZs began tendering out services through more of a market-based approach.

In children's services, a series of child protection scandals have attracted significant policy and media attention, with previous network-based approaches to children's services increasingly replaced with much more managed and hierarchical approaches (HM Treasury, 2003; Laming, 2009).

sectors). As an example of this, Alcock (2008, p 162) draws on the work of Billis (1989) to illustrate these relationships pictorially (*Figure 2.3*). As this portrayal suggests, the informal, voluntary, public and private sectors all have overlapping areas of responsibility and focus, with the boundaries between these spheres often very blurred around the edges. What is clear is that the public sector focus that may exist in the minds of the general public (and indeed in the minds of some practitioners and policy makers) is not an accurate reflection of the complex array of organisations and interests at stake in health and social care. For example, GPs have often portrayed themselves as a key part of the public sector ethos of the health service and yet have often been small business people selling their services to the NHS, while newer organisational forms such as foundation trusts, social enterprises, employee-owned organisations, independent living trusts and social work 'practices' might all be seen as hybrid forms in one way or another. It is also difficult to know how best to categorise the Coalition government of 2010– and it remains to be seen whether the emphasis on 'the Big Society' leads to genuinely new approaches or whether it may prove to be political cover for market-based reforms (see Chapter Three for further discussion).

Figure 2.3: *Mixed economy of care*

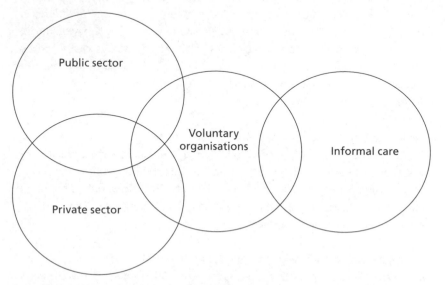

Source: Adapted from Alcock (2003, p 162); see also Billis (1989)

Summary

As a result of these trends and developments, current health and social care face a number of tensions and dilemmas:

1.   Both health and social care have developed from a very institutional and buildings-based background, and this legacy continues (both in terms of public association and attitudes, and in terms of current buildings and budgets). Despite significant changes in the 1980s and 1990s, a number of current problems relate to the high cost and the outmoded nature of some of this provision and the ongoing need to develop more community-based alternatives.
2.   Social care in particular has emerged from a history of considerable stigma, with deliberate attempts to make services as harsh as possible to prevent the 'feckless' from becoming dependent on formal 'support'. Thus, the Poor Law principle of 'less eligibility' has direct links to COS attempts to separate the 'deserving' from the 'undeserving' and even with more recent debates about alleged 'welfare dependency' (Murray, 1990, 1994) and whether or not to

give money to beggars (see **Box 2.4**). Similar debates are also taking place under the Coalition government around the future reform of social security. Against this background, the current role of social workers as gatekeepers to scarce resources using ever tighter eligibility criteria to ration services may not just be about concentrating on those with the greatest needs, but may also derive from a more controversial role in policing those on low incomes and in significant social need.

3. The 1948 separation of social care and social security may have reduced associations with the Poor Law, but also separated social support from financial assistance so that modern social care often lacks awareness of poverty issues (see also Chapter Six for further discussion).

4. Social work (as a unified entity) is a relatively new profession compared to some NHS equivalents, dating mainly from the 1960s and with significant changes to this infrastructure in the late 1990s. Against this background, the fragility of current social work discussed in Chapter Four is perhaps to be expected.

5. While both Seebohm and Barclay emphasised the importance of community-based, preventative services, both arguably failed to achieve this in practice. Given the almost identical aspirations of more recent reforms, there are very real questions about the extent to which current policies may be successful. Whether the more recent advent of clinical commissioning will be sufficient to resolve this longstanding issue remains to be seen (see also Chapter Three).

6. For the NHS, existing services and professions have evolved over many hundreds of years. In particular, the system has been dominated by the medical profession, which still retains considerable power and autonomy.

7. Because of this, other NHS professions (for example, nursing) have tended to be less powerful, have had to increase their status by adopting medical models of professional organisation (registration, self-regulation, university-based education etc), and have expanded their role by a policy of 'usurpation' (Baggott, 2004, p 42) – extending their remit to include work previously undertaken by doctors, but not challenging doctors' dominant position.

8. Despite considerable emphasis on the notion of a 'primary-care led NHS', the jury is still out on the extent to which this is an effective mechanism for changing behaviour in secondary care and rebalancing the current health care system, particularly with the Coalition's emphasis on clinically-led and GP commissioning (see Chapter Three).

As an interesting aside, it is also significant that so many changes in this chapter have followed periods of significant social change (and often periods of armed warfare). Although the power of ideas can sometimes be influential, it seems as though radical changes in thought or direction can often only occur when powerful social or economic changes prompt us to reconsider underlying assumptions.

> ## Box 2.4: Killing with kindness?
>
> You could be killing with kindness if you give to people begging on the capital's streets.
>
> Since 2003, Thames Reach has been urging well-meaning people that giving spare change to people who beg could help them to buy the drugs that kill them. Contrary to popular perception, most people who beg are not homeless, and are using the money they receive to fuel a drug or alcohol addiction.
>
> This campaign message has been taken up by both Westminster and Camden councils. In April 2006 Westminster placed 1,000 posters in London Underground carriages, bearing the campaign image of a dead body made up of spare change. These urged the public to give to homelessness charities rather than to people begging on the street.
>
> (www.thamesreach.org.uk/news-and-views/campaigns/giving-to-beggars/)

Further reading/relevant websites

For the history and development of social care, **Payne (2005a)** provides a fascinating account of the origins of social work (with important insights from international examples and a very comprehensive list of references and relevant websites). For more recent social care history, **Means and Smith (1998a)** and **Means et al (2002, 2008)** offer an accessible and invaluable account of postwar services.

For the NHS, introductory textbooks by **Ham (2009), Greener (2009)** and **Baggott (2004)** provide authoritative but accessible overviews, while **Abel-Smith (1964)** offers a more detailed historical account. **Smith and Goodwin (2006), Peckham and Exworthy (2003)** and the **King's Fund (2011)** provide an in-depth focus on the development of primary care services, while a basic but extremely helpful overview of current NHS structures and policy is provided by the annual NHS Confederation *NHS handbook*. For nursing, key sources include **Abel-Smith (1960), Dingwall et al (1988)** and **Kelly and Symonds (2003)**. For managers, **Walshe and Smith's (2011)** *Healthcare management* is a leading introductory textbook.

For more general social policy, **Alcock (2008)** is one of the leading introductory texts, while **Timmins' (2001)** *Five giants* is a fascinating and detailed account of the development of postwar welfare services.

For a brief summary of different professions and disciplines in health and social care, **Barratt et al (2005)** offer a series of edited chapters exploring the role and nature of key partners, from nursing to policing and from radiography to occupational therapy.

For a brief overview of the UK third sector, **NCVO's** annual *Civil Society Almanac* is an essential source.

In terms of websites, the following may be useful:

www.adass.org.uk
  Association of Directors of Adult Social Services, with policy documents,
  consultation responses and guidance
www.dh.gov.uk
  Department of Health, access to latest policy, legislation and press releases
www.districtnursing150.org.uk
  The Queen's Nursing Institute's District Nursing 150 website celebrates 150 years
  of district nursing, with histories, stories, pictures and archive film footage
www.nhsconfed.org
  The NHS Confederation is a membership network of NHS organisations, and its
  website (although for members only) contains details of the latest publications
  and press releases
www.workhouses.org.uk
  The Workhouse, pictures and a wide range of information about every aspect of
  the Poor Law and life in the workhouse

Reflection exercises

For social policy students
Given the history of health and social care presented in this chapter, what would you predict will happen in the next 20-30 years in terms of:

- Attempts to rebalance the health and social care system away from hospitals and other buildings-based services?
- The relationship between the medical profession and policy makers?
- Interprofessional working?
- The impact of clinical commissioning?
- Government attempts to promote a more preventative health and well-being agenda?

For health and social care professionals and students
How does an understanding of the origins of health and social care help to explain why your profession is the way it is? When working with other professions, what

aspects of their history may help to explain their professional value base, approach and perspectives?

In interagency settings
Compare your answers to the question above to those of colleagues from different professional backgrounds. Do they see your role and the history of your profession in the same way as you do, and do you agree with their assessment of their own profession?

For all readers
This chapter cites the popular view that 'the only thing we learn from history is that no one ever learns anything from history' – to what extent is this true of policy and practice in your own organisation/profession? What could future generations learn (positive or negative) from current policy and practice?

Current services

Overview

This chapter discusses:

- the introduction of market-based reforms in health and social care in the 1980s and 1990s;
- the election of a 'New' Labour government committed to principles of 'modernisation' and of 'third way politics';
- health and social care under the Conservative-Liberal Coalition;
- key changes and priorities in services for older people, for people with mental health problems, for people with physical impairments and for people with learning difficulties;
- the needs of people who cut across existing service structures.

By the late 1970s, health and social care in the UK were in difficulty. The NHS had initially been established on the basis that it would improve the health of the general population (and so would cost less in future once health status was generally higher). However, this neglected the fact that many people cured by the NHS (and who presumably might have died in the past) were brought back to full health and discharged from hospital, only to become ill again in the future. By improving the health of the population and by extending life expectancy, the NHS was thus a victim of its own success and its funding requirements far exceeded official assumptions. Following the devastation of the Second World War and with insufficient capital funds, proposed building programmes were limited in scope, and many former workhouses and infirmaries continued to be used in practice. Despite a national system, workforce planning seemed underdeveloped, and many of those areas that had traditionally lacked access to local services still seemed under-served. In spite of repeated attempts to develop more community-based services, the power of the institution continued to dominate and the resources to make a reality of community care never seemed to accompany the policy rhetoric (see **Box 3.6** for an example). A series of hospital scandals also brought to light the poor quality of many long-stay services for particular community care user groups.

In social care, the National Assistance Act 1948 had initially focused attention on residential forms of care, stating that 'it shall be the duty of every local authority ... to provide residential accommodation for persons who by reason of age, infirmity or any other circumstances are in need of care and attention which is not otherwise available to them.' In spite of more recent statutes, this remains the underpinning legislation for adult social care, with subsequent legislation building on rather than replacing this underlying framework (see Law Commission, 2010, 2011, for more recent reform proposals). Despite the power to provide community services and 'to make arrangements for promoting the welfare of persons ... who are blind, deaf or dumb, and other persons who are substantially and permanently handicapped by illness, injury, or congenital deformity', this remained significantly underdeveloped, with voluntary organisations meeting the majority of community needs. As a result, community services developed only piecemeal and, even after the Chronically Sick and Disabled Persons Act 1970 imposed a series of additional duties on local authorities, funding rarely followed the policy rhetoric. By the 1970s, therefore, adult social care was based around new generic SSDs (see Chapter Two), but was dominated by institutional approaches with insufficient capacity to deliver growing aspirations for more community-based services.

Outside health and social care, the wider welfare state was in something of a crisis amid widespread economic difficulties and ongoing industrial unrest. Following international oil crises, the postwar prosperity enjoyed over many years was increasingly replaced with a period of economic instability and of tighter financial constraints in the public services. Suddenly, Anthony Crosland's 1975 admission that 'the party is over' seemed a long way away from Harold Macmillan's 1957 claim that Britain had 'never had it so good'. Although the degree of cross-party consensus on postwar welfare policy should not be overemphasised, the period from 1945 till the mid-1970s had witnessed high levels of support for state-provided services and a commitment to full employment. With economic crisis came more radical alternatives, and 1979 saw the election of Margaret Thatcher as a prime minister committed to a philosophy of neo-liberalism. Strongly influenced by thinkers such as Hayek (1944), Friedman (1962) and later Enthoven (1985), neo-liberalism emphasised the importance of the free market, a reduced role for the state and the need for individual liberty and responsibility. As Alcock (1996, p 12) explains:

> [The New Right's] main argument was that state intervention to provide welfare services … merely drove up the cost of public expenditure to a point where it began to interfere with the effective operation of a market economy. They claimed that this was a point that had already been reached in Britain in the 1970s as the high levels of taxation needed for welfare services had reduced profits, crippled investment and driven capital overseas. [At the same time] the New Right also challenged the desirability of state welfare in practice, arguing that free welfare services only encouraged feckless people to become dependent upon them and provided no incentive for individuals and families to protect themselves through savings or insurance. Furthermore, right-wing theorists claimed that state monopoly over welfare services reduced the choices available to people to meet their needs in a variety of ways and merely perpetuated professionalism and bureaucracy.

In health and social care, this analysis led to a series of market-based reforms designed to make services more 'businesslike', more 'customer-focused' and more cost-effective. In particular, this included:

- The 1983 Griffiths Report: led by the managing director of Sainsbury's supermarkets, Roy Griffiths, this review was highly critical of the lack of clearly defined management functions throughout the NHS, recommending the development of general management at all levels. In addition to this, there was to be clearer leadership structures at a national level and greater medical involvement in management. Despite these changes, Griffiths (1992, p 65) later described the government's 'half-hearted' attempts to implement proposed changes.
- As government funding for the NHS increasingly fell behind the level of demand, an official review of NHS funding was carried out. Despite a consideration of alternative methods of funding, there was little public support for this and attention turned instead to mechanisms for improving efficiency and service delivery. As a result, the 1989 White Paper, *Working for patients* (DH, 1989a), heralded the introduction of an internal market and the introduction of a purchaser–provider split. Under the new system, health authorities and GP fundholders would commission services from a number of self-governing NHS trusts, who would increasingly have to compete for 'business'. Additional changes saw the introduction of

non-executive directors (appointed in their personal capacity and often bringing external expertise) and changes in primary care (with a new GP contract based around new targets and incentives to encourage GPs to be more patient-centred).

- A second (1988) Griffiths Report and the subsequent White Paper, *Caring for people* (DH, 1989b), introduced similar changes in social care, with SSDs given lead responsibility for planning and funding community care services. As such, local authorities were increasingly seen as purchasers, securing the provision of services from a much more mixed economy of care. These changes were particularly controversial given previous changes in social security (which had led to a massive increase in central funding for private sector residential and nursing care). Despite rhetoric around choice and empowerment, several commentators have seen the *Caring for people* reforms (and the subsequent NHS and Community Care Act 1990) as a deliberate attempt to transfer a rapidly escalating central budget on to local government (who would have to bring it back under control in order to stay within budget) (for further discussion, see Lewis and Glennerster, 1996; Glasby and Henwood, 2007). Additional controversy was caused by a subsequent insistence that 85% of the new funding received by local authorities had to be spent in the independent sector.
- *The patient's charter* set out a range of standards that patients could expect of NHS services and provided a means of comparing performance across the various indicators (DH, 1991).

Behind all these changes are a series of assumptions that remain problematic (see **Box 3.1**). While the research evidence is inconclusive (see, for example, Robinson and Le Grand, 1994; Klein, 1995; Maynard and Bloor, 1996; Le Grand et al, 1998) and certainly does not match the aspirations of policy makers at the time, it does suggest that the longest legacy of the 1990s may well be cultural. In the longer run, these changes seem to have altered the balance of power between hospital services and general practice and between doctors and managers (Ham, 2009), perhaps not dramatically, but enough to begin to challenge some of the traditional power of acute providers.

'Things can only get better': the election of New Labour

When the New Labour government was elected in May 1997, they argued that 'what counts is what works' (DH, 1997, p 11) and committed themselves to a 'third way' between the traditional left-wing emphasis on the state and new right preferences for the market. While this was a powerful and potentially popular image, it tended to define policy by what it is not

Box 3.1: Assumptions underpinning market reforms

- The market is the best way of driving down costs, raising standards and encouraging service providers to be responsive to the needs of people who use services. In practice, it.could be argued that markets often cost more to administer and police, that ensuring standards in a mixed economy is problematic, and that viewing users of health and social care as 'customers' implies a degree of financial power that most service users do not enjoy.

- The private sector is more efficient than the public sector. In contrast, some would argue that some private organisations tend to 'cream-skim' (that is, to work with people who have less complex needs or who offer the best financial return) and that private agencies differ mainly in their ability to offer worse terms and conditions to staff. At the same time, others would argue that there was rarely a level playing field, with an inbuilt bias towards public sector provision.

- GPs are the best people in the NHS to act as gatekeepers to scarce resources – by giving them financial flexibility and incentives to develop community-based alternatives to acute care, there is scope to improve patients' experiences and drive down costs. In practice, many GPs may not have entered their current profession with this in mind, and may not necessarily have the skills or inclination to take on this role.

- Cash-limited local authorities will have a financial incentive to stay within costs and bring the residential care budget under control. While local authorities arguably did this extremely successfully in the 1990s, they did it by driving down fees and by sometimes allowing 'good' as well as 'bad' homes to close.

(not the market and not the state). In practice, health and social care policy since 1997 saw some radical departures from the past coupled with the continuation (and indeed acceleration) of several aspects of the previous government's agenda. Thus, there were early commitments to staying within the previous government's spending limits (later replaced by large increases in funding) and attempts to abolish the internal market (but to replace it with a similar system of primary care-based commissioning). This has been described by Ham (2009, p 53) as 'eclectic', and acknowledged by the government itself as 'building on what has worked but discarding what has failed' (DH, 1997, p 10). In practice, changes in policy and key personnel meant that policy took a number of different forms over time, with New Labour's period in office capable of being separated into four main periods or approaches:

1. *Central control* and detailed performance management of additional funding. With financial investment came a series of measures to ensure that new money was not merely swallowed up in current services, but contributed to new ways of working. Thus, investment was accompanied by central targets and performance management, new NSFs for key conditions and user groups, and national bodies such as the National Institute for Clinical Excellence (NICE) (to develop guidance around clinical and cost-effectiveness).

2. *Shifting the balance of power* (DH, 2001a) towards localities, with a reduced number of (strategic) health authorities (SHAs) and new PCTs to commission services and control some three quarters of the health budget. In addition, high performing hospitals were enabled to opt out of NHS control and become new foundation trusts with less central interference and greater financial freedoms.

3. *Market-based approaches*, with greater plurality of provision and greater patient choice of provider. Over time, this involved a growing role for independent sector treatment centres, a system of payment by results (PBR) (whereby money follows the patient as they choose which hospital to attend for treatment), and changes in NHS provision (with a greater role for social enterprise and more integrated approaches with local government).

4. An emphasis on *quality*, *safety* and *clinical engagement*, perhaps epitomised in the NHS Next Stage Review conducted a leading clinician, Lord Darzi (2008). While these reforms were quickly overtaken by the 2010 general election, Ham (2009, p 72) observes that the new Prime Minister, Gordon Brown, 'did not share his predecessor's enthusiasm for market based reform' and that proposed changes were based more around 'empowering citizens, fostering a new professionalism and providing strong leadership' (p 72).

In adult social care, the same trends are recognisable to a degree, but the main policy priority (from 2007 onwards at least) was a commitment to 'transform' adult social care through a 'personalisation' agenda. This was captured in the 2007 'shared vision', *Putting people first* (HM Government, 2007), and continues to influence the way in which services are being delivered and reformed under the Coalition (see below for further discussion).

Overall, it seems as though New Labour made significant progress around some of its early priorities (particularly around waiting times, the built environment of some hospitals and particular clinical conditions). As the then Health Secretary noted in 2006 (DH, 2006b, p 1):

> The NHS has made significant strides since 1997. Waiting times
> have fallen to record lows, clinical outcomes for cancer and
> cardiac disease have improved ... and our facilities are cleaner
> and more modern.... We can however do much more.

With dramatic increases in funding, however, NHS productivity inevitably
declined, and a key question remains as to whether the improvements
made – while substantial – were sufficient to justify the extra resources
spent (see, for example, Wanless et al, 2007; ONS, 2008). Progress may
also have been more to do with increased funding and central targets
rather than market-based reforms (see, for example, Audit Commission/
Healthcare Commission, 2008; Ham, 2009). A number of commentators
have also argued that policy sometimes emphasised competition (for
example, to reduce hospital waiting times) and collaboration (for people
with cross-cutting needs in the community) – and that both collaborating
and competing at the same time requires very nuanced local relationships
(see, for example, Ham and Smith, 2010). Arguably this remains a difficult
balance to strike under the Coalition government that came to power in
2010. In adult social care, *Putting people first* set out a radical vision for a
more personalised adult social care system, and these concepts remain key
features of the reform process (see below for further details).

'We're all in this together': the Conservative-Liberal Coalition

After the 2010 general election failed to produce a single outright winner,
Britain witnessed the creation of what initially seemed an unlikely coalition
of Conservatives and Liberal Democrats. Faced with the aftermath of an
international banking and financial crisis, the new government began to
launch a series of health and social care policies which continued many
of the themes of the previous government but which also contained a
number of more radical departures (see *Box 3.2* for an overview). In
health care, one of the most controversial features of the *Liberating the
NHS* White Paper was the plan to abolish primary care trusts and strategic
health authorities, transferring responsibility for some £80 billion of public
spending to clinical consortia (DH, 2010a). In future, the NHS will be
overseen via a new National Commissioning Board, with previous PCTs
surviving temporarily on a 'cluster' basis. Public health will also transfer
to local government, and there will be greater patient choice (including
competition between different providers where appropriate). In adult social
care, the 2010 *Vision for adult social care* (DH, 2010b) emphasised seven key
principles (see *Box 3.2*) and set out the government's intention to review

the legal framework underpinning adult social care, reform the funding of long-term care, to publish a social care White Paper and to bring about new legislation (by spring 2012).

Box 3.2: Conservative-Liberal (2010-) policies

In 2010, the White Paper, *Liberating the NHS*, proposed a series of key reforms, including (DH, 2010a):

- the creation of a national commissioning board. Although described before the election as 'independent' of government, subsequent policy proposed a body that seemed subject to significant oversight by the Secretary of State;
- the abolition of PCTs and SHAs;
- the creation of new GP commissioning consortia, responsible for some £60-80 billion of NHS funding;
- lead role for local government in conducting an annual joint strategic needs assessment and leading a local health and well-being board;
- integration of public health into local government;
- abolition of a series of health and social care arms-length bodies and quangos
- reform of the economic regulator, Monitor;
- greater emphasis on services being provided by 'any willing provider'.

Following widespread protests, the last two proposals in particular were amended via an independent NHS Futures Forum established to review the 2010 White Paper. While increased choice and competition will be used where appropriate, there is also now greater recognition of the importance of integration and collaboration.

In adult social care, a new *Vision for adult social care* (DH, 2010b) set out a series of key themes and principles – many of them similar to New Labour's *Putting people first* concordat (HM Government, 2007):

- prevention
- personalisation
- partnership
- plurality of service provision
- protection for those at risk
- productivity
- people and a skilled, innovative workforce

Underpinning many of these more detailed policy measures were two additional priorities which critics have claimed might be mutually incompatible:

1. A key theme for Prime Minister, David Cameron, has been the creation of a 'Big Society'. While the definition of this approach has not always been clear (see ***Box 3.3*** for specific policy measures), the Cabinet Office has argued that (2010, p 1):

   > We want to give citizens, communities and local government the power and information they need to come together, solve the problems they face and build the Britain they want. We want society – the families, networks, neighbourhoods and communities that form the fabric of so much of our everyday lives – to be bigger and stronger than ever before.... Building the Big Society isn't just the responsibility of just one or two departments. It is the responsibility of every department ... and the responsibility of every citizen too. Government on its own cannot fix every problem. We are all in this together.

   Quite what this means in practice is arguably still unclear. While the government had claimed that this is a bold plan for a fundamental rethinking of how government, public services and society operate, critics have argued that this is little more than warm language to disguise deep-seated cuts in public services (see below for further discussion). On a more practical level, Alcock (2010) is surely correct in arguing that the devil is often in the detail:

   > It is how policy aspirations are translated into practical action that will concern analysts most.... Cameron's hope that the Big Society will be the kind of legacy that could be compared with the 20th-century welfare state is a big ask, in particular as it will be expected to flourish at a time when austerity within public finances is greater than throughout much of the that post-war welfare era. (Alcock, 2010, p 385)

2. Emphasised just as strongly as the 'Big Society' has been a commitment to reduce public spending and manage the economy following a global economic crisis. This has led to substantial changes in public spending – a 28% reduction in local government budgets and a requirement for the NHS (although its spending is ring-fenced) to reduce spending by some £20 billion in order to respond to rising costs and needs (for

Box 3.3: Big Society – overview

The Big Society is about helping people to come together to improve their own lives. It's about putting more power in people's hands – a massive transfer of power from Whitehall to local communities.

There are three key parts to the Big Society agenda:

- *Community empowerment*: giving local councils and neighbourhoods more power to take decisions and shape their area. Our planning reforms led by CLG [Communities and Local Government], will replace the old top-down planning system with real power for neighbourhoods to decide the future of their area.
- *Opening up public services*: our public service reforms will enable charities, social enterprises, private companies and employee-owned co-operatives to compete to offer people high quality services. The welfare to work programme, led by the Department for Work and Pensions, will enable a wide range of organisations to help get Britain off welfare and into work.
- *Social action*: encouraging and enabling people to play a more active part in society. National Citizen Service, Community Organisers and Community First will encourage people to get involved in their communities.

The Office for Civil Society, part of the Cabinet Office, works across government departments to translate the Big Society agenda into practical policies, provides support to voluntary and community organisations and is responsible for delivering a number of key Big Society programmes, namely:

The Big Society Bank: The government has committed to setting up a Big Society Bank to give social enterprises, charities and voluntary organisations access to greater resources. It will be set up using money from dormant bank accounts (those untouched for 15 years or more and available for spending in England) and will encourage investment in social change.

National Citizen Service Pilots: The National Citizen Service (NCS) scheme will bring 16-year-olds from different backgrounds together over the summer to take part in residential and home-based activities such as outdoor challenges and local community projects. Cabinet Office will run pilots for National Citizen Service in the summer of 2011 and 2012, involving 10,000 young people.

Community organisers: Over the lifetime of this parliament, the Community Organisers programme will identify, train and support 5,000 people who want to make a difference to their community. The organisers will have strong understanding of local needs and will catalyse social action.

Community First: Community First is a new fund that will encourage social action through new and existing neighbourhood groups. The fund will empower people in areas with high levels of deprivation and enable them to take more responsibility for their communities.

Available online via: www.cabinetoffice.gov.uk/content/big-society-overview. For further details, see Cabinet Office (2010). For early critiques, see Alcock (2010) and Coote (2010).

further discussion see Appleby et al, 2009, 2010; HM Treasury, 2010; Yeates et al, 2011; useful analysis is also provided via www.ifs.org.uk). For the foreseeable future, this might lead to very low or no real terms growth in NHS spending and active reductions in adult social care – an unprecedented situation for many managers and practitioners used to working in an era of plenty. This has been described by health economist John Appleby and colleagues (2010, p 4) as leading to a situation where we need to do 'more with the same' rather than 'more of the same'. Against this background, both health and social care will have to make some very difficult decisions about current and future services. For the government, these are unpalatable measures that have been forced on us by the international economic situation and, they might argue, by the actions of the previous government. For critics, the level of the cuts also supports suspicions that the 'Big Society' might be little more than a smokescreen for (much?) smaller government.

Services for older people

Throughout the 20th century, life expectancy in the UK increased from 45.5 (men) and 49 (women) to 74.4 and 79.7 respectively in the mid-1990s (Tinker, 1996, p 13). While such an ageing population is often portrayed as a problem, it is really a major sign of success and a key achievement of the welfare state (among other factors). However, demographic changes do mean that community health and social services will have to meet the needs of more and more older people in the future, and in particular work with an increasing number of people aged 85 and over (sometimes referred to as 'the oldest old'). According to official estimates (HM Government, 2008, 2009a):

- In the next 20 years, the number of people aged over 85 in England will double and the number of people over 100 will quadruple.
- In 20 years' time, there could be a funding gap of at least £6 billion (and this is if we only continued with current services that are already being criticised for being of insufficient quality and flexibility).
- If the current system remains unchanged, then the cost of disability benefits could rise by almost 50% in the next 20 years, while the cost of long-term care could rise by 17% by 2027/28.

Additional analysis by the Health Services Management Centre on *The case for adult social care reform* (Glasby et al, 2010) suggests that social care costs alone could double in 20 years without fundamental and ongoing reform. Faced with such pressures (and with a very difficult financial context), many health and social care services are now increasingly focusing on their services for older people – recognising that the numbers mean that all health and social care policy is essentially about older people.

To date, it is often argued that state services have added years to life, but that more now needs to be done to add life to years (that is, to maintain independence and increase quality of life). Within social care, the bulk of the budget is spent on care home placements, day care and home care, with the first two of these focusing on institutional forms of support and the third arguably focusing more on supporting people in their own homes rather than enabling older people to participate fully in community life. As one older person has remarked (personal communication), "even when someone is coming to deliver care in your own home, they can still recreate something of the asylum if their practice is disempowering and routinised." In the NHS, older people are major users of both GP and of hospital services, sometimes receiving the same services as the rest of the community and sometimes falling under the remit of more specialist 'geriatric' services (usually under a hospital-based consultant geriatrician). While such services often contain a broad range of expertise with regard to the needs and health of older people, there is also a risk that this somehow makes older people's needs seem different from the rest of the population, to be dealt with separately rather than as everyone's core business. In practice, the opposite may be true, with services that are good for older people arguably being good for everyone else too.

Underpinning current older people's health and social care is the 2001 NSF for older people (DH, 2001b). The third such framework to be produced by New Labour (after mental health and coronary heart disease), the NSF described itself as 'a ten year programme of action' (p i) with four main themes (see also *Box 3.4*):

Box 3.4: National Service Framework for older people

Standard 1: Rooting out age discrimination – NHS services will be provided, regardless of age, on the basis of clinical need alone. Social care services will not use age in their eligibility criteria or policies to restrict access to available services.

Standard 2: Person-centred – NHS and social care services treat older people as individuals and enable them to make choices about their own care. This is achieved through the single assessment process, integrated commissioning arrangements and integrated provision of services, including community equipment and continence services.

Standard 3: Intermediate care – older people will have access to a new range of intermediate care services at home or in designated care settings, to promote their independence by providing enhanced services from the NHS and councils to prevent unnecessary hospital admission and effective rehabilitation services to enable early discharge from hospital and to prevent premature or unnecessary admission to long-term residential care.

Standard 4: General hospital care – older people's care in hospital is delivered through appropriate specialist care and by hospital staff who have the right set of skills to meet their needs.

Standard 5: Stroke – the NHS will take action to prevent strokes, working in partnership with other agencies where appropriate. People who are thought to have had a stroke have access to diagnostic services, are treated appropriately by a specialist stroke service, and subsequently, with their carers, participate in a multidisciplinary programme of secondary prevention and rehabilitation.

Standard 6: Falls – the NHS, working in partnership with councils, takes action to prevent falls and to reduce resultant fractures or other injuries in their populations of older people. Older people who have fallen receive effective treatment and rehabilitation and, with their carers, receive advice on prevention through a specialised falls service.

Standard 7: Mental health in older people – older people who have mental health problems have access to integrated mental health services, provided by the NHS and councils to ensure effective diagnosis, treatment and support, for them and for their carers.

Standard 8: The promotion of health and active life in older age – the health and well-being of older people is promoted through a co-ordinated programme of action led by the NHS with support from councils.

Source: DH (2001b)

- respecting the individual
- intermediate care
- providing evidence-based specialist care
- promoting an active, healthy life.

More recently, there has been additional focus on services for older people with a national dementia strategy (DH, 2009) and high-profile debates about the future funding of long-term care (see also Chapter Four for controversial debates over the funding of long-term care). However, despite all this, an ongoing criticism of older people's services has been a failure to tackle discrimination, to root out ageism and to meet people's basic needs. In 2011, the Parliamentary and Health Service Ombudsman published a summary of 10 investigations into NHS care for older people (see *Box 3.5*). While these were individual stories in different parts of the country, there was a series of common themes: poor communication, lack of dignity and failure to pay attention to people's basic personal care needs. Although the Ombudsman acknowledged that there are many skilled and dedicated staff working with older people, she concluded that 'the investigations reveal an attitude – individual and institutional – which

---

Box 3.5: 2011 Ombudsman report

I encourage Members of both Houses [Commons and Lords] to read the stories of my investigations included in this report. I would ask that you then pause and reflect on my findings: that the reasonable expectation that an older person or their family may have of dignified, pain-free end of life care, in clean surroundings in hospital, is not being fulfilled. Instead these accounts paint a picture of NHS provision that is failing to respond to the needs of older people with care and compassion and to provide even the most basic standards of care. (p 5)

The difficulties encountered by the service users and their relatives were not solely the result of illness, but arose from the dismissive attitude of staff, a disregard for process and procedure and the apparent indifference of NHS staff to deplorable standards of care. (p 9)

My aunt's basic human rights ... were totally disregarded and neglected. I am certain that she was in great distress and felt totally alone and abandoned. It makes me feel so angry. (Mrs H's niece, p 20)

Source: Parliamentary and Health Service Ombudsman (2011; see also CQC, 2011)

---

fails to recognise the humanity and individuality of the people concerned and to respond to them with sensitivity, compassion and professionalism' (Parliamentary and Health Service Ombudsman, p 7). Nor did she feel that these were isolated cases – of the 9,000 complaints her office received in 2010, 18% were about older people. The Ombudsman accepted 226 cases for investigation – more than twice as many as for all the other age groups put together (p 8). These revealed similar themes to the 10 investigations, prompting the Ombudsman to include that 'these stories illustrate the gulf between the principles and values of [official policy] and the felt reality of being an older person in the care of the NHS in England' (p 7; see also CQC, 2011; Equality and Human Rights Commission, 2011).

On a more immediate and everyday level, current services for older people are focusing on a range of 'hot topics':

- As hospital lengths of stay have reduced and as acute care has become more focused on those with the most complex needs, many older people are discharged from hospital 'quicker and sicker' (Neill and Williams, 1992, p 17) – that is, with greater health needs than once would have been the case. With fewer beds and more rapid throughput of patients, the safe and timely discharge of older people has become a key policy issue, prompting significant amounts of government guidance and creating substantial inter-agency tensions (see Chapter Four for further discussion).
- With demographic changes and following the community care reforms of the early 1990s, the cost of care is rising (and local authorities are having to respond by trying to drive down the prices they pay). After multiple reviews (Royal Commission on Long-Term Care, 1999; Wanless, 2006; HM Government, 2009a, 2010a), this issue has not gone away and remains politically contentious (see also Chapter Four).
- In a similar manner, the boundary between (means-tested) social care and (free) NHS continuing health care has become equally contested, with a series of legal challenges and critical rulings by the Health Service Ombudsman (see Glasby and Littlechild, 2004, for an overview). In 2006, a new national framework for assessing continuing health care needs was launched (DH, 2006c), but doubts remain as to whether this is sufficient to resolve long-standing and underlying tensions in this area of policy (see Chapter Four for further discussion).
- A series of official policies stress the importance of a preventative agenda (see DH, 2005a, 2010b for examples). This has been described by the former Association of Directors of Social Services and the Local Government Association (2003) in terms of 'inverting the triangle of care' (see *Figure 3.1*) – at present, resources are most focused on a relatively small number of older people in crisis, with insufficient investment in

Figure 3.1: *Inverting the triangle of care*

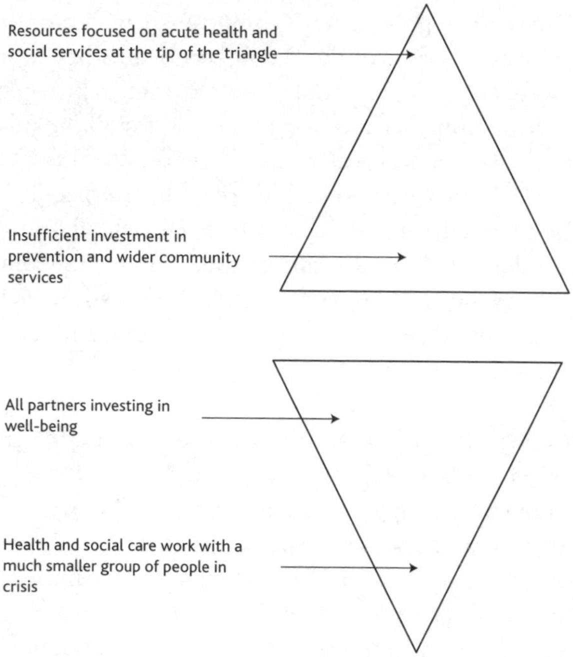

Resources focused on acute health and
social services at the tip of the triangle

Insufficient investment in
prevention and wider community
services

All partners investing in
well-being

Health and social care work with a
much smaller group of people in
crisis

preventative services. By inverting the triangle, it is hoped that services could begin to invest in preventative services for a larger number of older people, thus reducing future crises. Attractive though this model is intuitively, it remains largely aspirational, with insufficient evidence to back up claims made and with little sign of the long-term political (and financial) support that might be needed to make such a change (Allen and Glasby, 2010). Developing a more preventative approach has also been a stated aim of many governments over the years, and it is unclear why we might expect current and future policy to achieve this when previous attempts arguably failed.

Services for people with mental health problems

Although a much smaller and more specialist area of health and social care, mental health services have a potentially massive yet often neglected remit. Internationally, depression will be the second most common cause of disability (after ischaemic heart disease) by 2020, and mental/behavioural disorders affect more than 25% of all people at some stage during their lives (Lester and Glasby, 2010, pp 3-4). In the UK, mental health costs to society and the economy are estimated at £105 billion a year (Centre for Mental Health, 2010). In health and social care, mental health is the second most common reason for consultations in primary care and the sole reason for seeing a GP in 20-25% of consultations, nearly 11% of the secondary health care budget is spent on mental health and more than £2 billion is spent on social care for people with mental health problems (Lester and Glasby, 2010, p 65; HM Government, 2011a). Costs could also double within the next 20 years.

Despite this, mental health services in the UK have often been seen as one of the so-called 'Cinderella services' – low status, with considerable public and professional misunderstanding. In particular, the last third of the 20th century was characterised by ongoing attempts to move away from an asylum-based system to some form of community care. While the number of beds has reduced, progress has been slow and funding for community alternatives has not matched the policy rhetoric. Moreover, the cultural changes required to develop a more community-based approach should not be underestimated, as Enoch Powell's now famous 'water tower' speech suggests (see ***Box 3.6***).

Under New Labour, mental health was the first condition to have its own NSF (DH, 1999a; see ***Box 3.7***) and was the focus of an early government White Paper, *Modernising mental health services* (DH, 1998a). As a result of these changes, mental health services witnessed substantial investment and perhaps more political and managerial attention than has often been the case. In particular, broader changes in the NHS have tended to lead to the amalgamation of existing mental health trusts into much larger, more regional specialist services, and primary care mental health services were boosted by new primary care mental health workers (with 1,000 such workers promised in *The NHS Plan* [DH, 2000a] in order to treat people with common mental health problems via techniques such as anxiety management and cognitive behavioural therapy). In addition, the NSF (and subsequent implementation guidance) saw the development of new forms of community teams. This is often described as a move away from generic community mental health teams, towards a more *functionalised* approach, with a series of new services:

- *assertive outreach teams:* focusing on people who might otherwise need a hospital admission, assertive outreach teams have small caseloads (ideally 10:1) and provide intensive support;
- *crisis intervention teams:* also known as home treatment teams, these offer an alternative to inpatient care for people experiencing an acute mental health crisis;

- *early intervention teams:* targeted at people aged from 14 to 35 with first presentation of psychotic symptoms.

However, by far the most controversial aspect of recent mental health policy was the passage of the Mental Health Act 2007. After detailed and contested debates, the Act extended the definition of mental disorder (so that more people may fall under its remit), enabled wider preventative detention and introduced community treatment orders (to ensure those affected continue receiving medical treatment). Such measures were roundly criticised by a range of campaigners – service users, voluntary organisations, academics and professional groups alike – as being both impractical (difficult if not impossible to implement) and unethical (with disproportionate use of compulsion). Above all, the fear was that a greater emphasis on compulsion could drive people away from seeking support, thereby putting the public and people using services more at risk (see Lester and Glasby, 2010, for further background and discussion).

Box 3.6: Enoch Powell's 'water tower' speech

I have intimated to the hospital authorities who will be producing the constituent elements of the national Hospital Plan that in 15 years' time there may well be needed not more than half as many places in hospitals for mental illness as there are today. Expressed in numerical terms, this would represent a redundancy of no fewer than 75,000 hospital beds.... Now look and see what are the implications of these bold words. They imply nothing less than the elimination of by far the greater part of this country's mental hospitals as they exist today. This is a colossal undertaking, not so much in the new physical provision which it involves, as in the sheer inertia of mind and matter which it requires to overcome. There they stand, isolated, majestic, imperious, brooded over by the gigantic water tower and chimney combined, rising unmistakable and daunting out of the countryside – the asylums which our forefathers built with such immense solidity to express the notions of their day. Do not for a moment underestimate their powers of resistance to our assault. (Powell, 1961)

Above all, critics of recent policy have emphasised that media and public stereotypes about the link between mental health and crime are precisely that: stereotypes. As Sayce (2000, p 226) has argued, all the available evidence suggests that:

- most crime is committed by people without mental health problems;

Box 3.7: National Service Framework for mental health

Standard 1: Ensure health and social services promote mental health and reduce the discrimination and social exclusion associated with mental health problems.

Standards 2 and 3: Deliver better primary mental health care, and ensure consistent advice and help for people with mental health needs, including primary care services for individuals with severe mental illness.

Standards 4 and 5: Ensure each person with severe mental illness receives the range of mental health services they need; that crises are anticipated and prevented where possible; ensure prompt and effective help if a crisis does occur; and timely access to an appropriate and safe mental health place or hospital bed, including a secure bed, as close to home as possible.

Standard 6: Ensure health and social services assess the needs of carers who provide regular and substantial care for those with severe mental illness, and provide care to meet their needs.

Standard 7: Ensure that health and social services play their full part in the achievement of the target ... to reduce the suicide rate by at least one fifth by 2010.

Source: DH (1999a)

- people with mental health problems who do commit crimes tend to do so for the same reasons as everyone else (poverty, family problems, substance misuse);
- it is very rare for people with mental health problems to attack someone they do not know;
- people with mental health problems are more often victims than perpetrators of crime;
- people with mental health problems can usually be held responsible for their crimes.

Very few people with mental health problems commit homicides (around 40 or 50 incidents each year, compared to 600–700 murders committed each year, 300 deaths by dangerous driving and 3,500–4,000 deaths through road accidents; see Taylor and Gunn, 1999; see also Lester and Glasby, 2010, ch 6, for a summary). While even one homicide is clearly one too many, the very fact that there have been such high profile media cases surrounding crimes by people with mental health problems suggests that such incidents are actually very rare. As Taylor and Gunn (1999, p 13) observe:

> On average, every week someone in the UK wins the jackpot on the National Lottery. About 54,999,999 people do not. On average, rather less than one person a week loses their life to a person with mental illness, generally his/her mother, father, sibling, spouse, child or other close contact; 54,999,999 remain safe from this threat.

While the 2007 Act has been the most controversial aspect of recent mental health policy, current services are grappling with a series of additional dilemmas and tensions:

- Central to debates about the future of mental health services was a 1998 White Paper, and the clue was in the subtitle: *Modernising mental health services: Safe, sound and supportive* (DH, 1998a). Can services that are perceived as 'supportive' by service users be seen as 'safe' and 'sound' by the media, by policy makers and by the general public? The furore that greeted the Mental Health Act 2007 seems to suggest a resounding 'no' to this question. At the heart of this issue is whether the best way of reducing risk is to compel people to use services or to make services so close to what service users want that they actively choose to engage. While a balance may always be needed, the accusation of critics of recent policy is that the pendulum has swung too much towards the former at the expense of the latter.
- In spite of the development of functionalised mental health teams, the evidence base to underpin new ways of working remains underdeveloped. As is often the case with new teams, there is a danger that new ways of working simply identify and work with people who would not have accessed services before, and so do not free up time and resources in other parts of the system. While this is good news for patients and service users, it may mean that some of the reforms concentrate more on previously unmet (or badly met) need – not necessarily bringing some of the efficiencies and cost savings that such ways of working are often designed to achieve.
- Despite many changes in mental health policy and practice, significant and long-standing concerns remain about the quality of inpatient mental health beds (see, for example, Baker, 2000; Watson, 2001; Mind, 2004; NPSA, 2006; Healthcare Commission, 2008; Lester and Glasby, 2010). With fewer beds, higher turnover and people with more acute needs, there seems to be increasing pressure on acute services, with service

users in particular highlighting untherapeutic and sometimes dangerous conditions. In particular, it seems as though many of the same factors that contributed to some of the long-stay hospital scandals of the 1960s remain present in more recent acute mental health care, prompting serious concerns about quality of care (see *Box 3.8*).

• Government recognises that 'adults with mental health problems are one of the most excluded groups in society' (ODPM, 2004, p 3, 2006; see also *Box 3.9*). In particular, people with mental health problems face widespread stigma and discrimination – both in health and social care, and in wider society, the media and among the general public (see, for example, Sayce, 2000; Thornicroft, 2006). As a result, bringing about longer-term changes in mental health services may be less a matter of changing health and social care, as campaigning and educating to change deep-seated public beliefs, attitudes and perceptions. While this has been rsecognised in important contributions by the former Office of the Deputy Prime Minister (2004, 2006), more public debates about notions of risk and dangerousness undoubtedly undermine the impact of this work and run the very real risk of perpetuating long-standing fears and stereotypes. There is also a risk that changes to unemployment and disability benefits under the Coalition government could have a

---

Box 3.8: Concerns about the quality of acute mental health services

During the hospital scandals of the 1960s, key factors included (Martin, 1984):

• isolated services (both geographically and lack of visits by medical staff)
• closed, institutional settings and a tendency to suppress complaints
• focusing on maintaining order rather than on caring for patients (termed 'the corruption of care')
• poor leadership, staff shortages and inadequate training

In 2003, the former Commission for Health Improvement identified a very similar list:

• isolated services
• institutional environments and closed cultures
• low staffing levels/high use of agency staff
• poor clinical leadership and supervision

Source: For a summary see Lester and Glasby (2010, ch 5)

> ### Box 3.9: Mental health and social exclusion
>
> - Only a quarter of adults with long-term mental health problems are in work – the lowest employment rate for the main groups of disabled people.
> - People with mental health problems are at more than double the risk of losing their jobs than those without.
> - Two thirds of men under 35 with mental health problems who die by suicide are unemployed.
> - People with mental health problems are nearly three times more likely to be in debt.
> - One in four tenants with mental health problems has serious rent arrears.
> - People with mental health problems are three times more likely to be divorced.
>
> The five key reasons for the link between social exclusion and mental health are:
>
> - stigma and discrimination
> - low expectations by professionals
> - a lack of clear responsibility for promoting vocational and social outcomes
> - a lack of ongoing support to enable people to work
> - barriers to engaging in the community and to accessing (supposedly) universal services
>
> *Source:* ODPM (2004, pp 3-19)

negative impact on people with mental health problems (see later for further discussion).

Services for people with physical impairments and long-term conditions

In the UK, survey data suggests that there are some 11 million disabled adults – one in five of the population – as well as some 770,000 disabled children (see Prime Minister's Strategy Unit, 2005). Due to medical advances and other changes, these numbers are growing – the number of disabled adults increased by 22% between 1975 and 2002, while the number of disabled children grew even more rapidly (by 62%). By the early 21st century, the government was spending nearly £30 billion on disability benefits, with some 2.7 million people of working age claiming incapacity-related benefits. While these broad figures include people with a range of conditions, there is a smaller group of people with more complex needs who may need significant support from health and social care. As an example, around 80% of GP consultations and two thirds of hospital admissions relate to people whom the NHS describes as having 'chronic diseases' or 'long-term conditions' (often older people, but including younger disabled people as well) (DH, 2004a). The issue of long-term conditions is a crucial aspect of current policy, and is discussed in greater detail in Chapter Five.

Against this background, a potentially ground-breaking report by the former Prime Minister's Strategy Unit (2005), *Improving the life chances of disabled people*, aimed to ensure that, 'by 2025, disabled people in Britain should have full opportunities and choices to improve their quality of life, and will be respected and included as equal members of society' (p 53). While the deadline for this target is a long way off, there can rarely have been a more important and yet more ambitious aim. As the then Prime Minister explained in his foreword (p 5):

> Getting a job or education, travelling between home and work, going for a drink with friends are activities most of us take for granted. But for too many disabled people these ordinary aspects of life remain difficult to achieve.

In particular, the report identified widespread discrimination and exclusion, both in wider society (see *Box 3.10*) and in health and social care services. Above all, the latter tend to be influenced by:

- a culture of care and dependency (rather than of citizenship)
- fragmented and silo-based approaches to support
- assessments that focus on services rather than on needs
- cost constraints and a tendency to focus on expensive residential forms of service provision.

At the heart of the proposed changes was the notion of independent living (explored in more detail in Chapter Five): the idea that disabled people should be able to exercise the same choices and control over their lives as other people. In a health and social care context, this has led to an emphasis on a range of current service issues:

- In social care, the concepts of direct payments and personal budgets (sometimes described as a 'personalisation' agenda or as a form of 'self-directed support') have been developed to enable disabled people to receive cash payments instead of directly provided services. Despite ongoing barriers, both these ways of working offer potentially very

> ## Box 3.10: Experiences of disabled people
>
> - Disabled people are less likely to be in employment than non-disabled people, and the employment rate for disabled people is less than that of any other disadvantaged group (for example, lone parents or people from minority ethnic communities).
> - Disabled people's income is, on average, less than half that of non-disabled people. Despite this, disabled people face significant additional costs as a result of their impairment – for example, annual costs for bringing up a disabled child are three times greater than for a non-disabled child.
> - Disabled people are more likely to have no educational qualifications and less likely to have advanced qualifications.
> - Disabled people are more likely to experience hate crime and harassment.
> - Much of the housing stock and a significant proportion of public transport is inaccessible for disabled people.
>
> *Source:* Prime Minister's Strategy Unit (2005, ch 2)

different ways of responding to need, and are discussed in greater detail in Chapter Five.

- In the NHS, significant emphasis has been placed on meeting the needs of people with long-term conditions (see Chapter Five), reducing the number of emergency hospital admissions and promoting concepts such as self-care, care closer to home and greater joint working between primary/community services and hospital-based services.
- Despite these commitments, considerable concern remains about the discrimination and injustice built into current society and hence into health and social care services. Over time, these recurring issues have been highlighted by organisations such as the former Disability Rights Commission (2004), user-led organisations such as the National Centre for Independent Living (www.ncil.org.uk), campaigning groups such as 'Living with Dignity' and 'Not Dead Yet' (www.livingwithdignity.info/index.html and www.notdeadyet.org) and even the government itself (Prime Minister's Strategy Unit, 2005). Under the Coalition, moreover, there are wider concerns about the impact on the lives of disabled people of social security reforms, changes in housing policy and cuts in public service spending. As but one example, a group of disabled people, leading disability charities and their supporters have published a full page advert in *The Times* and launched a national 'Campaign for a Fair Society', arguing that the welfare state needs positive reform, but that recent policy has been both counter-productive and unfair (see www.

campaignforafairsociety.com). While the government has often argued that 'we're all in this together', the Campaign suggests that the cuts that have resulted will have a negative and disproportionate effect on disabled people, disabled children and people with learning difficulties.

Services for people with learning difficulties

Of all community care user groups, people with learning difficulties may well be the most neglected and most excluded. Like other groups, services have traditionally been based around long-stay hospitals, with hospital consultants responsible for almost every aspect of people's lives. Although sometimes justified in terms of protecting people from abuse, this was often derived from the eugenic belief that people with learning difficulties could 'contaminate the gene pool' if 'allowed' to 'breed' (and that there were genetic links between physical and mental impairments and crime, unemployment, sexual immorality and other social problems). Particularly associated with Francis Galton (a cousin of Darwin), this approach has often led to attempts to prevent the reproduction of such 'defectives' by a combination of sterilisation and segregation. While such attitudes seem very outdated, it is still possible to see the continued influence of such a philosophy around debates over current abortion laws and around the tendency for the public and professionals alike to ignore topics such as sex and sexuality with regards to people with learning difficulties. Even now, this history of segregation is hard to avoid, and some people with a learning disability still receive both their physical and mental health care from a learning disability psychiatrist, with some still living in NHS settings.

Following a 1971 White Paper on *Better services for the mentally handicapped* (DHSS, 1971), there was a gap of some 30 years before the next major policy statement – the 2001 White Paper, *Valuing people* (DH, 2001c). In contrast to many of the policy documents summarised in this chapter, this did not focus so much on health and social services, but on a broader vision for people's lives (and hence on the health and social care contribution to this vision). As a result, *Valuing people* was focused on achieving four main principles (with a series of more detailed objectives; see ***Box 3.11***):

- rights
- independence
- choice
- control

As *Valuing people* (DH, 2001c, p 23) noted: 'improving the lives of people with learning disabilities requires commitment nationally and locally to

---

Box 3.11: *Valuing people* objectives

Objective 1:   maximising opportunities for disabled children
Objective 2:   ensuring continuity of care during transition into adult life
Objective 3:   enabling people to have more control over their own lives
Objective 4:   supporting carers
Objective 5:   enabling people to have good health
Objective 6:   having greater choice and control over housing
Objective 7:   enabling people to live fulfilling lives
Objective 8:   enabling more people to move into employment
Objective 9:   ensuring the quality of service provision
Objective 10: to develop the health and social care workforce
Objective 11: to promote holistic services through effective partnership working

Source: DH (2001c, p 26)

---

strong principles, a firm value base and clear objectives for services. Each individual should have the support and the opportunity to be the person he or she wants to be.' This seems a very different message to that in other user group settings, where the emphasis has been more on the nature and quality of particular health and social care services, not so much on citizenship and on the lives of individual service users.

Underpinning *Valuing people* was a number of new mechanisms and enablers, including a national learning disability task force to advise government, a Valuing People support team to facilitate implementation and a national Learning Disability Development Fund of £2.3 million per year for three years. This was supplemented by the appointment of a national director for learning disabilities and a new learning disability 'tsar' (a person with learning difficulties to help lead government policy). At a local level, services are overseen by learning disability partnership boards, which bring together all key public, private and voluntary agencies, together with people with learning difficulties and family carers, to co-ordinate and develop local services. More recently, the initial Valuing People programme has been supplemented by a further three-year cross-government strategy, *Valuing people now* (HM Government, 2009b).

Central to health and social services for people with learning difficulties at ground level are three key ways of working that have potential relevance for other user groups:

- A key slogan for *Valuing people* (and the subject of a supplementary report accompanying the main White Paper; DH, 2001c) was the notion of 'nothing about us without us' (since taken up by the Coalition government as a more general principle for the reform of health and social care). While *Valuing people* itself drew on the active involvement of a broad range of people with learning difficulties, subsequent policy and practice was to involve people with learning difficulties at every stage in order to contribute to broader goals of rights, independence, choice and inclusion. While services for other user groups stress the importance of user involvement (see Chapter Seven), this is so central to services for people with learning difficulties that it is increasingly seen as the default position rather than as an exception.

- Person-centred planning (PCP) starts with the individual (rather than with services), asking how people would like their lives to be and seeking to focus formal services on meeting these aspirations (see, for example, Sanderson, 2000; Cambridge and Carnaby, 2005; Dowling et al, 2006). While there is a range of different approaches, it typically involves the people themselves and anyone who they feel is important to them (their 'circle of support') exploring what the person wants the future to be like, their hopes and fears, and the support needed to achieve people's desired lifestyles. In many ways, PCP links naturally to other concepts such as direct payments and personal budgets (which are discussed in greater detail in Chapter Five).

- Rather than seeking to meet the health needs of people with learning difficulties via specialist NHS services (as has often been the case in the past), the concept of health facilitation argues that specialist learning disability practitioners need to use their skills to help people with learning difficulties access mainstream primary care and hospital services (DH, 2002a). This is crucial, as all the available evidence suggests that people with learning difficulties have higher physical and mental health needs than the general population, yet have worse access to health care as a result of a combination of inaccessible services, discriminatory attitudes and a lack of accessible information (see below for further discussion).

Despite providing such an inspiring and admirable vision, *Valuing people's* main strengths were probably also its biggest limitation. Because its aspirations for people's lives were so bold and so principled, it was perhaps inevitably going to fail to meet some of its own very laudable targets and goals. In particular, the closure of some remaining long-stay hospitals (planned for April 2004) was delayed (see, for example, Turning Point, 2003), and concerns were raised about some 3,000 people with learning disabilities still living in NHS residential accommodation (known as NHS campuses – now to be closed). This may also have contributed to a rise in private sector institutional placements, which can be out-of-area, expensive and isolated from funding authorities, family and friends (see, for example, Brindle, 2004; DH, 2004b; Pring, 2004; Hunter, 2006, DH, 2011).

In addition to this, inspection data (CSCI, 2004a) summed up initial progress after *Valuing people* in terms of *much achieved, more to do*. Key topics and issues included a lack of funding for advocacy services, more work needed to improve the accessibility of information, scope to improve PCP and transitions into adult services, a poor record of supporting the employment of people with learning difficulties and insufficient choice for people with high support needs. For other commentators, the quality of health services available to people with learning difficulties remains problematic (Mencap, 2004; NPSA, 2004), and insufficient progress has been made around wider issues such as social inclusion, employment, education and friendships and family relationships (Emerson et al, 2005).

Under the Coalition, current services are particularly focused on a number of 'hot topics', including:

- The funding of services for people with learning difficulties. In future, services for people with learning difficulties will be commissioned by local authorities rather than by the NHS – and in theory this offers the chance to develop more community-based approaches. However, local authority budgets are to be reduced by some 28% as a result of the 2010 Spending Review (HM Treasury, 2010), and there remains a risk that this could stifle any attempt to promote independence and support people to lead chosen lifestyles. In a worst-case scenario, we could even see a process of 're-institutionalisation' where it becomes cheaper to provide large buildings-based services to people en masse rather than looking for more individual and personalised solutions. (For an alternative view, see the discussion of personalisation in Chapter Five.)
- Linked to this is the need to influence wider, supposedly universal, services. While so much of *Valuing people* focused on issues such as employment, feeling valued, housing and finances, the sad reality is that we live in a society that sees the needs of people with learning difficulties as being somehow 'specialist' and hence the responsibility of health and social care. Despite challenging this, *Valuing people* and subsequent policies have yet to find robust ways of ensuring that all public services see people with learning difficulties as part of their core business, and such cultural change may take a long time to embed.
- Despite all the policy proposals outlined above, there remain concerns about the quality of basic care provided by the NHS in particular. Similar to the 2011 Ombudsman report about older people's services summarised

in *Box 3.5*, there have been a series of high-profile investigations, stories and scandals that all point to a fundamental failure to meet the basic personal and health care needs of people with learning difficulties, whether in general hospitals or in some specialist learning disability services (see DH, 2011, for an example). There also remains a series of barriers to accessing high quality primary care and fears that tougher eligibility criteria for adult social care will deny people in genuine need access to support (see, for example, Mencap, 2004, 2007; DRC, 2006; Healthcare Commission/CQC, 2006; Healthcare Commission, 2007; House of Lords/House of Commons Joint Committee on Human Rights, 2008; Michael, 2008; Parliamentary and Health Service Ombudsman/Local Government Ombudsman, 2009).

People with cross-cutting needs

Although this chapter has focused on relatively discrete user groups, earlier discussion of the need for 'joined-up' approaches argued that the complexity of people's lives does not reflect the structures that we create in our welfare services. This is equally true here, with a series of groups with often complex health and social care needs that run the risk of falling between the gaps in existing services. Potentially part of everyone's business, they are often no one's specific responsibility or priority, and thus can easily get overlooked. Good examples here are the needs of offenders or of homeless people, both of whom may have higher physical and/or mental health needs than the rest of the population, but less access to services. Also relevant to this discussion are a range of other groups of people who do not sit neatly into existing service categories (such as disabled parents or families supporting disabled children; see *Box 3.12*).

However, one of the most important boundaries in current services is between adult and children's services (see Chapter Four for further discussion), and the impact that this can have on young carers. Due in large part to the work of the Young Carers Research Group at Loughborough University's Department of Social Sciences, the needs (and indeed even the existence) of young carers have become much more widely recognised. From being virtually invisible, young carers now have a much higher policy profile, and some receive support from a range of specialist young carers' projects across the country (see Chapter Eight). However, evidence suggests that children and young people provide a wide range of care and support to parents and families, including domestic tasks, personal and intimate care, emotional support and childcare (see, for example, Aldridge and Becker, 1993, 2003; Dearden and Becker, 1998, 2004). This can have a range of implications, including a negative impact on people's education,

Box 3.12: Groups with cross-cutting needs

The evidence around the needs of disabled parents suggests that this group may fall between services, with community care workers failing to see parenting as a part of their remit, and children's services focusing on the child rather than on the needs of the adult (see, for example, Goodinge, 2000; Wates, 2002; Morris, 2003; Morris and Wates, 2006, 2007; SCIE, 2009; see also www.disabledparentsnetwork.org.uk/).

People who have both learning difficulties and mental health problems may often be refused services by mental health providers (who sometimes say that they do not work with people with learning difficulties) and by learning difficulty services (who may lack the mental health expertise to address this aspect of the person's needs). This can result in demarcation disputes, with services arguing over which aspect of a person's life is the main 'problem' – their learning difficulty or their mental health problem (see Foundation for People with Learning Difficulties, 2004, for a self-assessment tool to help improve mental health support for people with learning difficulties).

People with physical impairments and mental health problems can often find that they fall between traditional services – with physical disability services lacking the skills and experience to work with people with mental health problems, and mental health services frequently inaccessible for people with physical impairments (Morris, 2004).

People who misuse substances may sometimes fall under the remit of mental health services, of the criminal justice system or of specialist substance misuse services. Often, however, substance misuse can be overlooked altogether, and it is significant how many mental health homicides involve someone who has consumed considerable amounts of alcohol or drugs (or both). While the focus is inevitably on the mental health status of the person concerned, it is at least arguable that attention to the person's substance misuse might be a more profitable way forward for everyone concerned.

Asylum seekers and refugees who have social care needs may face particular barriers when trying to access services, and little attempt is often made by service providers to take account of this group's distinctive experiences and needs (Patel and Kelley, 2006; see also www.scie.org.uk/socialcaretv/video-player.asp?guid=ecb33e43-419e-4442-8975-5434092b0dfc for a Social Care TV clip).

Although this chapter has already explored services for older people, older people with mental health problems can often find themselves working with older people's services in social care, and with specialist mental health services in the NHS – or often denied access to specialist support altogether (Barnes, 1997; see also Nichols, 2006, for practical guidance on assessing the needs of older people with mental health problems).

health and future lives (HM Government, 2010b). As services for children and for adults increasingly separate (see Chapter Four), this may become an even bigger fault line in the future, with an urgent need for a more holistic approach that can span the children–adult divide.

Summary

In the early 21st century, services for all community care user groups have moved away from long-stay hospital provision, yet still seem very unimaginative and a long way from what someone with any positive choice might want for themselves or a family member. Although a consensus has developed that 'care in the community' is a better way of doing things than providing support in institutions, there has been relatively little thinking about what 'community care' actually means. As a result, many of our current services – for example, day centres and group homes – still seem very institutional: smaller in scale than what went before and physically located within the community, but with little real change in the balance of power between services and users and in the underlying ethos of provision. Despite what look like significant changes in the nature of service provision, our underlying assumptions and approaches still seem very similar to those of the mid-20th century, and more progress may well be difficult to achieve without a profound shift in our thinking and values (see the postscript at the end of this book, Chapter Nine, for further discussion).

Despite a degree of pessimism, there are also grounds for optimism. Documents such as *Valuing people* and *Improving the life chances of disabled people* offer very different visions of what the world could be like (at least in theory), and policy rhetoric is changing to emphasise the importance of more personalised services that promote active citizenship and independent living. Whether this actually becomes reality is a more complex question, and Chapter Five explores these issues in more detail.

For several user groups, moreover, there is a tension between providing specialist services (with a view to meeting needs more effectively) and this becoming a way of downgrading the needs of that particular group and allowing more general services to view this as 'someone else's responsibility'. This seems particularly the case in learning difficulty services, where the health facilitation model discussed above is designed to harness specialist skills in order to enable people to access everyday mainstream services. However, similar dilemmas exist in other areas such as hospital-based 'geriatric' services and primary care-based mental health. A similar dilemma is evident in Chapter Six, around how best to meet the needs of groups experiencing discrimination.

Above all, this review of current services highlights the large numbers of people that fall under the heading of 'community care services'. While each specific group has been shown to experience discrimination and social exclusion, the overview of services provided here suggests that we are actually talking about many millions of people – a substantial proportion of the adult population. This is true now, and may be even more the case in the future, as a result of medical advances and current demographic trends. Although it is usually seen as a 'Cinderella service', community care is actually everybody's business – as practitioners, as policy makers, as taxpayers and as citizens. As potential users ourselves, this if nothing else should concentrate the mind and prompt us to rethink services that are undoubtedly well meant and provided with the best of intentions, but which many of us might hesitate to use ourselves if we were on the receiving end.

Further reading/relevant websites

This chapter has covered a broad range of services and policy changes, but more detailed material can be found in a range of additional textbooks and accounts. For a general overview, key texts include:

- **Means et al's (2008)** *Community care: Policy and practice*
- **McDonald's (2006)** *Understanding community care*
- **Mandelstam's (2008)** *Community care practice and the law*

For older people, key resources include:

- The **2006 Wanless** review of adult social care funding
- **Glasby and Littlechild's (2004)** *The health and social care divide*
- **Lymberry's (2005)** *Social work with older people*

For people with mental health problems, key resources include:

- A series of leading textbooks by **Rogers and Pilgrim (2001, 2003, 2010)**
- **Laurance's (2003)** *Pure madness*
- **Lester and Glasby's (2010)** introductory textbook on *Mental health policy and practice*
- **Tew's (2005)** *Social perspectives in mental health*

For disabled people, key resources include:

- *Improving the life chances of disabled people* **(Prime Minister's Strategy Unit, 2005)** – although it derives from the New Labour governments of 1997-2010, this remains one of the most challenging and comprehensive summaries of the

barriers that disabled people face, the factors that contribute to this and possible ways forward
- Although further resources are set out in Chapter Five, key textbooks are by disabled academics and campaigners such as Michael Oliver **(Oliver, 1990, 2009; Oliver and Sapey, 2006)** and Colin Barnes **(Oliver and Barnes, 1998; Barnes and Mercer, 2006)**
- **French and Swain's (2011)** *Working with disabled people in policy and practice: A social model*

For people with learning difficulties, key resources include:

- *Valuing people* **(DH, 2001c)** – still an inspiring vision of how all services can support people with learning difficulties to lead chosen, fulfilling lives
- **Cambridge and Carnaby's (2005)** *Person-centred planning and care management with people with learning disabilities*
- **Duffy's (2003)** *Keys to citizenship*
- **Williams' (2011)** *Learning disability and inclusion: Policy and practice*

For an exploration of the different theoretical approaches that underpin current health and social care, see:

- **Bury's (2005)** *Health and illness*
- **Jones' (1994)** *The social context of health and health work*
- **Payne's (2005b)** *Modern social work theory*

For an overview of policy and practice under the New Labour and Conservative-Liberal governments, see:

- **Powell's (1999, 2002, 2008)** New Labour 'trilogy'
- **Ham's (2009)** *Health policy in Britain*
- **Bochel's (2011)** *The Conservatives and social policy*

For a critical analysis of early Coalition policies and the 2010 Spending Review, see the **Social Policy Association's** *In defence of welfare* **(Yeates et al, 2011)**. A helpful analysis of the nature and implication of 'The Big Society' is provided by **Alcock (2010)** while a more politically-focused critique comes from the **New Economics Foundation** (Coote, 2010).

In terms of useful websites, there is up-to-date policy information available (usually free to download) from the DH (www.dh.gov.uk). Most leading voluntary organisations also have useful policy briefings, news updates and general information. See, for example:

www.ageuk.org.uk
  Age UK
www.carersuk.org
  Carers UK
www.learningdisabilities.org.uk
  Foundation for People with Learning Disabilities
www.mencap.org.uk
  Mencap
www.mind.org.uk
  Mind
www.rethink.org
  Rethink
www.turning-point.co.uk
  Turning Point

In addition, the following sites may also be helpful:

www.nhsconfed.org
  NHS Confederation
www.officefordisability.gov.uk
  Office for Disability Issues
www.scie.org.uk
  Social Care Institute for Excellence, includes free access to the Social Care Online database
www.valuingpeoplenow.dh.gov.uk
  Valuing people now
www.puttingpeoplefirst.org.uk/
  Government personalisation website

Reflection exercises

For social policy students
A number of commentators watching the 2010 general election and the televised leaders' debates seem to feel that the UK was adopting a more US style approach – with the key differences between the main candidates essentially around the ability to implement rather than ideological differences and based more around the politics of 'personality' rather than 'substance'. How true does this feel with regards to health and social care? How do the policies of the Coalition government (2010-) differ from those of New Labour? To what extent does the recent development of health and social care suggest continuity or more fundamental change?

For health and social care professionals and students

For students and practitioners living and working through these changes, what are some of the key underlying themes and issues that are shaping your work (irrespective of whichever government is in power at the time)? How different do current services feel from those in existence 10 years ago? How different do you think things will be in 10 years' time?

In interagency settings

Summarise the changes that are taking place in your own profession/organisation/ sector. Compare your answers with those of colleagues from other agencies and backgrounds. Which themes are consistent across health and social care and which seem profession- or agency-specific?

For all readers

If you were the Secretary of State, what policies would you devise to reform current health and social care? What policies would you suggest for:

- Older people?
- People with mental health problems?
- People with long-term conditions/physical impairments?
- People with learning difficulties?
- People with cross-cutting needs?

four

Partnership working in health and social care

Overview

This chapter discusses:

- the problematic nature of the health and social care divide;
- policy responses to try to promote more effective interagency working;
- key concepts such as professional culture, depth and breadth of relationship and the importance of focusing on desired outcomes;
- current hot topics such as delayed hospital discharge, continuing health care and ongoing debates about rationing and charging.

In most if not all developed countries, health and social services are beset by problems of fragmentation and insufficient interagency collaboration (see, for example, Meads et al, 2005; Kodner, 2006; Glasby and Dickinson, 2009). Whatever the exact structure of local and national services, health and social care tend to work with people with complex, cross-cutting needs, typically requiring a more coherent and 'joined-up' response from a range of agencies. As a result of this (and due also in part to a desire to find ways of organising services that are as cost-effective as possible), there is a national and international emphasis on partnership working – both between health and social care, and with other services and sectors of the economy (public, private, voluntary and informal). Against this background, this chapter reviews the current UK emphasis on achieving 'joined-up solutions to joined-up problems', focusing mainly on health and social care partnerships, but also acknowledging the importance of collaboration with other partners. After reviewing the policy context, a range of key concepts and theoretical frameworks are introduced to help make sense of the current partnership agenda, and a series of 'hot topics' are explored as case studies of the complexities surrounding the pursuit of more effective joint working.

More than many other areas of policy, the partnership agenda is justified in terms of a desire to provide better outcomes for service users and patients. While the evidence to support such aspirations can sometimes be problematic (see below for further discussion), there are very powerful examples of what can happen to people when the support they need is poorly co-ordinated or delayed. This is true in everyday health and social care settings, but can be even more the case when there are multiple agencies and very complex, cross-cutting issues involved. As an example, ***Box 4.1*** summaries a controversial but much broader example of what can happen in extreme cases when agencies and professions are not working effectively together. As well as illustrating the need for joint working, the example also touches on issues to do with prevention and with the personalisation agenda (see Chapter Five for further discussion). As the DH (1998b, p 3) long ago suggested in a very strongly worded critique of the failure to work in partnership:

> All too often when people have complex needs spanning both health and social care good quality services are sacrificed for sterile arguments about boundaries. When this happens people, often the most vulnerable in our society ... and those who care for them find themselves in the no man's land between health and social services. This is not what people want or need. It places the needs of the organisation above the needs of the people they are there to serve. It is poor organisation, poor practice, poor use of taxpayers' money – it is unacceptable.

Policy context

As outlined in Chapter Two, the current health and social care system in the UK remains heavily influenced by the legacy and structures of the postwar welfare state. In particular, current services are still based primarily on the ideas and assumptions underpinning two 1940s' pieces of legislation:

- the NHS Act 1946 (which led to the foundation of the NHS in 1948)
- the National Assistance Act 1948 (which set out the responsibilities and powers of local authorities).

Box 4.1: What can happen when the whole system isn't greater than the sum of its parts (an extreme example)

The ... high profile case of two young brothers from South Yorkshire graphically illustrates the problems [of silo-based working].... The brothers at the ages of 10 and 11 carried out a 90 minute attack on two other boys aged 9 and 11. The victims, who appeared to have been randomly chosen, were stripped, strangled, stamped on, hit with bricks, and forced to sexually assault each other. The brothers were sentenced in January 2010 to indeterminate sentences for public protection. The minimum term they will serve is five years.

The boys were members of a family with seven sons. The mother had depression and a drug dependency. The father was routinely cruel and violent to his wife and children. At their trial, the court was told that the boys were regularly witnesses to and victims of their father's extreme domestic violence, were allowed to smoke cigarettes and cannabis, drink alcohol and watch pornography, and were treated as adult confidants by their mother in relation to her personal and emotional needs.... The brothers along with the other 5 children in the family were well known to a number of agencies and the 10 and 11 year olds had, in fact, been taken into local authority care just 3 weeks before the attacks took place.

A serious case review found that various local agencies missed 31 opportunities to intervene with the family and [the] council subsequently apologised to the victims and their families for its failings.

Should there have also been an apology to the family of the two young perpetrators? An apology to their mother that no GP, midwife or health visitor throughout her 7 pregnancies and births asked the right questions about the life she and her children were living at home? They were each a victim of the 'hidden' crimes of domestic violence and child abuse. Yet the brothers are not clear cut victims. They had reached their tipping point and committed serious crimes; and, worryingly, organisations which exist to promote child welfare led the campaign for the sentences to be increased.

This case raises a number of questions which suggest the urgent need for alternative approaches to child offenders to be developed:

1. For an agency coming into contact with the family in 2009 any intervention, to be successful, would have had to have been drastic, long term and resource intensive. It is apparent that an intervention did take place as the brothers were taken into care but the very act of taking

the boys into care could have inflicted further damage. The 'placement' certainly did not last very long nor was it effective in reducing risk.

2. Taking the two young boys into care certainly did not address the fact that their mother and siblings were still living with a violent and abusive man and were daily victims of a serious crime within their own home. Providing a successful intervention which does not involve taking children into care is extremely challenging at such a late stage in a family's history, when patterns of behaviour are entrenched and children tip from being a vulnerable child into a dangerous adult.

3. It was obvious that members of the South Yorkshire family were at risk of offending as there had been many incidences of anti-social behaviour before the horrific attack took place. It is also clear that any intervention at such a late stage in the family's life would have had to be highly personalised and tailored not just to the meet the needs of each individual family member but the needs of the family unit as a whole. The first issue to be addressed would have been the safeguarding of the mother and the children as victims of the ongoing domestic violence. Identifying risk, needs, strengths and natural supports and subsequently creating an integrated, intensive 'family support plan and budget' would have been possible only through beginning to build a trusted relationship with the family.

Source: Extract from a paper on personalisation and criminal justice by Clare Hyde (2011, pp 20-1)

Under this approach, it was assumed that it is possible to distinguish between people who are *sick* (who are seen as having *health care* needs, met by the NHS free at the point of delivery) and people who are merely *frail or disabled* (who are seen as having *social care* needs that fall under the remit of local authority social services and that are frequently subject to a means test and user charges). Despite substantial policy changes, this 1940s' distinction remains largely intact, and although we have often blurred the boundary between health and social care, it remains enshrined in legislation and in the modern-day organisations and operating systems that flow out of these divisions (for a historical overview of the health and social care divide see Means and Smith, 1998a; Glasby and Littlechild, 2004). Arising out of this, contemporary health and social services have to overcome a series of barriers – organisational, financial, legal, professional and cultural – if they wish to work together more effectively (see *Table 4.1* for a summary of the key differences between health and social care).

Thus, any front-line practitioner, manager or policy maker wishing to develop more effective health and social care partnerships will immediately face a range of obstacles and complexities to do with the structure and history of services. When progress sometimes seems slow, it can often be because partnership working is extremely difficult, not necessarily because those involved do not want to collaborate (although as discussed below this can also be the case).

Table 4.1: *Health and social care divide*

	Health care	Social care
Accountability	National (to Secretary of State)	Local (to elected councillors)
Policy	Overseen by DH (which also has responsibility for social care policy)	Local government is overseen by the Department for Communities and Local Government
Charges	Free at the point of delivery	Means-tested and subject to charging
Boundaries	Based on GP registration	Based on geography and council boundaries
Focus	Individual (medical) cure	Individual in his/her wider context
Culture and training	Strongly influenced by medicine and science	Strongly influenced by social sciences

In response to this situation, successive governments have sought to find ways of delivering what is often described as 'seamless services' (in which users experience their contact with services as a coherent and joined-up whole rather than in a fragmented, disjointed manner). In other countries, too, there has been a similar quest for more collaborative working (typically focusing on older people, who are the largest user group and often have complex, cross-cutting needs – see ***Box 4.2*** for examples).

In the UK, the NHS Reorganisation Act 1973 placed a statutory duty on health and local authorities to collaborate with each other through joint consultative committees. Advisory rather than executive, these bodies were soon seen to be inadequate for the task in hand (Wistow and Fuller, 1982), prompting calls for further reform. In 1976, these arrangements were strengthened by the creation of joint care planning teams of senior officers and by a joint finance programme to provide short-term funding for social services projects deemed to be beneficial to the health services.

Box 4.2: International examples of integrated care

Integrated care can often be based around *horizontal integration* (for example, between health and social care) and/or *vertical integration* (for example, between primary and secondary services). Curry and Ham's (2010) review of the international evidence cites examples such as:

Kaiser Permanente, the largest non-profit-making health maintenance organisation in the US.

Veterans Health Administration, US

Geisinger Health System in north-east Pennsylvania comprises a hospital system of three acute hospitals and 12,000 employees, including a multispecialty group of 740 physicians. It serves a population of 2.6 million and is also insurer for about 30% of the patients who use its services.

The *Mayo Clinic* in Minnesota, the world's oldest and largest multispecialty group practice, including an affiliated regional system of clinics, hospitals and nursing homes serving 2.4 million people.

The US *Programme for All-inclusive Care for the Elderly* (*PACE*), an integrated provider model aimed at maintaining frail older people in the community for as long as possible.

SIPA (System of Integrated Services for Aged Persons), a demonstration programme in Canada to keep frail older people in the community using an integrated provider model. A similar model, *PRISMA*, co-ordinates rather than integrates care. Similar models exist in Europe via projects such as *Rovereto* and *Vittorio Veneto* in Italy.

Co-ordinated or integrated care pathways, such as Swedish *chains of care* or Scotland's *managed clinical networks*.

Underpinning some of these models are factors such as:

- the delivery of integrated care (often through integrating the provision and commissioning of care);
- a focus on chronic care and on preventing hospital admissions;
- promotion of self-management;
- a culture of measuring, reporting and improving performance (including the use of financial and non-financial incentives);

- a focus on evidence and research;
- high levels of clinical engagement and leadership, with a close relationship; between managers and clinicians and an emphasis on collaborative care;
- multi-disciplinary team working and active case management;
- high quality IT;
- a single entry point;
- financial incentives to promote more community-based services.

What remains debated is whether integrated structures per se can help joint working, or whether some of these underlying factors are more important, almost irrespective of the broader structures in place (see also Johri et al, 2003; Kodner, 2006). Further examples of integrated care for older people in the EU are available via www.euro.centre.org/interlinks

Despite growing criticisms of these mechanisms for joint working, formal arrangements for collaboration remained substantially unchanged until the community care reforms of the 1990s (Hudson et al, 1997; see Chapter Three, this volume).

Since 1997, the emphasis has arguably been more on creating local networks or partnerships between local agencies. Key policies include:

- The *Health Act 1999*: here, three new legal powers (or 'flexibilities') enabled health and social care to create pooled budgets, to develop lead commissioning arrangements or to create integrated providers (see Glendinning et al, 2002a).
- Creation of *care trusts* (NHS bodies with social care responsibilities delegated to them). With only a handful of such organisations currently in existence, this is the closest model to a full merger of health and social care (see Glasby and Peck, 2003; Miller et al, 2011).
- Creation of *children's trusts*: more virtual in nature than adult care trusts, these typically bring together a wider range of partners than just health and social care, and are local authority-based. Alongside these organisational arrangements, there is also an emphasis on a common assessment framework for children, greater information sharing, a lead professional to co-ordinate care and greater co-location of different professions working with children and young people (HM Treasury, 2003).
- The duty to conduct an annual *Joint Strategic Needs Assessment*, so that health and social care can jointly understand current and future needs of the local population (under the Local Government and Public Involvement in Health Act 2007).

- The piloting of *personal health budgets* (see also Chapter Five).
- The creation of an integrated health and social care inspectorate (Care Quality Commission, www.cqc.org.uk) and more joined-up approaches to registering health and social care professionals (via a new Health and Care Professions Council).
- A more integrated *public health* service, based within local government and overseen by a new national agency (Public Health England).
- The creation of *health and well-being boards* between local government and clinical commissioning consortia to develop an annual *Health and well-being strategy* (DH, 2010a).

As a result of these changes, services for children and those for adults are increasingly separate, and it may well be that future approaches are more integrated across the health and social care divide, but more fragmented across the children–adult divide. If so, this seems a case in point for one of Leutz's (1999) 'five laws' of integration: your integration is my fragmentation.

In recent years, political devolution has allowed a series of new approaches to develop in the different countries of the UK. While England is formally integrating some services via the care trust and children's trust model, Scotland developed a joint performance information and assessment framework to explore the outcomes (rather than just process issues) that whole systems working is achieving (see, for example, Hudson, 2005). In addition, rather than distinguishing between free health care and means-tested social care, Scotland provides all personal care free of charge, developing a new way of conceptualising needs that moves beyond the traditional health and social care divide (see 'Policy and practice dilemmas' below for further discussion). Wales has placed greater emphasis on strategic planning rather than more market-based commissioning reforms, and is exploring the scope to reorganise local strategic partnerships onto more of a regional level, thereby mirroring NHS boundaries (Independent Commission on Social Services in Wales, 2010). In contrast, Northern Ireland has long had integrated health and social care structures, although some commentators debate the extent to which this system is truly integrated at practice level and delivers different outcomes to other parts of the UK (see, for example, Hudson and Henwood, 2002; Hudson, 2003). In a more locally based, 'liberated' system, moreover, there may be additional scope for a greater range of models to emerge in individual health and social care communities, enabling a 'thousand flowers to bloom'. Whether or not such a localist agenda appears in practice remains to be seen.

Of course, many people who use services or who have complex needs require not only health and social care, but a broader range of services as well. As Chapter Three suggested, the various community care user groups may have significant contact with health and social services, but true inclusion and quality of life is probably more to do with housing, education, employment, income, transport, families and communities than it is with formal support services. Moreover, people with complex health problems may also find that their needs overlap and interact with each other to become greater than the sum of their parts. This is partly evident in current debates about how best to support people with long-term conditions (which is explored in more detail in Chapter Five), but is also illustrated by some practical examples in *Box 4.3*. Above all, partnership working is often seen as a key way of trying to tackle so-called 'wicked issues' – complex, cross-cutting problems where we do not really know the best way of responding, but where we know enough to realise that single agency approaches are unlikely to be successful (Rittel and Webber, 1973; Clarke and Stewart, 1997; Audit Commission, 1998). Thus, if policy makers are trying to reduce violent crime, tackle substance misuse, reduce teenage pregnancy, eradicate child poverty and promote social inclusion then some sort of multiagency response is going to be essential. In such situations, service responses also need to be greater than the sum of their parts if they are to be effective, and recent policy (DH, 2010b) recognises the need for health and social care to work in partnership with broader services as well as with each other.

Key concepts

Central to all discussion of health and social care partnerships is the notion of organisational and professional culture. Although many commentators struggle to define what they mean by 'culture' (see, for example, Scott et al, 2001), there is clearly something about the way organisations and professions function that makes one job and one setting potentially very different to another in terms of ethos, values and feel. As Ouchi and Johnson (1978) have suggested, one way of viewing culture is 'the way we do things round here'.

In the wider literature (for an accessible summary of these themes see Peck and Crawford, 2004; Anderson-Wallace and Blantern, 2005), culture is often seen as something an organisation *has* (that is, an attribute or component of the organisation that can be taught to new members). This is often portrayed in some of the less rigorous management textbooks, and often implies that it is possible for a (successful and dynamic) chief executive to identify 'the culture' of the organisation and intervene consciously to 'change the culture'. In the past, this has prompted attempts to identify cultural components from 'successful' companies (usually in the private sector) and import these components into UK organisations and into

Box 4.3: Cross-cutting needs and interagency working

An older person living alone with mental health problems may need support from health and social care, but they could also be living on a low income in poor housing in a neighbourhood where they feel afraid to go out. When they receive formal services, these could be provided by the public, private or voluntary sectors (or some combination of all three).

A young person with a mental health problem could be receiving support from mental health services, yet might be more concerned about their income, getting a job, meeting a partner and enjoying their social and leisure time.

A person with learning difficulties at a social services day centre may want to go to college, get married and have a family.

A disabled person may need support with some aspects of their personal care, but might be more concerned about being able to access public transport, being able to decide where they live and who they live with, and feeling fully included in society.

Offenders with health and social care needs are often seen as no one's priority, with their offender status used to deny them access to services (Williams, 2006). In prison, there are significant unmet mental health needs (Lester and Glasby, 2010), while older prisoners can be denied support with their personal care (Philpot, 2006).

Gypsies and travellers often have low health status, a higher likelihood of homelessness and a lower likelihood of accessing services (Warrington, 2006).

the public sector (for example, trying to introduce 'successful' techniques from firms such as Toyota). In contrast, another approach is to see culture as something an organisation *is* (that is, a much messier but potentially more helpful definition that sees culture as a more complex and ambiguous concept in which 'individuals share some viewpoints, disagree about some, and are ignorant and indifferent to others). Consensus, dissensus and confusion coexist' (Meyerson and Martin, 1987, p 637). Meyerson and Martin (1987) and Peck and Crawford (2004) offer a similar approach, and identify three different ways of thinking about culture (see *Box 4.4*). Of course, the net result of these debates is probably twofold:

- The 'how-to' management books that see culture as a component of an organisation and as something easily capable of being developed

Box 4.4: Different ways of understanding culture

- *An integration model:* this sees culture as something an organisation has and as an integrating force that holds organisations (and potentially partnerships) together.
- *A difference model:* this sees culture as more pluralistic with different interest groups and different cultures within organisations. This is something of a hybrid between notions of culture as something an organisation has or is.
- *An ambiguity model:* this sees culture as more local and personal, constantly changing over time and between different groups as they interact. This is closest to the notion of culture as something an organisation is.

Source: Meyerson and Martin (1987); Peck and Crawford (2004)

and changed in a planned way undoubtedly oversimplify a much more complex reality.

- Intervening in and trying to develop organisational cultures may be possible, but it is more subtle and harder to predict (for specific tools and approaches see Peck and Crawford, 2004; Peck, 2005).

As Parker (2000, pp 228-9) concludes:

> Cultural management in the sense of creating an enduring set of beliefs is impossible ... [yet] it seems perverse to argue that 'climate', 'atmosphere', 'personality', or culture of an organisation cannot be consciously altered.

In addition, one of the key lessons from the cultural literature is the limitations of relying on structural change alone as a means of trying to achieve positive change. This material is summarised elsewhere (see, for example, Fulop et al, 2002, 2005; Field and Peck, 2003; Edwards, 2010 Glasby et al, 2010), but key messages from research and from practice seem to suggest that:

- structural change by itself rarely achieves stated objectives;
- mergers typically do not save money – the economic benefits are often modest at best and are more than offset by unintended negative consequences such as a potential reduction in productivity and morale;
- mergers are potentially very disruptive for managers, staff and service users, and can give a false impression of change;
- mergers can stall positive service development for at least 18 months.

A more detailed discussion of partnership working and organisational culture is provided by Peck and Crawford (2004), and a helpful insight is provided by Dickinson et al (2006) in their review of the literature on leading organisations during mergers. Although most literature tends to focus on the process of the merger itself, the latter review suggests four key phases, with different approaches and styles of leadership appropriate at different times (see *Box 4.5* for a summary).

Perhaps crucial to these debates is the issue of clarity of roles and of relationships. When asked to work in partnership, it is always important to ask the question: 'partnership working with whom and for what?'. Put simply, it depends what you want to achieve as to who you need to work with and how you might want to work with them, and this is likely to vary, both over time and according to the nature of the task in hand. For Leutz (1999), the author of a classic commentary on partnership working, this can include three potentially very different ways of working or levels of integration:

- *Linkage:* appropriate for people with mild, moderate or new needs, linkage involves everyone being clear what services exist and how to access them, so that support is provided by autonomous organisations, but systematically linked.
- *Co-ordination:* with more explicit structures in place, co-ordination involves being aware of points of tension, confusion and discontinuity in the system and devising policies and procedures for addressing these.

Box 4.5: Managing and leading organisations during mergers

- *Pre-merger decision:* although public sector organisations tend not to have a choice over who they merge with, it is important to be aware of key cultural differences and similarities between the organisations.
- *Decision to merge:* leaders here have a key role to play in creating and communicating a vision that sets out the purpose of the merger.
- *During merger:* this phase requires a range of practical tasks to do with human resources, communication, new structures and helping staff to understand the implications of change.
- *Post-merger:* such change can have after-effects for at least three years, and it is important both to evaluate outcomes and to guard against the dangers of thinking that the job has been done once the merger is complete.

Source: Dickinson et al (2006)

- *Full integration:* for people with complex or unpredictable needs, full integration involves the creation of new services and approaches with a single approach and pooled funding.

A similar attempt to explore different levels of partnership working is also provided by Glasby (2005) and by Peck (2002), who identify different levels of *breadth* and *depth* of relationship (see **Figure 4.1**). According to their analysis, different services are starting from very different points on this matrix, with adult services having significant experience of close joint working between health and social care (through to and including full merger via care trusts), and with children's services working with a much broader range of stakeholders (but with much less experience of formal partnership working or of integration). At present, both sets of services seem to be trying to move to the top right-hand section of the matrix, achieving

Figure 4.1: Depth versus breadth

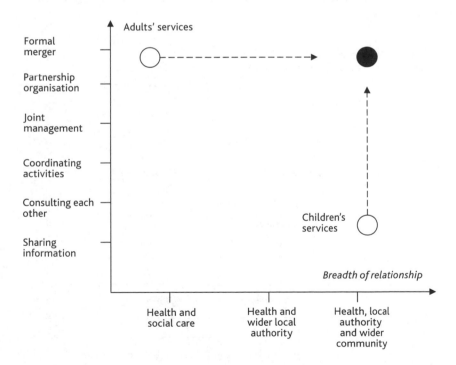

both depth and breadth (with adult services taking deep relationships and broadening them out, and children's services taking broad relationships and trying to deepen them). Whether it is necessary or even possible to achieve both depth and breadth at the same time remains to be seen.

Above all, however, the literature (and indeed current policy and practice) around effective partnership working tends to assume that partnership working is automatically a 'good thing' and that it somehow improves outcomes for service users and carers (see *Figure 4.2* for the assumed relationship between partnerships, services and outcomes). In practice, this remains a relatively untested assumption, with research (and indeed experience from practice) often struggling to link partnerships to improved outcomes (see, for example, Dowling et al, 2004; Audit Commission, 2005; Glasby et al, 2006a; Perkins et al, 2010). In particular, the literature tends to focus on issues of process (how well are we working together?) not on outcomes (does this make any difference to services or to users?).

As a result, more recent research and development work has emphasised the importance of focusing more on shared outcomes (see, for example, Dickinson, 2008). Given what we know about the limits of structural change, it seems particularly important that health and social care partners are clear about:

- what they are trying to achieve for local people;
- what partnership options exist to help them do this;
- why the partnership arrangements that they adopt are the best way of achieving desired outcomes;

Figure 4.2: Effective partnership working (in theory)

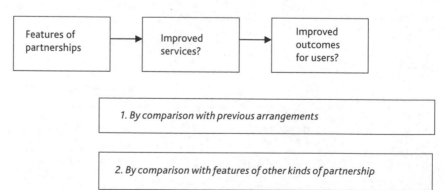

Source: Glasby et al (2006a)

- whether the proposed partnership is worth it (given the potential for a temporary reduction in staff morale, the amount of management time it will consume etc).

Unfortunately, keeping focused on these issues is difficult in a busy policy context and a pressured practice environment, and partnership working can easily become an end in itself rather than a means to an end. To guard against these dangers, *Figure 4.3* outlines a simple framework (adapted from the literature on realistic evaluation and theories of change; see Pawson and Tilley, 1997; Connell and Kubisch, 1998). Essentially, this reminds local partners to remain focused on what they want to achieve (outcomes), how well (or otherwise) they do this at present (context) and what needs to change to get from where they are now to where they want to be (process).

Figure 4.3: Focusing on outcomes

Policy and practice dilemmas

Of all the fault lines between health and social care, the issue of hospital discharge provides something of an acid test of the relationship between local partners. At discharge from hospital, someone with longer-term health and social care needs leaves the care of the hospital-based doctor and returns to community health and social care. Historically, this has tended to be viewed very much as a 'discharge', with one agency (potentially quite abruptly) ending its responsibility and this passing to others. However, more recent policy has started to describe this as more of a 'transfer of care'. As Henwood (1994, p 1) notes:

> Effective hospital discharge is dependent upon the various agencies involved acknowledging their complementary responsibilities. The benefits of getting it right can include maximising individuals' chance of recovery; improved hospital bed usage; more effective targeting of scarce assessment skills, and well informed community health staff knowing exactly what contribution they need to make to the care of the individual. The costs of getting it wrong include: a poor

service to patients, and unnecessarily slow recovery; GPs not knowing what has happened to their patients; social services staff receiving inappropriate referrals; disputes breaking out; un-planned readmissions, a general waste of resources, and the risk of bad publicity on bed blocking.

[Despite our traditional focus on hospital 'discharge'] … it is also apparent that a discharge from hospital is an admission – or transfer – to community care; and an admission to hospital is a transfer from the community. It is crucial, therefore, to recognise that actions and decisions made at any point in a care episode can have consequences for other parts of the health and social care system.

Unfortunately, all the available evidence suggests that hospital discharge continues to be a problematic area of policy and practice, with considerable interagency tension, fragmentation and negative outcomes for service users (see **Box 4.6**). In response, the Community Care (Delayed Discharges etc) Act 2003 introduced a system of 'reimbursement', with hospitals able to 'fine' SSDs when a discharge is delayed beyond an agreed period due to social care factors alone (currently £100 per day or £120 in London and the South East). While this initially coincided with a significant decrease in the rate of delayed discharge, it remains a controversial policy (see, for

---

Box 4.6: Negative experiences of hospital discharge

Over time, research identifies a range of recurring problems, including (Glasby, 2003; Henwood, 2004a, 2006):

- poor communication between hospital and community
- lack of assessment and planning for discharge
- inadequate notice of discharge
- inadequate consultation with patients and their carers
- over-reliance on informal support and lack of (or slow) statutory service provision
- a lack of support for carers
- the risk of premature discharge (and subsequent readmission).

More recently, concerns have been rising that premature or poor discharge could lead to a greater risk of emergency readmissions, with a series of policies from the Coalition government designed to penalise hospitals if patients are readmitted within the first 30 days of discharge.

example, House of Commons Health Committee, 2002; Glasby, 2003; CSCI, 2004b, 2005; Henwood, 2004a; McCoy et al, 2007; Godfrey et al, 2008). Although justified by government in terms of its success in tackling similar policy problems in Denmark and Sweden (DH, 2002b), doubts remain as to whether these systems are sufficiently similar for the approach to be transferable and about whether or not such an 'incentive' (or perhaps 'penalty'?) unfairly singles out one partner in what is undoubtedly a whole system problem.

Equally controversial has been the ongoing debate about the boundary between health and social care, and about who pays when someone has long-term needs. Over time, changes in this boundary have meant that the NHS now focuses more on acute care, providing much less support to people with long-term needs than was once the case (and with much of this care now being provided by social care). While this has raised concerns that NHS funding responsibilities may be gradually being passed onto social services (Royal Commission on Long-term Care, 1999), it particularly affects service users themselves, who now have to pay for services that were once free. In recent years, this disputed boundary has led to high profile legal cases, a Royal Commission on Long-term Care (1999), critical reports from the Health Service Ombudsman (2003) and the House of Commons Health Committee (2005) and a raft of government guidance (see, for example, DH, 1999b, 2001d, 2001e, 2003a, 2006c; Health Service Ombudsman, 2003). More recently there have been a series of Green/White Papers and a formal Commission on Funding of Care and Support chaired by Andrew Dilnot to explore the more general issue of funding for long-term care (see, for example, HM Government, 2008, 2009a, 2010a; Commission on Funding of Care and Support, 2011; see also *Box 4.7*). These issues became particularly controversial in the run up to the 2010 general election, with New Labour and the Conservatives each accusing the other of setting aside cross-party consensus in order to politicise these difficult debates for short-term gain (see Glasby, 2011a, for a discussion). Often, these controversies have centred on the difference between long-term care (funded by social care and means-tested), nursing care (now provided free to residents in nursing homes via a payment for nursing care costs direct to the home) and (often very tightly defined) NHS continuing health care (free NHS care for people with very complex medical needs; see also, Henwood, 2004b; Henwood and Waddington, 2005; Mackintosh, 2006) – with critics frequently questioning how meaningful these categories are in practice. As the House of Commons Health Committee (2005, pp 3, 54) argues:

> Current arrangements for funding long term care are beset with complexity, and lack of clear Government guidance has

> **Box 4.7: The Dilnot review**
>
> In 2011, the Commission on Funding of Care and Support headed by Andrew Dilnot recommended that:
>
> - the current system is 'not fit for purpose and needs urgent and lasting reform' (p 5);
> - people's lifetime contribution to the cost of their care should be capped (perhaps at £35,000);
> - the threshold beyond which people are fully responsible for the cost of their own care should be raised to £100,000;
> - people should pay a standard amount for their food and accommodation (perhaps £7,000-£10,000).

led to widespread variations across the country. The artificial barriers between health and social care lie at the heart of the problems surrounding access to continuing care funding.... The funding of long term care is a policy area that has, for ten years, been characterised by confusion, complexity and inequity. Despite the considerable investment by Government in recent years in researching, reviewing and changing systems for the funding of long term care, it seems that we are no closer to a fair and transparent system that ensures security and dignity for people who need long term care, and which promotes their independence.

Interestingly, a very different model now exists in Scotland, where older people receive free personal care at home and in care homes (a recommendation of the 1999 Royal Commission on Long-term Care that was rejected in England but taken up by the Scottish Executive; for more details see Bell and Bowes, 2006; Dickinson and Glasby, 2006). However, underneath all these rather detailed debates is a more fundamental issue about charging and ongoing issues about universalism and selectivity. For all previous attempts to promote more effective interagency working, the current system still assumes that it is ultimately possible to distinguish between health and social care, with the former free at the point of delivery and available on the basis of clinical need, and the latter subject to means testing, charging and tight eligibility criteria. While all of the above policy and practice dilemmas relate to organisational boundaries and professional cultures, they also relate to the very basic fact that one service is free and general, while the other is targeted and requires services to pay (see ***Box 4.8*** for international examples of other approaches to these issues).

Box 4.8: International approaches to charging, universalism and selectivity

In Germany, a 1994 care insurance scheme provided a number of non-means-tested benefits for home care, day care, respite care and institutional care. A new home care cash benefit was meant to be handed directly to informal carers, and the scheme pays the pension and accident insurance of a carer. The scheme was financed by additional social insurance contributions and by the loss of one day's statutory paid holiday. Claimants can also choose whether to receive formal services or to receive around half the amount in cash to pay an informal carer (see also Chapter Five, this volume).

In the Netherlands, the system is firmly rooted in a universalistic tradition, with health care funded through taxation and health insurance, and with long-term care funded by a national care fund.

In Finland, municipalities receive funds from central government for primary and secondary health services, with service users paying about 10% of the health service budget in charges. Local taxation makes up the remainder. Municipal social welfare services can be subject to charging, although the extent of this varies from area to area (but with plans to extend charges to all activities except health promotion and to increase these by up to 30-40% in social welfare and by 20% in health care).

In Denmark, there is a commitment to universal, comprehensive and tax-financed services, with medical care provided free of charge, free home nursing and home help services, and people contributing their full state pension and 60% of other income for nursing homes.

Source: Glendinning (1998)

Summary

Despite a long-standing emphasis on interagency working, UK welfare services are founded on an underlying assumption that it is possible to distinguish between health and social care, and two very different systems continue to exist to meet these needs. For all that this boundary has been blurred and has shifted over time, it still exists and continues to shape current services. While this causes significant practical difficulties for workers and for service users alike, there is a much wider issue about citizenship and about rights that lies at the heart of this problematic area of policy and practice. For all the current emphasis on public and patient involvement (see Chapter Seven), we have never really had a proper debate about how best to meet health and social care needs within scarce resources, what should be free to all as citizens and taxpayers, and what we should be expected to pay for (see *Box 4.7* for a recent incarnation of this broader debate). As a result, integrated teams that are funded with a pooled budget, managed by a single joint appointment and provide joined-up health and social services, still have to disaggregate what they do into 'health care' and 'social care' for charging purposes. Returning to the DH's (1998b, p 3) diagnosis at the start of this chapter, the critique offered in 1998 seems as true now as it was then:

> All too often when people have complex needs spanning both health and social care good quality services are sacrificed for sterile arguments about boundaries. When this happens people, often the most vulnerable in our society ... and those who care for them find themselves in the no man's land between health and social services. This is not what people want or need. It places the needs of the organisation above the needs of the people they are there to serve. It is poor organisation, poor practice, poor use of taxpayers' money – it is unacceptable.

Further reading/relevant websites

Key partnership textbooks include the following introductions and studies:

- **Barnes et al's (2005)** *Health action zones*
- **Barrett et al's (2005)** *Interprofessional working in health and social care*
- **Glasby and Littlechild's (2004)** *The health and social care divide*
- **Glendinning et al's (2002b)** *Partnerships, New Labour and the governance of welfare*
- **Meads et al's (2005)** *The case for interprofessional collaboration in health and social care*, Oxford: Blackwell/CAIPE.
- **Pollard et al's (2010)** *Understanding interprofessional working in health and social care*

For a detailed and authoritative introduction to some of the key theory and research on partnership working, one of the best books is **Sullivan and Skelcher's (2002)** *Working across boundaries*. In addition, two special editions of international academic journals focus specifically on the issue of partnership working – **Rummery's (2006a)** 'Partnerships, governance and citizenship' (*Social Policy and Society*) and **Glasby et al's (2006a)** 'Partnership working in health and social care' (*Health and Social Care in the Community*). Useful journals include:

- *International Journal of Integrated Care* (see below for further details and website)
- The UK's *Journal of Integrated Care*
- *Journal of Interprofessional Care*

For organisational culture and organisational development, **Peck's (2005)** *Organisational development in healthcare* is essential reading, as is a shorter Integrated Care Network discussion paper on *'Culture' in partnerships* **(Peck and Crawford, 2004)**.

In terms of useful websites, the following may be helpful:
www.caipe.org.uk
   The Centre for the Advancement of Interprofessional Education (CAIPE) is a national body dedicated to supporting education and training that helps workers from different backgrounds to come together to learn from and with each other
www.ijic.org
   The *International Journal of Integrated Care* is a free online journal with articles from a range of different countries and continents
http://interlinks.euro.centre.org/project
   EU-funded project exploring the provision of integrated health and social care for older people in the EU, including an interactive online resource of practice examples from different European countries

Reflection exercises

For social policy students
Imagine you were to settle on a new planet and design your ideal welfare services from scratch – how would you design and pay for health and social care on your new inter-galactic 'utopia'? If you were the current Secretary of State how would you reform the current system (given that you are not starting with a blank sheet of paper)?

For health and social care professionals and students
Using the framework in *Figure 4.1*, what kinds of relationships do you need with which local partners to achieve desired outcomes for the user group with whom you work?

Which of these relationships do you have already and how could you build links over time to develop the kind of partnerships you need to be successful?

In interagency settings

Compare your answers to the question above with colleagues from different agencies and backgrounds. To what extent do you interpret current relationships in the same way, and where do your views differ? Using the model in **Figure 4.3**, can you agree what outcomes you are each trying to achieve for local people?

For all readers

Think of a situation where you have needed to co-ordinate the activities of as range of different agencies. This could be a health and social care example or it could be from everyday life (moving house, changing phone provider etc). Where this went well, what was it that helped to produce a co-ordinated outcome? Where it didn't work, how did it feel to be on the receiving end of services that weren't joined up and why did it go wrong?

five

Independent living and the social model of disability

Overview

This chapter discusses:

- disabled people's experiences of the health and social care system;
- the tendency of underpinning legislation and our implicit assumptions to focus on a culture of 'care' and of dependency, rather than on promoting independent living;
- examples of policies and statutes that constrain disabled people's lives;
- recent policy responses, including direct payments/individual budgets in social care and the long-term conditions agenda in the NHS;
- key concepts such as a social model of disability and issues of dependence/ independence;
- the potential applicability of a social model to other user groups.

In Chapter Three, an overview of services for disabled people briefly introduced the concept of independent living, highlighting the importance of social care policies such as direct payments and NHS priorities such as the long-term conditions agenda. This chapter explores these themes in more detail, placing such issues in a broader context and developing key concepts such as a social model of disability and issues of dependence/ independence. In the process, this involves an important discussion about the potential breadth of the independent living movement, and the extent to which a social model of disability can be applied to other user groups (for example, people with learning difficulties and people with mental health problems). Like each of the substantive chapters in this book (Chapters

Four to Eight), however, this account begins with a real–life case study (***Box 5.1***) in order to illustrate the significance of the subsequent discussion. While theories are important, they matter so much because of the ability they give us to understand and respond to very significant real–life issues.

> **Box 5.1:** A personal hospital account, by Jane Campbell
>
> I have had the best of times and the worst of times at the hands of the NHS. When I was born my mother was told to take me home and enjoy me because I would be dead within the year. Well here I am at 45 defying all the medical predictions! But it should be said that my survival is a combination of bloody-mindedness and fantastic health care. Particularly dispensed by one of the best respiratory units in the country and my fantastic consultant who celebrates disabled people's lives. But it hasn't always been that way. Let me tell you a story about an experience I had.
>
> In January 2003 I was rushed in to A&E with severe pneumonia in both lungs. I was very ill. The consultant who was treating me said to me: "You're very ill. If you go into respiratory failure I presume that you won't want to be resuscitated with a ventilator." I was a little taken aback by this and said, "Well, why?" He replied that the chances of weaning me off would be very remote – "And you wouldn't want to live on a ventilator." When I said that meant I would die and of course I want to be ventilated, he looked a little puzzled but let it drop. I thought that was the end of the matter.
>
> The next day I was in intensive care when another consultant in a very senior position said the same thing. "If you go into respiratory failure – and this looks likely – then I'm sure you won't want to be anywhere near a ventilator." Again I protested but by now I was very scared. My husband tore home, got a picture of me in my graduation gown receiving my doctorate, came back to the hospital and screamed that "This is my wife, not what you think she is and has. You do everything for her just as you would for anybody in this situation. She is young and has everything to live for." Then they changed their minds. Surely extreme measures should not be needed for me to access life-saving treatment. This should be my right – a right to life. Nevertheless I forced myself to stay awake for the next 48 hours, fearful that if I went to sleep I'd never wake up.
>
> So why was my experience 18 months ago so different from an able 44-year-old professional entering A&E at the peak of his or her career? Some of the answers lie in the negative beliefs about severe disability that are still so prevalent in our society. Sadly society still sees disabled people as tragic victims of their condition or diagnosis. And in my case without dignity because I need all

physical tasks done for me. It is not unusual for me to hear "I would rather be dead than live like that." Views such as these are just as likely to be held by the medical profession as anyone else. After all they are just people drawn from a cross-section of society, subject to the same influences and negative stereotyping around disability as anyone else. It takes incredible strength to rise above these stereotypes and not to perceive them as fact. Some of us are fortunate enough to be able to challenge these assumptions. But stop and think: what if I couldn't speak up for myself, if I had no partner or carer that night to fight for my right to live?

Progress has been made but there is still a long way to go before prejudices of the kind I've described are eliminated. I would like to leave you with three messages:

1. That we start from the premise that all life is of equal value.
2. The best health care must be based on clinical need. It must not be dispensed on the basis of views about a patient's quality of life.
3. Options regarding treatment should be imparted to the patient and his/ her supporters in a neutral, calm manner using open non-prejudicial language. People can only make appropriate choices when they have clear honest information.

I believe that acceptance and celebration of diversity at this level is absolutely necessary for disabled people's equality and feelings of self-worth and safety. So long as society continues to see us in terms of our diagnosis, we will never have equal access to, or choice about, health care.

Source: Jane Campbell (2004, www.livingwithdignity.info/)

Policy context

Underpinning experiences such as those cited in ***Box 5.1*** is a legislative and policy context frequently shaped by implicit and (until recently) often unchallenged assumptions about disabled people's quality of life and about their position within society. As the former Prime Minister's Strategy Unit (2005, p 73) has argued:

> Independent living initiatives are constrained by a welfare system which assumes dependency.

> The National Assistance Act 1948 underpins later community care legislation and provides the legal definition of a disabled person [as] … someone who is 'blind, deaf or dumb, or who suffers from mental

disorder ... and persons who are substantially and permanently handicapped by illness, injury or congenital deformity...'. This definition is out of date, offensive and does not provide a useful starting point for enabling disabled people to fulfil their roles as citizens. Disabled people themselves have insisted that it is not impairment or illness in itself that determines their life chances but the social, economic and environmental barriers they face.

One of the most significant barriers to enabling disabled people to be full citizens is the culture of care and dependency within health and social care structures. Associated with this 'culture of care' is a failure to see expenditure on independent living as a form of social and economic investment. Instead of meeting disabled people's additional requirements to enable them to improve their life chances, resources are used in ways that maintain and create dependency.

While notions of care and dependency are explored in greater detail in the section on 'Key concepts' below, the results of these assumptions can be seen in a wide range of statutes and policies that shape large sections of disabled people's lives (see **Box 5.2**; see also Law Commission, 2010, 2011, for a more general critical review of community care legislation). Even where policy has had an inclusive intention, it has frequently failed to deliver such aspirations, and has ultimately tended to reinforce rather than challenge traditional assumptions.

More recent policies, in particular direct payments/individual budgets in social care and the long-term conditions agenda in the NHS, are explored in more detail below.

Key concepts

Central to any discussion of disabled people's experiences of health and social care is the concept of independent living (see also Chapter Three). As the former Disability Rights Commission (2003) explains, independent living is:

> All disabled people having the same choice, control and freedom as any other citizen – at home, at work, and as members of the community. This does not necessarily mean disabled people 'doing everything for themselves', but it does mean that any practical assistance people need should be based on their own choices and aspirations.

Box 5.2: Key policies shaping the lives of disabled people (prior to the NHS and Community Care Act 1990)

- 1940s legislation was the first to focus specifically on disabled people as a single group (for example, the Disabled Persons (Employment) Act 1944, the 1944 Education Act, the NHS Act 1946 and the National Assistance Act 1948). However, some of the egalitarian aspects of the Employment and Education Acts failed to deliver employment rights for disabled people and provided the legal mechanism for the creation of segregated special schools. Similarly, local authorities were not required to provide services, and most disabled people had to go without support or enter residential care. In the NHS, little was offered beyond acute care and long-term care (usually in a 'geriatric' ward).
- The Abortion Act 1967 enabled selective abortion for unborn children with impairments (where 'there is a substantial risk that if the child were born it would suffer from such physical or mental abnormalities as to be seriously handicapped').
- The Chronically Sick and Disabled Persons Act 1970 was intended to secure additional rights for disabled people, yet largely failed to impose additional duties on local authorities – even a list of services that local authorities should make available only needed to be provided where it was 'practical and reasonable'.
- The Education Act 1976 contained a section that would have given disabled children the right to attend mainstream schools, but this was never implemented.
- The Disabled Persons (Services, Consultation and Representation) Act 1986 was never fully implemented, and initial commitments to a right to an advocate and to a written statement of the person's needs assessment were subsequently scrapped.

Source: Oliver and Barnes (1998)

Originally developing in the US in the 1970s, what became known as the Independent Living Movement had its origins in the first Centre for Independent Living (CIL), founded in 1972 in Berkeley, California. Managed by disabled people, the role of the CIL was to provide access to peer support, advocacy and other forms of support. From here, CILs spread throughout the developed world, and began to reach Britain in the early 1980s through early projects in Hampshire and Derbyshire (see, for example, Evans, 1993; Oliver and Barnes, 1998; Barnes and Mercer, 2006). Over time, CILs and the broader Independent Living Movement have been a crucial source of new ideas and of challenge, pioneering new ways of working such as direct payments (see below for further discussion).

Closely linked to the notion of independent living is the concept of a social model of disability. Rather than seeing disability as an individual medical condition or limitation (often referred to as a medical or personal tragedy model), a social model distinguishes between a (medical) *impairment* and a (socially constructed) *disability* (see, for example, Oliver 1990; Swain et al, 2004). Thus, a person is disabled not by their impairment (their physical, psychological or mental condition), but by the way in which society discriminates against people with impairments. This is particularly well illustrated in two classic definitions of disability – with a medical model espoused by the WHO (1978) and a social model developed by disabled people's organisations (see *Box 5.3*). While a medical definition of disability concentrates on trying to cure or alleviate the individual medical condition, a social model changes the focus to the social, environmental and attitudinal barriers to disabled people enjoying full participation in social life. Nowhere is this more starkly illustrated than on the front cover of Michael Oliver's (1990) classic *The politics of disablement*, which depicts a man in a wheelchair unable to enter a polling station to vote because of a flight of steps into the building. Arguably, a social model is not only an important move away from 'blaming the victim' (someone is unable to participate because of their impairment, not because society is not geared up for people with impairments), but is also potentially more effective – if someone in a wheelchair cannot reach a light switch because it is too high, we could either invest in genetic research with a view to curing the person's impairment (an individual, medical model) or we could simply move the light switch (a social, environmental approach).

Unfortunately, all the available evidence suggests that both health and social care, although they may sometimes pay lip-service to a social model, remain heavily influenced by an individual, medical model of disability (see *Boxes 5.1* and *5.4*). In particular, progress towards a more social model approach has been limited by the tendency of formal services to create and reinforce dependency (rather than promote independence) and by the expectation that disabled people will fit into services (rather than services being personalised and responding to individual need) (Prime Minister's Strategy Unit, 2005). As Oliver and Sapey (2006, p 189) reflect in the third edition of their seminal critique of *Social work and disabled people*:

> The first edition of this book was written in the early 1980s, in the hope that the social model of disability would provide a useful basis for constructing an effective social work practice with disabled people. In the years since then, economic and

political changes, coupled with a less than inspired professional leadership of the social work profession, has meant that many of our earlier hopes have not materialised.... In this third edition of the book, we have reviewed the changes that have taken place over ... the past two decades, and concluded that the individual model of disability is so embedded in social work practice that in its current form the profession is unlikely to retain its role of working with disabled people as citizens. The citizenship approach to welfare seeks to change fundamentally the relationship that disabled people have with the welfare state, and this requires the administrators of welfare also to change fundamentally.

That this is the case is to be deeply regretted, as the contribution of the disabled people's movement has led to genuinely new understandings of disability and very real alternatives to traditional statutory services. With non-disabled allies in health and social care, this movement for more independent living could become an even more powerful force for change. As part of this process, some commentators have suggested that current professions are so dominated by medical approaches to disability that only a fundamental shift in professional culture will be sufficient to bring about longer-term change. For Finkelstein (1999a, 1999b) in particular, there is an urgent need to move away from traditional notions of professionals allied to medicine (or allied health professions) towards a new notion of 'professions allied to the community'. Committed to a social model and immersed in a disability culture, these workers would focus on disabled people's aspirations (rather than on 'care') and would be resources on which disabled people could draw (not experts who 'know best').

Central to the notion of independent living and to a social model of disability is a critique of current concepts of dependence/independence and of 'care'. While most people make a sharp distinction between independence (being able to do everything for yourself) and dependence (being reliant on others to do things for you), everyone is in reality interdependent (that is, in a modern industrial society, no one is completely independent and we all rely on other people to help meet different physical, social, emotional, financial and other needs). Thus, as Oliver (1990, p 84) argues, 'the dependence of disabled people therefore, is not a feature which marks them out as different in kind from the rest of the population but different in degree.' In practice, moreover, dependency is not the result of physical attributes, but of social processes (and we tend to talk about dependency as being socially constructed). In developing this line of reasoning, Oliver (1990) identifies three main ways in which this occurs:

Box 5.3: Medical and social models of disability

The WHO's international classification of impairments, disabilities and handicaps (1980) – a 'medical model':

IMPAIRMENT: an impairment is any loss or abnormality of psychological, physiological, or anatomical structure or function.

DISABILITY: a disability is any restriction or lack (resulting from an impairment) of ability to perform an activity in the manner or within the range considered normal for a human being.

HANDICAP: a handicap is a disadvantage for a given individual, resulting from an impairment or disability, that limits or prevents the fulfilment of a role that is normal (depending on age, sex, social and cultural factors) for that individual.

The Disabled People's International definition (1982) – a 'social model':

IMPAIRMENT: is the functional limitation within the individual caused by physical, mental or sensory impairment.

DISABILITY: is the loss or limitation of opportunities to take part in the normal life of the community on an equal level with others due to physical and social barriers.

The Union of the Physically Impaired Against Segregation definition (1976) – a 'social model':

IMPAIRMENT: lacking all or part of a limb, or having a defective limb, organ or mechanism of the body.

DISABILITY: the disadvantage or restriction of activity caused by a contemporary social organisation that takes little or no account of people who have physical impairments and thus excludes them from participation in the mainstream of social activities.

Source: For more detailed extracts from some of these documents see Oliver and Barnes (1998)

Box 5.4: Dominance of the medical model in health and social care

- There is a tendency to focus on (medically) 'curing' the impairment or working with the individual to help them 'come to terms' with it. As Oliver and Barnes (1998, p 15) suggest, 'people with impairments become objects to be treated, changed, improved and made "normal."' Thus, the emphasis is on medical intervention, rehabilitation and psychological adjustment, rather than on campaigning for broader social change.
- This has led to an over-medicalisation of disability and to doctors having considerable control over disabled people's lives. As Brisenden (1986, p 176, quoted in Oliver and Barnes, 1998, pp 15-16) argues: 'in the past, doctors have been too willing to suggest medical treatment and hospitalization, even when this would not necessarily improve the quality of life for the person concerned.'
- Health and social services tend to be dominated by professional views of 'what is best', with the expert being seen as the practitioner, not the person with experience of living with the particular condition. Although several official policies now emphasise the importance of ensuring the economic well-being of service users, most health and social care services have not used their positions as a major local employer to tackle widespread unemployment and poverty among disabled people (let alone recognising that having experience of living with an impairment could be a good preparation for supporting others).
- Arising out of this, services are often dominated by a narrow focus on health and social care (and on eligibility criteria, needs assessment and professional gatekeeping), rather than on the things that disabled people say are important to them (and indeed to all of us): employment, education, income, adequate housing, meaningful relationships etc.

- An *economic* basis for the creation of dependency – with industrialisation and urbanisation, emphasis on paid work has increased, and new mechanisms (such as the workhouses and the Poor Law described in Chapter Two) were needed to control those deemed economically unproductive. Even after the end of the Poor Law, disabled people are often denied access to employment and hence kept financially dependent.
- A *political* basis for the creation of dependency – with a patronising political emphasis on helping those who cannot help themselves ('looking after' the dependent), rather than on giving rights to disabled people.
- A *professional* basis for the creation of dependency – with institutional practices, segregated provision and a failure to involve disabled people

in decision making in meaningful ways. Even the notion and language of the professional–client relationship is dependency creating, and emphasises the power imbalance that exists in the system. This quickly leads to an overemphasis on 'care' – doing things *to* and *for* disabled people rather than working *with* them to ensure that they are able to fulfil their citizen rights to choice and control over their own lives. Of course, such professionally created dependency is more than a little ironic as it is arguably the professionals who are most dependent on disabled people (for their careers, their salaries and their quality of life).

Despite the important insights that a social model provides, questions remain about the extent to which such an approach can be applicable to other user groups. Historically, the social model is most associated with younger people with physical impairments, and the Independent Living Movement is sometimes seen as not being as inclusive as it might be for groups such as older people, people with learning difficulties and people with mental health problems. On the one hand, there is significant strength in numbers, and each of these groups undoubtedly has a shared experience of discrimination and exclusion in common. While service responses to such groups tend to be dominated by individual, medical approaches, a broader social model could move the debate away from some of the impairment-specific factors that divide people to a wider and more inclusive focus on challenging oppression and asserting civil rights. As Peter Beresford (2000, 2002) has argued, people with mental health problems have much in common with people with physical impairments:

- a tendency by services to 'lump' (Beresford, 2000, p 169) these groups together (whether they like it or not);
- significant overlaps between the two groups (with some people having both physical impairments and mental health problems – see Morris, 2004, for an excellent study on this topic);
- a shared experience of discrimination and oppression.

However, there are also key differences, including some disabled people not wanting to be associated with people with mental health problems, some people with mental health problems not viewing themselves as having an impairment, and some key texts and writings of the disabled people's movement seeming to pay little attention to mental health. Similar debates and challenges also exist in other service settings. Thus, some older people and some people with learning difficulties feel that they can be excluded from the wider disability movement, and that the social barriers they face are inherent to their impairment (Chappell et al, 2001; Williams and Heslop, 2005).

Overall, however, there seems to be considerable potential for a broader approach to 'disability' that is inclusive in nature and that focuses not on individual medical diagnoses so much as a social model of disability and the social processes by which 'disabled people' (in the broadest sense) are discriminated against and excluded (see, for example, Chappell et al, 2001; Beattie et al, 2005; Gilliard et al, 2005; Race et al, 2005; Williams and Heslop, 2005). A good example of such potential is Shaping Our Lives – the national user-led organisation – whose work is cited in *Box 5.5*. Ultimately, as Gilliard et al (2005) suggest:

> Disability rights activists were initially slow to include people with cognitive impairment within the social model and the disability rights movement and it continues to largely exclude people with dementia. It may be that the social model can go

---

Box 5.5: Shaping Our Lives

Shaping Our Lives National User Network is an independent user-controlled organisation. It started as a research and development project but became an independent organisation in 2002....

Shaping Our Lives National User Network's vision is of a society that is equal and fair where all people have the same opportunities, choices, rights and responsibilities. A society where people have choice and control over the way they live and the support services they use.... We work with a wide and diverse range of service users. We do not discriminate on the basis of race and ethnicity, sexual orientation, gender, age, or religious belief. Here are some of the people we work with:

- people with physical and/or sensory impairments
- people with learning difficulties
- users and survivors of mental health services
- young people with experience of being 'looked after'
- people living with HIV/AIDS
- people with life-limiting illnesses
- older people
- people with experience of alcohol and drug services

Source: www.shapingourlives.org.uk

some way to inform our understanding and practices, but it is not yet sufficiently all-embracing.... However, our research findings underline how important it is to continue trying to situate our understandings of dementia care issues within a social model. As Oldman and Beresford (2000) argue, the social model is *the* way to get professionals to stop arguing that nothing can be done because a condition is chronic.

Policy and practice dilemmas

Against this background, current health and social care policy and practice have remained relatively resistant to the challenges of the Independent Living Movement (see *Box 5.4* earlier). As a result, many of the most exciting developments in recent policy and practice have come not from policy makers or front-line professionals, but from organisations of disabled people developing alternative approaches (see Chapter Seven for further discussion of user-led alternatives to statutory services).

In social care, a classic example is provided by direct payments – with the Community Care (Direct Payments) Act 1996 described as holding out 'the potential for the most fundamental reorganisation of welfare for half a century' (Oliver and Sapey, 1999, p 175). Under this legislation – long campaigned for by organisations of disabled people – local authorities could give cash sums to disabled people (initially aged 18-65) to purchase their own services or hire their own personal assistants (PAs). Initially discretionary, this later became mandatory, was a key performance indicator for SSDs and was extended to older people, carers, younger disabled people and people with parental responsibility for disabled children. Although the UK scheme has distinctive features, this is part of a broader move away from directly provided services towards more personalised forms of provision and greater user control (what the US calls 'consumer-directed care') (see *Box 5.6*). Overall, the available evidence suggests that direct payments can lead to greater choice and control, greater satisfaction, greater continuity of care and fewer unmet needs, with direct payment recipients frequently designing support that is more creative and innovative than the direct services that a local authority could provide (for a summary of the evidence see Leese and Bornat, 2006; Glasby and Littlechild, 2009; Carr, 2010).

From the beginning, it was disabled people who advocated for this way of working, lobbied Parliament for legislation, commissioned independent (and highly effective) research to explore the issues at stake and now provide much of the guidance and support to make direct payments work. As set out above, a crucial aspect of direct payments has been the role of CILs, organisations of disabled people providing peer support, positive role

Box 5.6: International examples of 'consumer-directed care'

Within the UK there are at least three different approaches to self-directed support (the Independent Living Fund, direct payments and In Control's system that includes the concept of an individual budget).

Within the US there are numerous initiatives and there are significant variations within these models, not only between states, but also at county level. Moreover there are many such systems in other countries:

- Germany's Social Insurance scheme enables people to take their funding as cash.
- France's *Prestation Spécifique Dépendance* gives cash to disabled people for support.
- Austria has an individualised funding programme called Cash Allowance for Care.
- There are several Canadian initiatives, for example, the Individualised Quality of Life Project in Ontario.
- There are some Australian programmes, for example, Future for Young Adults in Victoria.
- New Zealand has an Individualised Funding programme.
- In Sweden the Personal Assistance Act created a system of direct funding for support.
- In the Netherlands there is a system of personal budgets (*persoosgebondenbudget*).

To date, most schemes tend to have a limited focus: some serve older people while others are just for younger adults. People with learning difficulties are often excluded altogether. This tendency to limit approaches to service-defined labels has the impact of reinforcing traditional, system-focused models of care delivery. (See, for example, Halloran, 1998; Robbins, 2006; Glasby and Littlechild, 2009.)

Source: O'Brien and Duffy, 2009, p 144

models and practical advice to other disabled people. While the pattern is not always uniform, those authorities with successful direct payments schemes often seem to have a well-funded and active CIL, and the evidence suggests that the presence of user-led support services can be a key factor in shaping the uptake of direct payments (see Glasby and Littlechild, 2009, for an overview). Unfortunately, recent evidence suggests that this way of working is increasingly under threat. Although the former Prime Minister's

Strategy Unit (2005) recommended that each local authority should have a user-led organisation (modelled on existing CILs) by 2010, the most comprehensive review to date of current user-led organisations found that many face significant financial pressures and were also running the risk of alienating their funders through broader campaigning and awareness-raising work (Barnes and Mercer, 2006). In a difficult financial context, there remains a clear danger that service user-led organisations providing peer support and critical challenge could be hard hit by cuts in public spending.

More recently, the concept of direct payments has been developed into the broader and potentially even more exciting notion of personal budgets. Rather than assessing someone's needs and selecting services from (an often fairly limited) menu of options, personal budgets start by placing each individual into a cost band and being up front about the resources available. Knowing how much money is available to spend on their needs then allows the person and their circle of support to make decisions about how this money could best be spent (via direct services, direct payments, public services, the independent sector, paying family and friends or any combination of the above). Although initially a small pilot programme with people with learning difficulties in six local authorities, this way of working has since been championed by successive governments, who have committed to ensuring that all adult social care will be delivered via personal budgets in future (except in an emergency). There are also pilots taking place in health care and in children's services, as well as broader debate about scope to extend these concepts to other sectors (including criminal justice, tax and benefits, education, housing and beyond; see Glasby and Littlechild, 2009, for an overview in adult social care and Needham, 2010, 2011, for a broader study of the spread of personalisation; see also **Box 5.7**). By September 2010, it was estimated that some 244,000 people with ongoing support needs had a personal budget (ADASS, 2010), and by mid-2011 the figure was believed to be around 340,000 people.

In health care, policy and practice is much less influenced by service user-led alternatives, and remains dominated by the imperative to reduce emergency hospital admissions and improve support for people with long-term conditions (sometimes referred to as chronic disease management). With the NHS weighted towards acute, episodic care, people with multiple long-term conditions often receive poorly co-ordinated support, with services fragmented between health and social care and between the community and hospital. In recent years, there is growing evidence that poor management of chronic diseases can lead to a waste of scarce resources and can consume significant proportions of current NHS time and expenditure. Indeed, the DH estimates that one in three members of the population have a long-term condition, but that 70% of the primary

Box 5.7: Debi and Ryan's story

Ryan has various complex needs and has been receiving direct payments for his care for around a year. Previously we were receiving respite – or 'stresspite' as we called it – and as a family we felt it wasn't working and making us feel very isolated. As a working mum I needed more flexibility and choice in how we were supported.

The introduction of direct payments for Ryan's care gave us the choice and control we needed. We can ensure Ryan is involved with mainstream life and we have been able to build and expand our community network.

We now have two personal assistants for Ryan, with whom he has built strong relationships and we are able to do much more. Ryan is getting grounded in his own community and gaining real life experiences for his journey throughout life. Ryan is a valued member of society who can give something back and best of all we are ensuring he is part of 'mainstream life'.

I remember recently Mo's (one of Ryan's personal assistants) mum saying since she had Ryan in her life she has built more relationships with neighbours and people on her street than in the last 20 years because with Ryan's outgoing lively nature nobody can walk past him in the garden without talking to him and enjoying him! Ryan gives so much back.

Recently Ryan's school asked for our consent for him to take part in a 'casting' day for the BBC who were looking for children who were confident in front of a camera and talked spontaneously. This was Ryan's moment and being a very chatty boy he actually got a part in a new programme on CBeebies called Mr Bloom's Nursery.

We have held such a positive attitude and high expectations for Ryan from a young age and we are so proud of him being a person in his own right. Anybody who meets him would say what a 'character' he is and now he actually gets paid to perform!

For this and other personal stories, visit: www.in-control.org.uk/support/support-for-individuals-family-members-carers/personal-stories.aspx

and acute budget in England is spent on the care and treatment of people with long-term conditions. Thus, two thirds of the NHS budget is spent on one third of the population (see *Box 5.8*).

In response, successive governments have promoted policies designed to improve support for people with long-term conditions. This ranges from an NSF (DH, 2005b) to a greater emphasis on supporting people to self-care (DH, 2001f, 2004c, 2005c, 2005d, 2005e, 2005f, 2006d) and from greater use of new technology to case management and more integrated teams (DH, 2005g, 2006a). However, central to recent policy has been the lessons drawn from a North American not-for-profit organisation, Kaiser Permanente, which suggest that Kaiser is able to use around one third of

---

Box 5.8: Ten things you need to know about long-term conditions

1. Around 15 million people in England, or almost one in three of the population, have a long-term condition. This number has fallen in recent years: as people become better able and supported to manage their condition, some no longer report having one.

2. Half of people aged over 60 in England have a long-term condition.

3. While the number of people in England with a long-term condition is likely to remain relatively steady, the number of people with comorbidities is expected to rise by a third in the next 10 years.

4. People with long-term conditions are the most frequent users of health care services. Those with long-term conditions account for 29% of the population, but use 50% of all GP appointments and 70% of all inpatient bed days.

5. It is estimated that the treatment and care of those with long-term conditions accounts for 70% of the primary and acute care budget in England. This means around one third of the population account for over two thirds of the spend.

6. 7.1 million people have clinically identified hypertension. It is estimated that the same number again have unidentified hypertension, meaning that over a quarter of the population has the condition.

7. Common mental health problems affect about one in seven of the adult population, with severe mental health problems affecting one in a hundred.

8. The proportion of people with a limiting long-term condition in work is a third lower than for those who don't.

9. Long-term conditions fall more heavily on the poorest in society: compared to social class I, people in social class V have 60% higher prevalence of long term conditions and 60% higher severity of conditions.

10. Around 170,000 people die prematurely in England each year in total, with main causes being cancers and circulatory diseases. And those with long-term conditions are likely to have a lower quality of life.

Source: www.dh.gov.uk/en/Healthcare/Longtermconditions/tenthingsyouneedtoknow/index.htm

the bed days utilised by the NHS as a result of a range of factors, including (Ham, 2005, 2006; Curry and Ham, 2010; see also ***Box 5.9***):

• *Integrated care* across the community–hospital divide, with specialists working alongside generalists in the community and patients able to move easily from community to hospital and back again.

Box 5.9: International approaches to long-term conditions

In the US, key approaches include models developed by Kaiser Permanente, EverCare and Pfizer, with the former focusing on integrating services and removing distinctions between primary and secondary care, and the last two approaches concentrating on targeting those at highest risk of hospitalisation.

In France, support for people with long-term conditions is based around regional systems, with an emphasis on population-based prevention, continuity of care and physician involvement in decision making, and with a combination of specialised medical care, assistive technology and home support.

In Denmark, institution-based long-term care services are being remodelled into national home-based and community-based services, drawing on the internationally recognised chronic care model (among other sources).

In Germany, initial medical opposition is now giving way to a greater emphasis on disease-specific programmes and on new incentives to co-ordinate care for people with long-term conditions.

In the Netherlands, a system of 'transmural care' is designed to bridge the gap between hospital and community services.

In Australia, there have been various trials of co-ordinated care models, and a new national strategy for long-term conditions is being developed.

In Singapore, a new chronic care framework is placing emphasis on primary care and self-care.

A key factor is the promotion of self-management, whether this be via the Expert Patients Programme in England, the Sharing Care Initiative in Australia or Care Plus in New Zealand.

Source: Ham (2005, 2006); Singh and Ham (2006); Powell Davies et al (2009)

- A focus on *chronic disease management*, with a combination of prevention, self-management, disease management and case management for more complex needs. This is often portrayed in terms of a triangle of care (see **Figure 5.1**), with different responses appropriate at different degrees of need.

Figure 5.1: *Long-term conditions triangle of care*

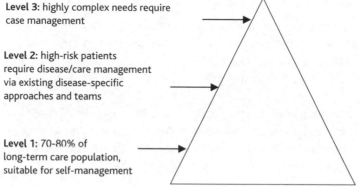

Level 3: highly complex needs require case management

Level 2: high-risk patients require disease/care management via existing disease-specific approaches and teams

Level 1: 70-80% of long-term care population, suitable for self-management

Source: Adapted from DH (2005f, p 10)

In the UK, this has been taken forward via an official long-term conditions model based around (DH, 2010c):

- *Case management*: dedicated one to one support for people from a highly skilled health professional (e.g. a community matron) with regular face to face contact.
- *Personalised care planning*: placing the person at the centre of decision making about their care and agreeing a plan of how that care will be delivered.
- *Support people to self care*: providing people with information and skills to make day to day decisions about the way they manage their health. This has included developing the Expert Patients Programme.
- *Assistive technology*: using emerging telecare and telehealth technology and telephone coaching arrangements to support people to remain independent and self care for as long as possible.

Despite this welcome extra focus on long-term conditions, it remains to be seen whether current models and approaches are sufficient to rebalance the whole health and social care system, and whether new case managers can link sufficiently with mainstream health and social care services to begin to deliver the high hopes that have been placed on them. After all, genuinely responding to the needs of people with long-term conditions might require a fundamental rebalancing of the health care system away from current hospital-based provision towards care closer to home – and hospital-based services have often shown themselves to be powerful players able to resist significant calls for change (see Chapter Two). At the same time, the focus to date on 'community matrons' and 'chronic disease' has given the long-term conditions agenda a strong NHS flavour, and there is much less certainty about the role of social care. As a classic example, there is currently little clarity about how the government's long-term conditions model (*Figure 5.1*) fits those developed in social care around the preventative agenda (see *Figure 3.1* in Chapter Three). There is also little recognition that this NHS policy draws heavily on previous case management pilots in social care (see, for example, Challis et al, 1995, 2002), which in many ways were the inspiration for the NHS and Community Care Act 1990. Indeed, the system of 'care management' introduced in 1990 was initially to be called 'case management' until patients complained that they were not 'cases' to be managed by professionals and the name was changed.

Away from health and social care, a further issue for disabled people's services is the reform of social security and a range of recent policies designed to support disabled people to enter paid employment. With access to work a key priority for the previous New Labour government, disabled people have previously been able to access the government's New Deal for Disabled People and Pathways to Work pilots. More recently such measures have been accompanied by changes to the social security system in order to reduce the number of claimants of Incapacity Benefit (now Employment Support Allowance), a new, more stringent Work Capability Assessment, greater use of private companies to support people back to work and claims in the press that 'half a million "sick" are fit to work' (Hennessy, 2011). While proposed changes have been criticised by those concerned about an overly punitive approach and the financial consequences on the lives of disabled people on low incomes, one of the major limitations of the reforms seems to be the emphasis on changing the perceived behaviour of the disabled person, rather than on tackling the attitudes of employers, the physical environment in the workplace and access to public transport. Once again, it seems, a policy that emphasises that 'ensuring citizens have the right to enter the world of work is a fundamental responsibility of any government' (DWP, 2006, p 2) quickly retreats back into individual explanations, and the chance to promote more radical social, political and environmental change may not be taken up. This seems even more of a danger in a difficult international economic context, making finding work hard for growing numbers of people whether or not they have a physical impairment.

Summary

Services for people with physical impairments and with long-term conditions are an important policy priority, yet there seems to be two different (and potentially incompatible) contributing factors:

- On the one hand is an Independent Living Movement committed to civil rights and to full participation in society for all disabled people. It is this group of people who developed and promoted the notion of a social model of disability, who are reaching out to other user groups to develop broader coalitions, who successfully campaigned for direct payments and who support other disabled people through CILs. In many ways, this perspective is best illustrated by the ground-breaking *Life chances* document produced by the former Prime Minister's Strategy Unit (2005).
- On the other hand is an approach more associated with the NHS and with the DH, which sees support for disabled people and people with long-term conditions as a key way of reducing emergency hospital admissions and reducing current and future costs.

In many ways, a similar tension was evident during the mid-1990s' debate about the introduction of direct payments, with an uneasy alliance of civil rights campaigners (keen to promote the rights of disabled people) and neo-liberal policy makers (keen to role back the frontiers of the welfare state) both seemingly in favour of direct payments. Over time (and hardly surprisingly), these groups later began to diverge, and a series of underlying tensions began to emerge (for a summary see Glasby and Littlechild, 2009). Under the Coalition and in a difficult financial context it is possible that the same could happen again with the more recent concept of personal budgets, which again can be taken up from a citizenship perspective or from more of a neo-liberal desire to 'roll back the boundaries of the welfare state' (see Spandler, 2004; Rummery, 2006b; Ferguson, 2007, for more critical discussion; see also Needham, 2011 for a study of the spread of personalisation and the ways in which difficult stakeholders perceive this agenda). More broadly, there remains an ongoing tension between official NHS policies focused on 'chronic disease management' and emergency hospital admissions on the one hand, and a civil rights movement which seeks to achieve choice, control and independence on the other. Central to this debate is whether or not the lives of disabled people are best improved by more and better health and social services, or by rights, inclusion and greater choices and control. While both stances may be cloaked in the same language, they tend to adopt very different definitions of 'disability', take very different approaches and hence might be expected to lead to very different outcomes.

Further reading/relevant websites

Central to any analysis of independent living and a social model of disability are textbooks by leading disabled campaigners and academics such as Michael Oliver, Colin Barnes and Jane Campbell. See for example:

- **Barnes and Mercer's (2006)** *Independent futures: Creating user-led disability services in a disabling society*
- **Campbell and Oliver's (1996)** *Disability politics*
- **Oliver's (1990)** seminal *The politics of disablement*
- **Oliver and Barnes' (1998)** *Disabled people and social policy*
- **Oliver and Sapey's (2006)** *Social work with disabled people*

Also useful is the broad overview provided in **Swain et al's (2004)** *Disabling barriers – Enabling environments* and the inter-agency focus of **French and Swain's (2011)** *Working with disabled people in policy and practice: A social model*

For direct payments and individual budgets, key resources include:

- **Leese and Bornat's (2006)** *Developments in direct payments*
- **Glasby and Littlechild's (2009)** *Direct payments and personal budgets*
- **SCIE's (2010)** *Personalisation: A rough guide* **(Carr, 2010, revised edition)**
- Work by **Catherine Needham (2010, 2011)** on the nature and spread of personalisation

For long-term conditions, see:

- The **DH's (2004a)** *Chronic disease management*
- Summaries of national and international models and developments by **Ham (2005, 2006; Singh and Ham, 2006), Parker (2009)** and **Powell Davies et al (2009)**
- **The Health Foundation's (2011)** review of the evidence on self-management

Key websites include:

www.centreforwelfarereform.org
   The Centre for Welfare Reform, a think tank run by Simon Duffy, pioneer of the concept of personal budgets and former founder of In Control
www.ukdpc.net/index.asp
   UK Disabled People's Council – the umbrella organisation for disabled people's organisations

www.in-control.org.uk
> In Control, a national social innovation network which pioneered the concept of personal budgets

www.leeds.ac.uk/disability-studies
> The leading UK Centre for Disability Studies, University of Leeds, also houses an online Disability Archive with open access to a large collection of key material (including early campaigns and writings by disabled activists that are unavailable elsewhere)

www.livingwithdignity.info
> The website of Baroness Jane Campbell, a leading disabled activist and campaigner, with information on independent living and news on the campaign against euthanasia and proposed legislation on assisted dying

www.ncil.org.uk
> The National Centre for Independent Living, a national disabled person's organisation with resources on direct payments and independent living

www.officefordisability.gov.uk
> The government's Office for Disability Issues, with full details of government policy and publications

www.puttingpeoplefirst.org.uk
> An official website hosting a range of policy and practice documents about personalisation

Reflection exercises

For social policy students

List the key policies that affect the lives of disabled people – which are influenced by a medical model and which by a social model? How would current health and social care policy be different if it was genuinely underpinned by a commitment to a social model of disability?

For health and social care professionals and students

Which models of disability are you taught when your profession is training, and which models do you see in action in your daily work? Does this differ for other professions and, if so, how? Talk to some of the disabled people and people with a long-term condition with whom you work – what models do they use and/or make sense to them?

If you are not already familiar with the concepts of direct payments and personal budgets, find out how your area approaches these issues. How many direct payment/personal budget recipients are there, what do disabled people say about the pros and cons of these approaches and what support do they receive?

In interagency settings

Compare and contrast the models of disability which predominate in different health and social care professions and the language used in official policies and procedures. How does each model influence your practice, and how might you practise differently if your agency or profession was more influenced by a social model of disability? Wherever possible, explore these issues in a multidisciplinary team setting.

For all readers

To what extent and in what ways do the approaches of the previous New Labour and the current Coalition government differ, and what impact might these have on the lives of disabled people?

If you were a government minister, where would you focus in order to have the maximum impact on the lives of disabled people and people with long-term conditions – health care, social care, social security, housing, income, civil rights etc?

six

Anti-discriminatory practice and social inclusion

Overview

This chapter discusses:

- the founding principles of the UK welfare state and the long-standing commitment to equality and to treating equal need in the same way;
- the importance of recognising that people do not start equal and so treating everyone the same way can perpetuate or exacerbate existing inequalities;
- the experience of various groups who face discrimination and the policy measures developed to respond to this;
- the importance of theoretical approaches that focus on the process and experience of discrimination, rather than individual manifestations of it (for example, racism, sexism etc);
- current key issues, such as discrimination in mental health services, accusations of institutional racism and more recent shifts away from preventing discrimination to more positive duties to promote equality.

Challenging discrimination is a key element of many health and social care professions (at least in terms of their formal codes of conduct – see *Box 6.2*) and is enshrined in legislation, in government policy and in organisational policies and procedures. However, in practice, the achievements of health and social care in this area have been mixed, and much more remains to be done. Against this background, this chapter explores the current policy context, before focusing on some useful theoretical frameworks that help to explore issues of discrimination and reflect on current policy and practice dilemmas. In order to provide something of a 'human face' to some of the theoretical and policy issues below, ***Box 6.1*** begins with an everyday example of some of the issues at stake.

Box 6.1: Discrimination in practice: a case study

James is an older Afro-Caribbean man starting to need help form health and social care as he becomes more frail. When trying to access local services, he found that most staff and other service users were from a white UK background, that it was difficult to cater for his dietary needs and that some service users subjected him to racist remarks. He often found that staff did nothing to stop this, and sometimes even joined in – seeing this as 'gentle teasing' and 'banter' rather than anything worse. Many other service users were also women and he was keen to find some male friends as well.

Policy context

A core and enduring feature of the UK welfare state is its commitment to equality and to treating people on the basis of need rather than of ability to pay. Nowhere is this more apparent than in the foundation of the NHS itself, with the NHS Act 1946 pronouncing that:

> The NHS Act 1946 provides ... a complete and medical service free of charge at the time it is required for every citizen. (Introduction to the NHS Act 1946)

These beliefs are firmly held, and have been constantly repeated throughout the history of the NHS. Thus, the trade union Unison (2002, p 3), in writing about *What's good about the NHS*, emphasised that the aim of the NHS is 'to provide to the entire population of the UK health care free at the point of delivery. Its aim was to treat all alike on the basis of need and not the ability to pay.' Similarly, the former *NHS Plan* (DH, 2000a, p 2) reiterated that:

> The NHS is the public service most valued by the British people. Ever since its creation in 1948, the NHS has been available when we've needed it and has removed the fear of paying for treatment when we are ill. Its founding principles of providing access to care to all on the basis of need, not ability to pay, remain as important today as in 1948.

Nor does this apply merely to the ability to pay – in many ways health and social care are underpinned by notions of 'unconditional positive regard' (see, for example, Thompson, 2005, pp 119-20) in which practitioners seek to work constructively with all service users (not just those they approve of). Arising out of this, the professional codes and guidance of many of the health and social care professions emphasise the importance of treating everyone the same and of guarding against the dangers of discriminating against particular groups or individuals (see *Box 6.2*). The NHS Constitution (NHS, 2010, p 18) is also clear that:

Box 6.2: Professional commitments to preventing discrimination

The General Social Care Council (GSCC) (2010, p 13) code of practice emphasises that social care workers should 'protect the rights and promote the interests of service users and carers'. This includes:

- Treating each person as an individual
- Respecting and, where appropriate, promoting the individual views and wishes of both service users and carers...
- Promoting equal opportunities for service users and carers
- Respecting diversity and different cultures and values

The duties of a doctor registered with the General Medical Council (GMC) (2006) include a requirement to 'make the care of your patient your first concern' and 'treat patients as individuals and respect their dignity' (www.gmc-uk.org/guidance/ethical_guidance/7162.asp). Additional guidance for doctors makes it clear that doctors must respect their patients' life choices and beliefs and must not unfairly discriminate against patients by allowing their personal views to affect adversely their professional relationship with them or the treatment they provide or arrange. This includes views about a patient's age, colour, culture, disability, ethnic or national origin, gender, lifestyle, marital or parental status, race, religion or beliefs, sex, sexual orientation, or social or economic status (www.gmc-uk.org/about/valuing_diversity_index.asp).

The Nursing and Midwifery Council (NMC) (2004, p 5) code of professional conduct is clear that nurses 'must treat people as individuals and respect their dignity', 'must not discriminate in any way against those in your care' and 'must demonstrate a personal and professional commitment to equality and diversity' (www.nmc-uk.org/Nurses-and-midwives/The-code/The-code-in-full).

> You have the right not to be discriminated against by the NHS based on your gender, race, religion or belief, sexual orientation or disability (that includes learning disability or mental illness).

While health and social care state their commitment to avoiding discrimination, the universalism on which the welfare state is founded is problematic in two key areas:

- Treating everybody the same does not recognise the fact that different groups start from unequal positions. Rather than leading to equality, treating everybody equally could actually perpetuate existing inequalities.
- Despite our commitment to treating people on the basis of need, many of our services have been designed from the perspective of dominant groups within society (often white, middle-class, heterosexual men), and (perhaps unwittingly) discriminate against other groups (see the example in **Box 6.1**).

More recently, the public spending cuts being implemented by the Coalition government have been criticised by a range of commentators for the ways in which they may damage equity and hit the poorest hardest. Despite government claims that 'we're all in this together', key concerns have been raised by groups as diverse as the Institute for Fiscal Studies (Elliot, 2010), the Social Policy Association (Yeates et al, 2011) and the Campaign for a Fair Society (www.campaignforafairsociety.org) (see HM Government, 2011b, for an alternative view).

Against this background, there is considerable evidence to suggest that various marginalised groups within UK society can have negative experiences of health and social care, which perpetuate or even exacerbate the discrimination they face in wider society. While this is dealt with in detail elsewhere (see, for example, Langan and Day, 1992; Bytheway, 1995; Ahmad and Atkin, 1996; Oliver and Barnes, 1998; Morris, 2004), some examples from mental health services – a key area of recent debate – are set out in **Box 6.3** (and explored in more detail in 'Policy and practice dilemmas' later).

In response to situations such as this, there have been a series of statutes and policies that have sought to challenge discrimination, now brought together in the Equality Act 2010 (see **Box 6.4**). Of course, similar issues also exist in other countries, and some international examples are set out in **Box 6.5**. However, over time, UK policy (and the response of various marginalised groups) has shifted between different approaches. This is often characterised in different ways, but the framework provided by Dominelli (2002) is a helpful way of exploring this issue. For Dominelli, powerful groups within society can respond in one of three ways:

Box 6.3: Discrimination in UK health and social care: an example from mental health

In mental health services, all the available evidence suggests that black people are more likely to experience more coercive forms of treatment (such as compulsory admission to hospital, admission via contact with the police, excessive use of drug treatments etc).

Women may also be disproportionately represented in some sections of the system – more likely than men to be treated for conditions such as depression and anxiety, less likely to receive prompt treatment as a result of a tendency to focus on the needs of men (who are perceived as being more potentially violent) and often having experienced some form of sexual or physical abuse (or both). Despite the latter, inpatient mental health services in particular have been the subject of ongoing allegations of sexual harassment.

Unlike other areas of the health system (where people in higher socioeconomic positions tend to have more contact with services), those from lower social classes are over-represented in mental health services. Above all, the evidence suggests that poorer people are more likely than richer people to experience coercive rather than voluntary forms of treatment and biological rather than psychological interventions. While social stresses may contribute to the incidence of mental ill health, it is also possible that a 'cultural gap' between some mental health workers (who may come from very different class backgrounds) and their patients may have a part to play.

Although legalised in 1967, homosexuality continues to be seen as a form of mental illness by some groups, and people's sexuality is often inappropriately seen as a contributing factor to their mental health problem. All the evidence suggests that gay men, lesbians and bisexual people can experience discrimination and victimisation in mental health services and that services sometimes try to 'cure' their sexuality or to use it to explain their mental distress.

As explored in earlier chapters, disabled people frequently experience physical and attitudinal barriers when trying to access mental health services, people with learning difficulties can be denied access to specialist mental health provision altogether and older people with mental health problems can often be seen as no one's priority at all.

Source: Summarised in Lester and Glasby (2010, ch 9)

- *Demarcationist:* powerful groups adopt a hierarchical view, focusing on keeping power for themselves and sustaining the status quo (viewing issues in terms of 'us' and 'them') – at the extreme end of this approach is a policy like Apartheid.
- *Incorporationist:* emphasises assimilation into the dominant group. This maintains the privileged position of the elite, but allows other groups to enter its ranks as long as they 'know their place' and 'keep their distance'. This can lead to small-scale change, provided it does not challenge the existing order.

Box 6.4: The Equality Act 2010

The Equality Act 2010 brings together a number of existing laws into one place so that it is easier to use. It sets out the personal characteristics that are protected by the law and the behaviour that is unlawful.... The 'protected characteristics' under the Act are (in alphabetical order):

- Age
- Disability
- Gender reassignment
- Marriage and civil partnership
- Pregnancy and maternity
- Race
- Religion and belief
- Sex
- Sexual orientation

Under the Act people are not allowed to discriminate, harass or victimise another person because they have any of the protected characteristics....

- Discrimination means treating one person worse than another because of a protected characteristic (known as direct discrimination); or
- Putting in place a rule or policy or way of doing things that has a worse impact on someone with a protected characteristic than someone without one, when this cannot be objectively justified (known as indirect discrimination).
- Harassment includes unwanted conduct related to a protected characteristic which has the purpose or effect of violating someone's dignity or which creates a hostile, degrading, humiliating or offensive environment for someone with a protected characteristic.
- Victimisation is treating someone unfavourably because they have taken (or might be taking) action under the Equality Act or supporting somebody who is doing so.

Source: www.equalityhumanrights.com/advice-and-guidance/new-equality-act-guidance/ten-key-questions-about-the-act/

> ## Box 6.5: Discrimination in an international context
>
> The Treaty of Waitangi is New Zealand's founding document, and establishes a special relationship between the Crown and Maori. Current health services are based on a series of key principles, including a commitment that Maori should have at least the same level of health as non-Maori and that Maori cultural concepts, values and practices should be protected (see www.maorihealth.govt.nz).
>
> In Western Australia, the Office of Aboriginal Health works in partnership with Aboriginal communities and Torres Strait Islander people to develop culturally appropriate health care services (see www.aboriginal.health.wa.gov.au).
>
> In the US, there are some four million people who can claim American Indian or Alaska Native ancestry, living on nearly 300 reservations in 48 states and speaking more than 300 languages. With worse health than the general population, this community can be difficult to reach because of its diverse and dispersed nature (for a web resource on American Indian health see http://americanindianhealth. nlm.nih.gov/).

- *Egalitarian:* seeks to change the system to be more egalitarian and inclusive of difference on an equal basis.

In the same way, those on the receiving end of discrimination can adopt a similar threefold approach (see Chapter Seven for further discussion):

- *Acceptance:* endorsing the status quo and accepting one's position uncritically.
- *Accommodation:* mildly critiquing the current system, but seeing one's interests best served by maximising opportunities within the current order (and may accept the system if it works consistently in their favour).
- *Rejection:* fully rejecting and devising alternatives to the current social order, based on a vision of a more just society.

Key concepts

Central to many of these issues is the notion of social divisions. As G. Payne (2000, p 1) suggests:

> It is impossible to begin to think about people without immediately encountering 'social divisions'. We automatically perceive other human beings as being male or female, black

or white, older or younger, richer or poorer, sick or well, or
friend or foe. In forming a perception of them, we place them
in pigeonholes, adapting our behaviours and attitude to them
in terms of the slots into which we have placed them.

In such a situation, there are two common responses: the development
of *typifications* and the development of *stereotypes*. Whereas the former is a
helpful shorthand or set of characteristics that we associate with a particular
group (and thus a helpful way of making sense of the world), the latter
is often negative and is based on assumptions that we continue to apply,
even when we have evidence to challenge our preconceived ideas. If we
hold negative views about black people, for example, we might continue
to hold them about black people in general, viewing one black person that
we meet as 'the exception to the rule' (Thompson, 2006).

While many social divisions may appear to be biological categories, they
are often social constructions. Thus, differences between men and women
may be biological (their sex), but can also be social (gender or the roles that
we ascribe to men and women in our particular society and point in time).
Similarly, 'race' is often portrayed as a biological category, yet is actually
social in its origins – there are more biological differences between people
of the same 'race' or skin colour than there are between different 'races'
(see, for example, Blackburn, 2000). In Chapter Five, a similar distinction
was drawn between (biological) impairment and (socially created) disability.
Thus, underpinning many forms of discrimination can be an assumption
that something is 'natural' and inevitable, when often it is social and capable
of being changed. Also at stake is the difference between a statistical norm
and an ideological norm – as Thompson (2006, p 34) observes, for example,
the ideological norm of the nuclear family is often portrayed as a statistical
norm, when in reality only 22% of households follow this pattern.

Historically, a common response to discrimination has been for
marginalised groups to come together to campaign for change. This has been
extremely powerful, and we have seen various social movements that have
been at the forefront of change (feminism, anti-racism, the disabled people's
movement etc). However, a limitation with traditional approaches has been
the tendency to focus on a single form of discrimination (for example,
racism), arguing that the group concerned is particularly marginalised
compared to others and therefore deserves special consideration. While
this can sometimes be effective in terms of identifying injustice and raising
public awareness, it runs the risk of portraying the group concerned as
helpless and in need of support (rather than arguing that more dominant
groups need to change their attitudes and approach). At the same time, it

can also bring different groups into direct conflict with each other, each arguing that they are the most excluded.

In contrast, one way of preventing these limitations and of bringing different groups with common experiences of discrimination together is Thompson's (2006) notion of anti-discriminatory practice. Rather than concentrating on a single manifestation of discrimination (sexism, racism etc), the focus is on discrimination itself. Instead of claiming that they are the most marginalised and the most deserving of support, this means that minority ethnic communities, women, older people, disabled people and others can now have common cause, tackling discrimination in all its forms. At the same time, this also recognises that individuals have multiple identities and rarely define themselves according to a single aspect of their lives. Thus, a black man may have very different experiences to a black woman, while a rich, older woman may have very different experiences again to an older woman from a working-class background. Often, this is expressed in terms of *jeopardy* – the single jeopardy that a minority ethnic community might face, the double jeopardy that a black older person may face and the triple jeopardy that a black older person from a low socioeconomic position might face (see, for example, Norman, 1985).

Also helpful is the focus of anti-discriminatory practice on different levels of discrimination (see *Figure 6.1*). When someone acts in a discriminatory way, it is seldom the result of an individual's actions or beliefs alone. More often, individual beliefs are created and reinforced by discriminatory attitudes and values in the wider society and culture. Thus, discrimination can exist at a personal (P) level (of individual thoughts, actions, feelings and attitudes). However, this aspect of discrimination takes place within a

Figure 6.1: Thompson's (2006) PCS model

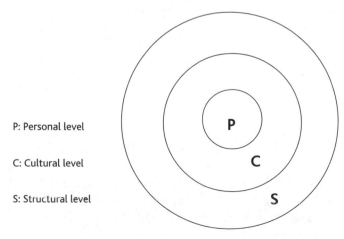

P: Personal level

C: Cultural level

S: Structural level

cultural context (the C level of common values and shared ways of seeing, thinking and doing). This in turn is embedded in a structural (S) level (the established social order and accepted social divisions). As a result, action is needed at all three levels if discrimination is to be tackled – focusing on the individual alone will not be enough (for further discussion and models see Dalrymple and Burke, 1995; Dominelli, 1997).

In seeking to tackle some of these issues, considerable effort has gone into making sure that services do their best to ensure that everyone is treated the same (a doctrine often described as one of 'universalism'). However, this is a notion of equality that prioritises *equality of input* (giving everyone access to the same service). A classic example of this are the ongoing debates in policy about the need to avoid a 'postcode lottery', with access to services depending not on need but on where you live. In contrast, an alternative approach is to focus on *equality of outcomes* (see also Chapter Four for a discussion of outcomes) – working with different groups in different ways to ensure that they experience similar outcomes. In race relations, for example, the universal principles that underpin UK welfare are often described as 'colour-blind' – treating black and white the same irrespective of the fact that different groups start from different places and may have different needs. As Blakemore and Boneham (1994, p 119) explain:

> A basic flaw in universalistic and 'colour-blind' philosophies is that … services can never treat individuals in like fashion if they are imbued with the culture and values of one group, white service providers and welfare professionals. The idea that … services are, or should be, culturally neutral is therefore questionable…. Defined more imaginatively, equality means treating individuals and groups sensitively, and sometimes differently, in order to achieve similar outcomes.

Under the Coalition government, there has been a stated commitment to focusing on 'outcomes' rather than more process-based targets, to greater fairness and to greater localism. As the government's social mobility strategy suggests (HM Government, 2011b, p 5):

> A fair society is an open society, one in which every individual is free to succeed. That is why improving social mobility is the principal goal of the Government's social policy. No one should be prevented from fulfilling their potential by the circumstances of their birth. What ought to count is how hard you work and the skills and talents you possess, not the school you went to or the jobs your parents did.

Whether or not all this actually develops into an approach which allows a genuine focus on equality of outcomes at local level remains to be seen.

Policy and practice dilemmas

Of all the service areas reviewed in this book, the one that has hit the headlines most consistently for its poor track record in tackling discrimination is mental health. While an overview is provided in ***Box 6.3*** earlier, two specific examples illustrate the complex and deep-seated nature of the issues at stake:

• *Allegations of 'institutional racism'* (see ***Box 6.6***): following the Macpherson inquiry into the racist murder of the black teenager, Stephen Lawrence, critics and campaigners have levelled similar allegations at mental health services. While there is a long literature on the negative experience of minority ethnic communities within UK mental health services (see, for example, Wilson and Francis, 1997; Bahl, 1999; Pierre, 1999; National Schizophrenia Fellowship, 2000; Sainsbury Centre for Mental Health, 2002), these issues came to the fore during an inquiry into the case of David Bennett, an African-Caribbean man who died in a medium secure unit after being forcibly restrained by staff (Norfolk, Suffolk and Cambridgeshire SHA, 2003). While this was a complex case, it led to a statement from the then chief executive of the National Institute for Mental Health in England that the NHS is racist in parts and that 'institutional racism was a true accusation that should be levelled at the NHS who should have no tolerance of it' (Norfolk, Suffolk and Cambridgeshire SHA, 2003, p 43). In response, mental health services have witnessed a stream of policy documents and guidance on issues of ethnicity and cultural sensitivity (see, for example, DH, 2003b, 2005h, 2005i; NIMHE, 2003a, 2004; see also McKenzie and Bhui, 2007 for further discussion), with one particularly hard-hitting report entitled *Inside, outside* (NIMHE, 2003b) as a way of emphasising the need to

Box 6.6: Institutional racism

Institutional racism is the collective failure of an organisation to provide an appropriate and professional service to people because of their colour, culture, or ethnic origin. It can be seen or detected in processes, attitudes and behaviour which amount to discrimination through unwitting prejudice, ignorance, thoughtlessness and racist stereotyping, which disadvantage minority ethnic people. (Norfolk, Suffolk and Cambridgeshire SHA, 2003, p 43) work *inside* services to make them more culturally appropriate, while also working *outside* services to build capacity within the voluntary sector and within communities for dealing with mental ill health. Despite all this, significant questions remain about the extent to which recent policy has been translated into practice, and about the commitment of some policy makers to take issues of discrimination seriously (see, for example, Samuel, 2006). Certainly, black people remain over-represented in mental health acute inpatient care (CQC/NMHDU, 2011).

- *The risk of abuse for women in inpatient settings:* while allegations of harassment and abuse have continued to surface for many years (see, for example, Feinmann, 1988; Cohen, 1992; Copperman and Burrows, 1992; Payne, 1998; Warner and Ford, 1998; Fleischmann, 2000), ongoing concerns about sexual safety remain (NPSA, 2006). This is despite the fact that a substantial proportion of women mental health inpatients have experienced abuse either as a child or as an adult (or both), and there is a clear danger that such abuse could be replicated in inpatient services. In spite of government guidance and pledges around the provision of women-only services (see, for example, DH, 2002c, 2003c; RCN/CSIP/NIMHE, 2008), the former National Patient Safety Agency (2006, p 41) has claimed that 'there needs to be greater awareness of the risks of sexual vulnerability of mental health inpatients and greater protection for patients.'

While raising specific issues about mental health services, these examples illustrate a more complex underlying dilemma about the best way of tackling discrimination. In particular, the concept of working both 'inside' and 'outside' services at the same time seems a helpful way of recognising the interconnections between discrimination in health and social care, and wider societal attitudes and structures. In addition, there remains a tension between responding to such issues by developing *specialist services* and responding by making discrimination a core part of everyone's role. In many ways, this is similar to the dilemma facing learning disability health facilitators in Chapter Three – while specialist services might make things better for particular groups in the short term, they run the risk of presenting discrimination as something that is only the responsibility of a particular area of the organisation. In the case of discrimination, this can often be a member of the group concerned, so that black workers can become unfairly labelled as experts on ethnicity, women are expected to tackle all gender issues and gay workers are seen as experts on sexuality. This not only exploits these staff members, but also takes away responsibility from other workers and from the organisation as a whole for dealing with these issues. Ultimately, tackling discrimination may require some specialist services, but it should also be core business for all services and workers – both 'inside' and 'outside' the organisation, and in both specialist and generic settings.

Linked to this, more recent equality legislation has started to adopt a very different approach to tackling discrimination. Whereas previous measures sought to *prevent* public services from discriminating against people from minority ethnic communities, more recent policies give public bodies a *positive duty* to promote equality. This turns the responsibilities of health and social care services from a negative and passive requirement into a much more positive and proactive duty, and potentially offers an exciting way forward. At the same time, this emphasis on a positive duty to promote equality coincides with a wider shift away from traditional notions of discrimination towards a consideration of broader human rights. Under the Human Rights Act 1998 there is a move away from rooting out discrimination against specific groups to a more rights-based approach, which safeguards the rights of *all* to family life, to liberty and security, and to freedom of expression (for further discussion of human rights and citizenship see Chapter Seven). As part of this process, previous equality bodies (such as the Commission for Racial Equality, the Equal Opportunities Commission and the Disability Rights Commission) have been replaced with a single, over-arching Equality and Human Rights Commission. While this may help to promote common cause between different groups with a joint experience of discrimination, it also runs the risk of diluting existing campaigns and expertise with regard to specific forms of discrimination. Like the discussion above about balancing specialist and generic approaches, therefore, the success of a single Commission may ultimately depend on how well it can continue to focus on the experience of particular marginalised groups, while also recognising people's multiple identities and the multifaceted nature of discrimination.

Of course, above and beyond the social divisions discussed above is the often neglected issue of poverty. In health care, there has been a long-standing recognition of the links between poverty and ill health, dating back at least as far as the public health reforms of Edwin Chadwick in the 1840s. In particular, this has been captured in Tudor Hart's (1971) 'inverse care law', with the availability of NHS services argued to be inversely proportionate to the level of need (and with poorer areas tending to have worse health services). Landmark studies from *The health divide* (Whitehead, 1987) and the *Black Report* (Black, 1980) to more recent documents such as the *Marmot Review* (2010) have also provided very detailed and hard-hitting evidence of the links between ill health and poverty, albeit that official responses have often fallen short of the initial diagnosis and progress has often been slow.

In contrast, social care has arguably seen a growing lack of 'poverty awareness' (Becker, 1997, p 93), with an apparent failure to recognise that the vast majority of service users are also people living in poverty (Becker and MacPherson, 1988; Becker, 1997). Where poverty is acknowledged at all, it is often seen as the responsibility of the social security system and not as a social care concern. Where attempts have been made to respond to these issues, it has often been via specialist welfare teams, and many of these have since closed or are no longer seen as a core feature of social care. Given social care's history (see Chapter Two) and given its tendency to view the individual in a wider social context, this seems ironic to say the least, and it may be that some of the current focus on employment, inclusion and well-being in the wider policy context gives social care an opportunity to renew its commitment to tackling the problems of poverty (see, for example, Glasby et al, 2010, for an example of ways in which social care could be seen not just as a basic safety net but as a form of social and economic investment). Whatever happens, the fact remains that both health and social care could do more to respond to the poverty of so many of their service users, and that the discrimination and exclusion highlighted in this chapter are unlikely ever to be resolved until this happens.

Summary

Underlying the debates in this chapter are two key issues that will make uncomfortable reading for policy makers and for practitioners:

- In many ways, health and social care reflect the views and beliefs of wider society – if we live in a racist, sexist society then we should not be surprised to see similar issues in health and social services.
- Against this background, the basic rule for health and social care should be to try not to make the experiences of already marginalised groups worse and, if at all possible, make some of their experiences a little better. While policy and practice state their ongoing commitment to tackling discrimination, the evidence reviewed in this chapter suggests that, in some key areas, formal services may be failing to do this, and might sometimes be considered part of the problem rather than part of the solution.

These are complex, controversial and long-standing issues, and the logic of the frameworks presented in *Figure 6.1* earlier is that deep-seated and multifaceted issues such as these require equally sustained and multifaceted responses if progress is to be made. While there is much that is positive in the current policy context, and in health and social care practice, there is much that remains problematic, contested and underdeveloped. As a result, it is difficult to be optimistic about prospects that the underlying principles of the welfare state – treating everyone equally on the basis of need alone – can ever be achieved in practice.

Above all, the insight offered by notions of anti-discriminatory practice move beyond the experiences of individual groups to consider how best to tackle discrimination in all its forms, recognising the multiple identities that exist and the way in which individual forms of discrimination interact. However, as health and social care embrace these notions more fully than ever before, there seems an alarming gap between policy rhetoric and the lived experience of various excluded user groups on the ground. In the longer run, a question clearly remains as to whether health and social care can tackle issues of discrimination from within, or whether the time is right to move beyond more traditional (incorporationist) approaches to consider wider changes in state welfare to tackle issues of exclusion, stigma and disempowerment (for example, notions of citizenship explored in Chapter Seven, a re-examination of social work's role in anti-poverty strategies, the scope of community development and neighbourhood renewal to engage with health inequalities etc). What is clear, however, is that 'treating everyone the same' – while seemingly egalitarian – does little more than perpetuate existing inequalities (at best).

Further reading/relevant websites

Introductory reading on the more theoretical aspects of anti-discriminatory practice includes:

- **Dominelli's (2002)** *Anti-oppressive social work theory and practice*
- **G. Payne's (2006)** *Social divisions*
- **Thompson's (2006)** *Anti-discriminatory practice*
- **Thompson's (2011)** *Promoting equality*

For more detail on specific groups and on health and social care, the following are helpful:

- **Butt's (2006)** *Are we there yet? Identifying the characteristics of social care organisations that successfully promote diversity*
- **Dominelli's (2008)** *Anti-racist social work*
- **Langan and Day's (1992)** *Women, oppression and social work*
- **Oliver and Barnes' (1998)** *Disabled people and social policy* and/or **Oliver and Sapey's (2006)** *Social work with disabled people*

- **S. Payne's (2006)** *The health of men and women*
- **Shaw et al's (1999)** *The widening gap: Health inequalities and policy in Britain*
- **Victor's (2010)** *Ageing, health and care*
- **Wilton's (2000)** *Sexualities in health and social care*

For specific examples of multiple identities and of the ways in which different forms of discrimination interact, see:

- **Abbott and Howarth's (2005)** *Secret loves, hidden lives?* on sexuality and people with learning difficulties
- **Arber and Ginn's** *Gender and later life* **(1991)** and *Connecting gender and ageing* **(1995)**
- **Blakemore and Boneham's (1994)** *Age, race and ethnicity*
- **Fernando's (2010)** *Mental health, race and culture*
- **Morris' (2004)** *'One town for my body, another for my mind'* on mental health and physical impairment and *Pride against prejudice* **(1991)** on disability and gender
- **Norman's (1985)** *Triple jeopardy* on age, race and class
- **Patel and Kelley's (2003)** *The social care needs of refugees and asylum seekers*

For further reading on poverty and on cash and care, see:

- **Alcock's (2006)** *Understanding poverty*
- **Becker's (1997)** *Responding to poverty*
- **Glendinning and Kemp's (2006)** *Cash and care*

Key websites include:

www.equalityhumanrights.com
The Equality and Human Rights Commission, official body promoting and monitoring human rights. See www.equalityhumanrights.com/advice-and-guidance/new-equality-act-guidance/equality-act-starter-kit for a 'starter kit'/practical material (including video clips, online modules and an e-bulletin) on the implications of the Equality Act 2010. Guidance and good practice is available via www.equalityhumanrights.com/advice-and-guidance/new-equality-act-guidance
www.equalities.gov.uk
Cross-government unit responsible for equality strategy and legislation. See www.homeoffice.gov.uk/equalities/equality-act/ for details of the Equality Act 2010

Reflection exercises

For social policy students
Although welfare services often claim to treat everyone the same, how well do they manage this in practice? Even if they could achieve this, what impact would it have on the lives of people from marginalised groups?

In what ways might different welfare policies (for example, health, housing, social security etc) interact and what impact (positive or negative) might this have on the needs and lives of these groups?

Is there ever a justification for trying to treat some groups differently in order to achieve equality of outcomes rather than equality of inputs, or is this itself unfair?

What impact would it have if we shifted the focus from preventing discrimination to promoting equality?

For health and social care professionals and students
How well do your current services respond to the needs of some of the groups discussed in this chapter (for example, people from minority ethnic communities, older people, women etc)?

How representative are local staff of the communities they serve?

What could be done to improve access to and the quality of services for all groups?

In interagency settings
After reading this chapter, meet with a colleague from a different professional or organisational background who has also read it. Do both your professions approach issues of discrimination and equality in the same ways? Are there lessons you could learn from each other?

What would patients and service users say about the way in which they experience your professions if you asked them?

For all readers
These are longstanding issues, yet numerous problems seem to remain. If you were the Secretary of State for Health, what policies would you peruse to try to resolve these issues once and for all? What might prove key barriers and success factors and how successful do you think you would be?

seven

User involvement and citizenship

Overview

This chapter discusses:

- the growing policy and practice focus on user involvement (in social care) and public and patient involvement (in the NHS), together with changes in public expectations with regards to professional power;
- gaps between rhetoric and reality, with aspirations for meaningful involvement frequently outstripping the infrastructure, funding and organisational commitment available;
- different models of involvement and empowerment;
- the danger of tokenism and cynicism with regard to more passive forms of 'consultation';
- the issue of 'representation';
- human rights and broader approaches to user involvement;
- the extent to which involvement has led to meaningful change in health and social care.

Forty years ago most people did exactly what the doctor (and other professionals) told them, and those who could remember the pre-welfare state system in particular were grateful for the support they received. In the early 21st century, doctors still enjoy considerable professional power, but attitudes have changed, and patients and the public expect to have a greater say – both in their own care and in the way in which services more generally are organised and funded. From passive recipients of welfare services, patients and service users have increasingly been recast as 'customers' or 'clients', and even more recently as active citizens and as 'micro-commissioners' of their own services, with both 'rights and responsibilities'. In several key areas of policy and practice, service user movements are even developing their own alternative services and ways of working, directly challenging traditional and often very paternalistic statutory approaches.

Against this background, this chapter reviews the growth of user involvement in social care and of public and patient involvement in the NHS, highlighting underlying theoretical assumptions about people who use services as consumers, citizens, 'expert patients' and/or service providers in their own right. In addition to reviewing recent policy shifts, progress to date and different types and models of involvement, the chapter also considers the role of a human rights–based approach to health and social care, moving beyond previous notions of 'involvement' to more recent attempts to improve the position of service users and patients via campaigning and a direct appeal to civil rights, direct action and social and political change. While there are still many areas where individuals would want to draw on the expertise of a trained medical professional (or other skilled worker), the terms on which this encounter takes place have started to shift dramatically (see, for example, *Box 7.1*).

> ## Box 7.1: User and public/patient involvement: a case study
>
> Tom (not his real name) is a person with a learning disability who had previously lived in a long-stay institution, was frequently medicated and was diagnosed as having 'challenging behaviour.' With support from friends and other people with learning difficulties, he was eventually able to move out of the hospital and start living in a shared house. He now works as a trainer, using his experiences to help public sector workers to deliver more person-centred services to people with learning difficulties. This has given him a role, increased his income, brought him into contact with friends and colleagues – and helped to use negative experiences of services to make things better for others in future. In one sense, he now helps to train the workers who once kept him against his will in the hospital and his status, friendships and outlook are now fundamentally different.

Policy context

Traditionally, notions of involvement have tended to focus around long-standing concerns about the perceived 'democratic deficit' within the NHS. With the NHS accountable nationally to the Secretary of State for Health, there have been various attempts to strengthen the accountability of local health services to local people and local communities (through, for example, various different mechanisms for including elected local politicians on the governing boards of NHS bodies – for a recent incarnation of this debate see Glasby et al, 2006b). Perhaps the best example of this was the introduction in 1974 of community health councils to advise and represent local people and to be consulted about NHS services and changes. However, during the early 1990s, the consumer focus of the then Conservative government led to a series of attempts to introduce private sector models of customer service into public sector health and social care. Thus, this decade witnessed the advent of a patient's charter (DH, 1991) to set out clear service standards and expectations that patients should have of services, the creation of formal complaints systems, the introduction of quasi-markets (see Chapter Three) to enable service users and patients (in theory) to exercise greater choice about services, and a series of pieces of guidance on developing strategies for involving patients in health service planning (see, for example, NHS Executive, 1992, 1996). In many ways, this emphasis on consumerism and involvement was a growing international phenomenon, with a similar direction of travel in several developed countries (for an example of different approaches to involving the public in decision making see *Box 7.2*).

Box 7.2: International approaches to public involvement in health care decision making

Ham and Coulter's (2001) review of public involvement in decisions about health rationing describes a series of different models of involvement, including:

- Oregon's use of public hearings, community meetings and telephone surveys as part of work to identify a list of priorities for public health care funding;
- Dutch public discussion (reaching one third of the population) about choices in health care;
- Swedish public surveys to guide the work of the Parliamentary Priorities Commission;
- New Zealand's community consultation exercises to explore which services should be publicly funded.

In addition to these, often very technical, approaches, some countries place an emphasis on enabling people to become involved in wider political processes in an open and transparent manner. Thus, membership of New Zealand district health boards is determined through direct public elections (Cumming and the Health Reforms 2001 Research Team, 2003). In contrast, Fairfax County, Virginia, is governed by an elected board of supervisors (which establishes county government policy, passes resolutions and ordinances, approves the budget, sets tax rates, approves land use plans and makes appointments). These actions are taken in open meetings that citizens are encouraged to attend. Members of the public are allowed to speak at the board to express their views on issues of concern. Board meetings are shown live on cable television and the board's agenda is published 10 days in advance in a free newspaper mailed out to citizens. Elsewhere in the US, board members often run online consultations and chairs often appear in chat rooms on websites made available through local cable services. For further information, visit www.fairfaxcounty.gov

Under New Labour, this emphasis on involvement continued, with a renewed emphasis on what increasingly came to be known as 'public and patient involvement' (DH, 1999c, 2000a). Over time, this led to the abolition of community health councils and the introduction of a raft of new organisations tasked with promoting involvement at different levels of the health service, including Patient Advice and Liaison Services (PALS) to respond to patient questions and concerns, a greater role for local government in scrutinising the work of local health services and the creation of local involvement networks (LINks). Under the Coalition, key developments include a stated commitment to much greater shared decision making and public engagement – summed up under the mantra of 'nothing about me without me' (DH, 2010a). In practice, policies include a much greater emphasis on access to meaningful information (described as 'an information revolution', (DH, 2010a, p 13), greater use of existing tools such as patient-reported outcome measures (PROMs), greater choice of provider and the replacement of LINks with new local HealthWatch organisations (supported nationally by HealthWatch England within the health and social care inspectorate, the Care Quality Commission).

Throughout all this, there has been constant change, considerable rhetoric about the importance of involvement and not insignificant progress in some areas, but ongoing questions about the priority that is genuinely attached to patient involvement by policy makers, the funding available and the effectiveness of some of the structures established. There is also concern that repeated reorganisation and rebranding may actually weaken involvement rather than strengthen it. The choice of slogans by the Coalition government is also particularly interesting, with policies that still seem very focused on choice and consumerism (see below for further discussion) badged using a variant of the phrase 'nothing about us without us' (often most associated with radical, service user-led movements of people with learning difficulties). Whether this represents a radical departure from previous engagement policies or more of an appropriation of the language of radical service user–led campaigning for a more limited set of approaches remains to be seen.

Despite ongoing support for user involvement in national policy and local practice, a number of barriers remain to more meaningful dialogue and relationships between health and social care and people who use such services. These have been explored in detail in most accounts of user involvement, and common themes are summarised briefly in **Box 7.3**. However, an additional factor to consider here is the very different experiences of different user groups. Whereas some user groups have a long and active history of collective action and of campaigning within and outside services for change (see, for example, accounts of the disabled

---

Box 7.3: Commonly cited barriers to more meaningful involvement

- Professional resistance to involvement and a reluctance to share power and knowledge more equally.
- A lack of meaningful and accessible information about current services, about what is possible in practice, and about opportunities for involvement.
- The time and resources it takes to involve people appropriately and on their own terms.
- Practical difficulties in enabling people to become involved (for example, organising meetings in accessible community-based venues at convenient times, paying service users to recognise their time and expertise – see, for example, DH, 2006e).
- The need to invest extra effort in hearing the voices of 'seldom heard' groups (while these are often referred to as 'hard to reach', the term 'seldom heard' places the onus on services to do more to engage these groups, rather than blaming the groups themselves for being 'difficult' to access).
- Concerns that involvement can often be tokenistic (see below for further discussion).
- A tendency to speak to the same small number of people (which can place significant pressures on these individuals and lead to burnout) – as an example, Brodie (2003) provides a powerful first-hand account of what it feels like 'being involved' as a service user and the tensions and complexities this can entail.
- Barriers to meaningful involvement for people from minority ethnic communities (Begum, 2006).
- The practical and ethical dilemmas that can be raised when trying to involve people who are involuntary users of services (for example, in inpatient mental health or forensic services; see, for example, Barnes et al, 2000).

people's movement in Chapter Five), other areas of service provision have been much slower to develop a user movement, and their voices have often been downplayed (see, for example, the work of Barnes and Walker, 1996, with regard to older people). Of course, different levels of involvement may also be desirable and/or possible in different areas of service provision – while user involvement may be crucial in services for people with long-term conditions (where people may want to be involved in decisions about their own services and about services more generally), it may be very different in acute care (where individual patients may be more concerned about the respect with which they are treated by staff and the extent to which they are involved in decisions about their treatment).

Centrally linked to the rise of user and public/patient involvement has been the changing nature of professional expertise (see Chapter Two for further discussion of professional power). With a less deferential public and with growing government regulation of the professions, traditional assumptions that health and social practitioners 'know best' and only have their service users' interests at heart have been increasingly challenged. Drawing on Wilding (1982), M. Payne (2006, pp 147-52) summarises this in terms of:

- *Excessive claims and limited achievements*: for all their claim to expert knowledge, some professions may well have overemphasised their contribution or been subject of unrealistic expectations, ultimately being perceived as failing to deliver.
- *Failures of responsibility*: in both health and social care, a series of scandals have undermined the image and reputation of professions. Examples here include long-standing concerns about the quality of care provided in long-stay hospitals (Martin, 1984) and a series of childcare scandals and mental health inquiries (see, for example, Stanley and Manthorpe, 2004), as well as more recent events such as the organ retention scandal at Alder Hey hospital (BBC, 2000), child deaths following cardiac surgery at the Bristol Royal Infirmary (BBC, 1999) and the infamous case of GP Harold Shipman (BBC, 2006).
- *The claim for neutrality*: despite claims to a scientific evidence base, both health and social care are based on a broad range of approaches, which can include formal research evidence, but which are also influenced by traditional practice and assumptions, professional self-interest and national policy (which may or may not be evidence-based).
- *Neglect of rights*: in spite of formal complaints procedures, there are ongoing concerns that workers in both health and social care can override the rights of their patients and service users in day-to-day practice. A good example here is the ongoing concern about people with learning

difficulties and mental health problems being kept in locked buildings, even when being treated as 'voluntary' patients (see the Bournewood case later, p 153).

- *The service ideal*: although supposedly altruistic and based around notions of public service, professions can also be self-interested and can sometimes put their own priorities and preferences above those of the people they are there to serve. An example of this might be the very collegiate nature of medical practice, and a traditional NHS culture that is sometimes perceived as 'covering up' for individual mistakes or errors rather than eradicating these in the interests of patient safety (see, for example, HM Government, 2005).
- *Social control/disabling effects*: as well as being sources of support, health and social care professionals also have a role in controlling behaviour (for example, sectioning someone under the Mental Health Act or taking someone's children into the care of the local authority). Even in everyday practice, professions can encourage dependence rather than independence (see Chapter Five).
- *Lack of accountability*: despite complaints systems, many professions regulate their own members' conduct, and these processes can seem slow, opaque and geared towards supporting the professional rather than the patient.

Thus, the recent emphasis on involvement may come both from changing public expectations and from a growing tendency to question traditional assumptions about professional power and expertise.

Key concepts

Underlying current attempts to involve service users in decisions about their own treatment and services more generally are a (contested) series of models and concepts. While each of these may initially point in a similar direction (and hence add impetus to the current emphasis on greater involvement), they do so for different reasons and to a different extent. Ultimately, therefore, questions must remain as to how compatible these different approaches are in the longer term. In many ways, this seems similar to the dilemmas explored in Chapter Five, where the emergency admissions agenda and the citizenship agenda are both focusing attention on the needs of people with long-term conditions, but with very different values, approaches and desired outcomes.

For Barnes and Walker (1996), for example, a key distinction is between involving people in their capacity as 'consumers' (that is, with users as customers in a health and social care market) and involving people because they are citizens (that is, with a series of rights to involvement and to high quality services). Whereas the neo-liberal ideology of the Conservative government (1979–97) tended to emphasise the former, Barnes and Walker focus on the need for an empowerment model (see ***Table 7.1*** for the key differences between consumerism and empowerment; see also ***Box 7.4*** for the concept of citizen rights).

Table 7.1: *Consumerism versus empowerment*

Consumerism (and bureaucratic approaches to involvement)	Empowerment (and citizenship approaches)
Service/provider orientated	User orientated
Inflexible	Responsive
Provider-led	Needs-led
Power concentrated	Power sharing
Defensive	Open to review
Conservative	Open to change
Input orientated	Outcome orientated

According to Rogers and Pilgrim (2010), service users (in this case in mental health services) can be seen in one of four different ways, each of which implies a different understanding of the purpose and nature of involvement:

- as patients, viewed as passive recipients of professional (and often medical) intervention;
- as customers, viewed as capable of exercising choice between different services or products;
- as survivors, with the mental health service user movement increasingly viewing individuals as having 'survived' the psychiatric system, and using the term 'survivors' to denote their rejection of medical models of mental illness and to portray a positive image of people experiencing mental distress;
- as providers themselves, developing user-led alternatives to statutory provision, often in the voluntary sector, and promoting alternative understandings of and responses to mental distress.

Arising out of these different approaches are a number of different ways of involving people and different levels of involvement (see also Newman and Vidler, 2006, for additional discussion). These are often portrayed in terms of a spectrum, with different levels of power sharing along a continuum between the service user/patient as a passive recipient of services to user-led alternatives to current (professionally dominated) services. Of all these frameworks, one of the most famous is that of Arnstein (1969), whose 'ladder of citizen participation' is frequently quoted and often used as the basis for more recent incarnations of similar concepts. According to this typology, participation can vary from non-participation (with users viewed passively as people who are there to be 'educated' or 'cured') through tokenistic involvement (where users can at least have some voice, but often lack power to ensure that their views are heeded) to citizen power (where users are seen as citizens with the power to be involved in genuine decision making) (see *Figure 7.1*).

Box 7.4: Citizenship

Marshall (1950) defined citizenship rights as comprising:

- Legal or civil rights that enable the individual to participate freely in the life of the community. These rights include property and contractual rights, and rights to freedom of thought, freedom of speech, religious practice, assembly and association.
- Political rights that entitle the citizen to participate in the government of the community: the right to vote and to hold political office.
- Social and economic rights to the circumstances that enable the individual to participate in the general well-being of the community. They include rights to health care, education and welfare.

Source: Barnes and Bowl (2001, p 14)

Linked to notions of involvement are the equally complex issues of power and of empowerment. While there is little consensus on how best to define 'empowerment', the term implies gaining greater control over one's life and challenging discrimination and stigma. While power is often seen as something that one person can give to another (thereby reducing their own power), a more helpful approach is offered by Thompson (1998, p 9, quoted in Thompson, 2005, p 125):

> It is commonly assumed by many that empowerment involves taking away the worker's power. However, if this is done, it will of course make him or her less effective and therefore of less value. Empowerment is a matter of helping people gain

Figure 7.1: Arnstein's (1969) 'ladder of citizen participation'

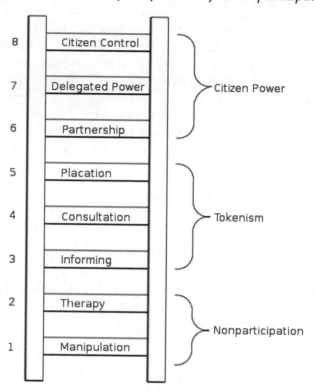

Source: Arnstein (1969) (www.partnerships.org.uk/index.htm)

greater control over their lives, helping them to become better equipped to deal with the problems and challenges they face – especially those that involve seeking to counter or overcome discrimination and oppression.

As Dominelli (2002) argues, moreover, 'power' can be understood in terms of 'power over' (the ability of a dominant group to maintain its position, to normalise its worldview and to portray others as different and subordinate), 'power to' (the ability to take action to achieve certain ends) and 'power of' (groups coming together to exercise collective strength). Returning to the above discussion about consumerism and citizenship, Means and Smith (1998b) supplement this debate by identifying different forms of empowerment – each of which implies a different level of power sharing. Drawing on the work of Hirschman (1970), this includes:

- *Empowerment through 'exit'*: with service users seen as consumers and able to switch services if not satisfied. This seems a limited concept in health and social care, where many service users may lack meaningful information about alternatives, may not be in a position to switch providers, have no guarantee that an alternative provider would be any better and may not even be a voluntary user of services at all. As Rogers and Pilgrim (2001, p 169) point out:

> Many psychiatric patients do not ask for what they get – it is imposed on them. Various sections of the 1983 Mental Health Act, like its legal predecessors, are utilised to lawfully impose restraints and treatments on resentful and reluctant recipients. In such circumstances, mental patients could be construed to be consumers if being dragged off the street and force-fed was a feature of being a customer in a restaurant.

- *Empowerment through 'voice'*: with service users able to contribute their views about services to discussions about future provision. As outlined below, this can become a cynical process if there is no genuine desire to hear and act upon what users say.
- *Empowerment through 'rights'*: with service users seen as citizens (see **Box 7.4** earlier) with a series of political, legal and social rights. In many ways, this is encapsulated in the slogan 'Nothing about us without us', popularised by people with learning difficulties following the publication of the *Valuing people* White Paper (DH, 2001c; see Chapter Three). Despite considerable rhetoric, however, significant areas of health and social care remain based on professional discretion and control, rather than on formal rights.
- *Empowerment through 'struggle'*: with service user movements (such as the disability movement explored in Chapter Five) developing user-led alternatives to current professionally led services and campaigning for social and political change. In the wider academic literature, such groups are often described as 'new social movements' (Byrne, 1997; Barnes and Bowl, 2001; Martin, 2001).

Interestingly, these discussions of power and empowerment link directly to earlier discussions about anti-discriminatory practice (see Chapter Six). In particular, Dominelli's (2002) earlier categorisation summarises how more powerful groups can vary between maintaining the status quo (demarcationist), assimilating new groups into the current system without challenging underlying power relations (incorporationist) and changing the system to make it more equitable (egalitarian). Similarly, those experiencing discrimination can respond through acceptance (uncritically accepting the status quo), accommodation (working within the current order for some changes) or rejection (dismissing the status quo and developing more radical and more just alternatives) – and this may be exactly the same for people using health and social care services.

Finally, it is important to stress that notions of empowerment and involvement can include both individual and collective action. As one example, Hoggett (1992, p 9, quoted in Means and Smith, 1998b, p 89) distinguishes between the degree of participation/control available to the individual and whether they are involved as an individual or through collective action (see *Figure 7.2*). While empowerment through 'voice' and through 'exit' are primarily individual in their focus, empowerment through struggle in particular is a collective notion, which involves people with shared interests coming together to make sense of their experiences and campaign for change. Although individual approaches can make a difference, there is evidence that collective forms of involvement can be particularly helpful in terms of building confidence, sharing experiences and helping personal empowerment to become a form of social or political empowerment (see, for example, Barnes and Walker, 1996; Barnes and Bennett, 1998; see also Tom's story in *Box 7.1* earlier).

Policy and practice dilemmas

Despite the growing influence of people who use services, a key question remains as to how meaningful much current 'involvement' is in practice. In spite of the policy rhetoric (and despite some very real changes), much activity that is labelled as 'involvement' in health and social care may sometimes seem very tokenistic (see, for example, Rose et al, 2002; Carr, 2004). At its worst, such activity involves more passive notions of 'consultation', and typically can entail little more than asking service users about decisions that have already been taken (or asking about users' priorities but failing to act on the results). In some circumstances, there are even suggestions that individual managers can 'consult' service users with a view to selecting views that will most bolster their own preferred course of action and using this in power struggles with fellow managers (often referred to as 'playing the user card'; see Rose et al, 2002, p 12). When involvement is abused and misused in this way, it is little more than placation (at best) or cynical manipulation, and can quickly lead to disengagement by staff and service users alike. Put simply, if those in authority asking the question do not really want to listen to the answers, then why would anyone want to waste their time by becoming 'involved'?

Figure 7.2: User involvement

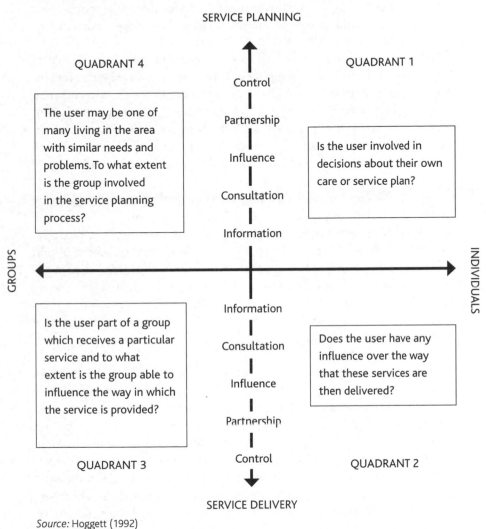

SERVICE PLANNING

QUADRANT 4

QUADRANT 1

Control

Partnership

The user may be one of
many living in the area
with similar needs and
problems. To what extent
is the group involved
in the service planning
process?

Influence

Is the user involved in
decisions about their own
care or service plan?

Consultation

Information

GROUPS

INDIVIDUALS

Information

Is the user part of a group
which receives a particular
service and to what
extent is the group able to
influence the way in which
the service is provided?

Consultation

Does the user have any
influence over the way
that these services are
then delivered?

Influence

Partnership

QUADRANT 3

Control

QUADRANT 2

SERVICE DELIVERY

Source: Hoggett (1992)

Although tokenism is a potential risk, an alternative view is to emphasise
the symbolic importance of user involvement. While it is important to
ensure that attempts to involve service users are meaningful and lead to
genuine change, particular forms of user involvement can also have symbolic
functions. Thus, a mental health service user sitting on the board of an
integrated health and social care trust felt that their views were downplayed
and that their contribution ran the risk of tokenism. In contrast, some
commentators see this as highly significant – irrespective of whether the
service user or the board actually 'did anything' or 'made decisions', the fact

that a mental health service user was also a member of the board sent out a powerful message about user involvement, the organisation's commitment to this way of working and the strengths and skills of people with mental health problems (see Peck et al, 2002; Brodie, 2003).

In all forms of health and social care involvement, a key issue is that of 'representation' (and staff struggling to think through how best to involve people with experience of using services will often become concerned that the users they seek to involve are 'representative'). While it is important that all people with experiences and views to contribute have a means by which their voices can be heard (and while more work is required to support seldom heard groups), the issue of 'representation' is undoubtedly overemphasised (and can even be used as a way of dismissing views that challenge the status quo). While a more detailed critique of the notion of 'representativeness' is provided in *Box 7.5*, there is a danger that genuine service user concerns can be ignored, that users can be caught in a 'catch-22' situation (perceived as either too well or too ill to be representative) and that service users may unfairly be asked to 'represent' others when none of the professionals involved are asked to be representative of anyone else other than themselves (Rose et al, 2002). In fact, many service users involved in health and social care are elected by user organisations, or have well established mechanisms for seeking and feeding in user views, so in one sense are often more representative than anyone else.

Despite a growing focus on user involvement in health and social care services, there are a range of other equally significant areas in which service users can make a meaningful contribution. While the emphasis within front-line practice is typically on users' experiences of the services they receive and how this can be used to bring about change, other avenues for involvement are arguably just as significant in terms of influencing organisational culture and the context within which services are provided. A range of different approaches to involvement and empowerment are explored elsewhere (see, for example, Barnes and Warren, 1999; Kemshall and Littlechild, 2000), but examples include user involvement in staff recruitment, in research, in training and in governance (see *Box 7.6* for examples of broader approaches to involvement). People with experience of using services can also be employed within services, and hence have multiple identities as both 'user' and 'professional'. More recently, moreover, there has been growing debate about the role of service users with regards to current notions of evidence-based practice. Although this is often viewed in terms of basing policy and practice on formal research evidence, there is a growing concern that this should also include not only the practice wisdom of health and social care professionals, but also the lived experience of users and carers (Beresford and Branfield, 2006; Glasby and Beresford, 2006; Beresford, 2007; Glasby,

Box 7.5: User involvement and 'representation'

As Lindow (1999, p 166) suggests in a long but important quote:

When workers find what we [users] are saying challenging, the most usual strategy to discredit user voices is to suggest we are not to be listened to because we are too articulate, and not representative. Workers seem to be looking for someone, the 'typical' patient, who is so passive and/or drugged that they comply with their plans. We are developing our own strategies to respond to these challenges in an attempt to reveal to such workers their double standards:

- We ask how representative are they, and the others on the committee? We point out that as they are selected for their expertise and experience, so are we. Indeed, we are more likely to have been selected by a group than they are.
- We ask, would workers send their least articulate colleague to represent their views, or the least confident nurse to negotiate for a change in conditions?
- We ask, if a person's criticisms are valid, what relevance has representativeness?
- We point out that it is very rude to suggest that someone is not a 'proper' service user (that is, so disempowered and/or medicated that they cannot speak). We could ask, but do not, that the challenger produce his or her credentials, their certificates of qualification.

Similarly, Crawford (2001, p 85) argues that:

Concerns are sometimes expressed about whether those who represent the views of service users do so accurately – how can one know whether or not the views of a service user reflect those of users more generally? This problem is not specific to those representing the views of service users. The same question could be asked of those representing the views of local general practitioners, psychiatrists etc.... Some user group representatives ... are democratically elected. Others receive training that involves considering one's own views and those of others. Central to the concept of user involvement is the understanding that someone who has experienced services has developed an informed view that is of value to those developing and assessing services. Concern about the representativeness of service users must not be used to undermine the criticisms of service users.

2011b). In this way, user views and experiences are no longer seen as merely a form of 'anecdotal evidence' (and thus dismissed as unrepresentative), but as 'human testimony' (Lindow, 1999), and hence as a potentially important and valid way of understanding the world in its own right.

Box 7.6: Broader approaches to user involvement

User involvement in staff selection is increasingly common (see, for example, Townsley et al, 2002), and evidence suggests that this can lead to a different approach to recruiting staff that can be more effective at identifying some of the human skills of candidates. In one example, provided by Newnes et al (2001), professionals commenting on the involvement of service users in recruiting a clinical psychologist acknowledged that 'she [a service user] came up with questions none of us professionals would ever have thought of and got a much stronger sense of what the candidate was like as a person.'

Service users are increasingly represented on the governing boards of health and social care organisations (see, for example, Brodie, 2003; Hasler, 2003), providing a user perspective on the work of the organisation and making an important symbolic statement about the importance of involvement.

User involvement in education and training can be a particularly important way of learning and of influencing the values and attitudes of health and social care professionals (see, for example, Levin, 2004; Barnes et al, 2006; Taylor and Le Riche, 2006).

User-led research often asks different questions to studies carried out by non-service users, and user researchers can often establish more of a rapport with service user interviewees as a result of their common experiences (see, for example, Rose, 2001; Turner and Beresford, 2005a).

Service users are also employed in health and social care, and there are a broad range of examples to demonstrate ways in which both organisations and individuals can benefit from this approach (see, for example, Brody, 2006; Seebohm and Grove, 2006).

In recent years, current progress around user involvement has been boosted by an increasing emphasis on human rights. With the passage of the Human Rights Act 1998, public authorities must act compatibly with the European Convention on Human Rights (which emphasises various rights to life, to liberty and security, to a fair trial, to respect for private and family life, to freedom of expression and to other civil and social rights). Since 1998, there has been growing interest in applying these broader legal principles to health and social care, and a number of legal challenges have been successful in prompting significant changes to particular areas of mental health and learning disability services in particular (for an online guide see www.

yourrights.org.uk/your-rights/the-human-rights-act). A classic example is the notorious Bournewood case (which revolved around whether people who are deemed to lack capacity can be admitted to hospital as 'informal' or voluntary patients) (see, for example, *Community Care*, 2006b). While case law is still emerging, one of the main effects of the Human Rights Act to date seems to have been to accelerate the move away from notions of consumerism to a more rights-based, citizenship-orientated notion of involvement. In many ways, all this links to debates in Chapter Five about the personalisation agenda, where one view of recent policy is that it could shift our thinking away from health and social care as a form of 'professional gift' towards a situation where the person is seen as a citizen with an entitlement to choice and control over their services and hence over their lives. Thus, concepts such as direct payments and personal budgets (often described as a form of 'micro-commissioning' using the official jargon) might not just be a matter of promoting individual choice and competition, but *could* also contribute to a broader citizenship agenda.

Above all, however, a key question remains as to whether user involvement has made a difference to services and to the lives of people who use services. While there is a broad consensus that user involvement is a 'good thing' (for a range of practical, ethical and political reasons), there is much less evidence about the actual impact of involvement. This is the focus of a key report from SCIE, which asks: *Has service user participation made a difference?* (Carr, 2004). Building on reviews of involvement in services for older people, children and young people, people with learning difficulties, disabled people and people with mental health problems, the report concluded that considerable activity is under way but that potential change and improvement has yet to be fully monitored and evaluated. A little like earlier discussions of health and social care partnerships (Chapter Four), participation to date may have had a clearer impact in terms of process (how individual users experience attempts to involve them) rather than outcomes (what difference this makes). For all recent progress, therefore, we may still know more about some of the barriers than we do about the best way forward.

Summary

With changing public expectations, a reduction in professional power and the rise of consumerism in public services, user involvement has become a central feature of health and social care (at least in theory). From a position where 'doctor knows best', we have moved to a situation where the concept of user and public/patient involvement is broadly accepted as a 'good thing', espoused by national policy and (to varying degrees) promoted locally. In spite of this, a series of underlying barriers remain, and the extent to which practice matches policy rhetoric remains open to question. Ironically, it may well be that the combination of a range of different movements and ideologies (neo-liberalism, civil rights campaigners) that has created such a powerful momentum for change may also sow the seeds of its own destruction. Underlying current attempts to 'involve' service users are so many potentially incompatible interpretations of what 'service users' are and why we should 'involve' them, that there is scope for considerable confusion, tokenism and dispersal of effort. If these ambiguities are not tackled, then further progress may be slow.

Above and beyond these issues, current debates around user and patient involvement centre around a fundamental tension. While users have become much more involved in decisions about their own treatment and about services more generally, they have arguably made much less progress in terms of broader inclusion within society (see Chapter Three) – for example, in terms of social inclusion, gaining meaningful employment, combating stigma and rooting out discrimination. This mismatch seems ironic to say the least, and it may well be time to focus less on (health and social care) 'user involvement' and more on broader campaigning and human rights in order to challenge the position of 'service users' within society more generally. In reality, of course, a more feasible approach may well be the 'inside–outside' concept introduced in Chapter Six – working *inside* services to make them more responsive to users' needs, while also working *outside* services to tackle the wider determinants of the exclusion and stigma that so many community care user groups undoubtedly face.

Further reading/relevant websites

For a more detailed exploration (both practical and theoretical) of the issues raised in this chapter, useful summaries are provided by:

- **Baggott et al's (2005)** *Speaking for patients and carers*
- **Barnes et al's (2007)** *Power, participation and political renewal*
- **Carr's (2004)** *Has service user participation made a difference to social care services?*
- **Greenhalgh et al's (2010)** *User involvement in health care*
- **Kemshall and Littlechild's (2000)** *User involvement and participation in social care*

For information on specific user groups and user movements, see:

- **Barnes and Bowl's (2001)** *Taking over the asylum* (on mental health) and papers by Marian Barnes and colleagues on an early and innovative project to involve frail older people in decisions about health and social care (see, for example, **Barnes and Bennett, 1998**).

- **Thornicroft's (2006)** book on stigma is an excellent account of the discrimination and barriers experienced by people with mental health problems
- **Begum's (2006)** *Doing it for themselves: Participation and black and minority ethnic service users*
- **Campbell and Oliver's (1996)** *Disability politics*
- **Williams' (2012)** *Learning disability and inclusion: Policy and practice*

For service user contributions to research and to generating valid knowledge about 'what works' in health and social care, see:

- **Barnes and Mercer's (1997)** *Doing disability research*
- **Beresford's (2003)** *It's our lives*
- **Branfield et al's (2006)** *Making user involvement work*
- **Glasby and Beresford's (2006)** 'Who knows best?' (*Critical Social Policy*)
- **Turner and Beresford's (2005a)** *User controlled research*

For guidance on making payments to enable service users to become involved, see **Turner and Beresford's (2005b)** *Contributing on equal terms* and subsequent **DH (2006e)** guidance. Broader guidance on involvement is available via the **Department of Health's (2008)** *Real involvement: Working with people to improve services*.

Key websites include:

www.healthtalkonline.org
  HealthTalk Online is a database of personal and patient experiences compiled from research by the Health Experience Research Group at the University of Oxford (see also www.youthhealthtalk.org)
www.involve.org.uk/
  Involve is a national body delivering research and training around public involvement
www.jrf.org.uk
  The Joseph Rowntree Foundation publishes a series of research studies on involvement (free to download from the website in full and also available via helpful 'Findings' summaries)
www.pickereurope.org
  Picker Institute Europe is a leading national/international not-for-profit organisation developing the evidence base around patient-centred care, patient engagement and patient experiences
www.scie.org.uk
  The Social Care Institute for Excellence is fully committed to user involvement in all its work, and publishes a range of free research reports on good practice in user involvement

www.shapingourlives.org.uk
   Shaping Our Lives is the national user-controlled organisation seeking to support
   the development of user involvement and to provide a shared voice for user-
   controlled organisations

Reflection exercises

For social policy students
Reflect on the approaches to involvement and engagement outside health and social
care, using Arnstein's ladder of participation. How does the track record of health and
social care compare? Compare and contrast different areas of the welfare state in
terms of Means and Smith's concepts of exit, voice, rights and struggle.

For health and social care professionals and students
Look at local organisational policies and the website of your professional body. What
do these say about the importance of involvement and what types/level/degree
of involvement do these imply? If possible, talk to a local involvement lead about
the work they do and to local service users/patients about their experiences. How
committed to involvement do local organisations seem to be in practice? How do
they go about trying to involve people? What do they do with the results? What
difference does this make?

In interagency settings
Debate the models and issues raised in this chapter with a colleague from a different
organisation or profession. What similarities and differences are there in your models
of and approaches to involvement, and what role do you see for service users and
patients? What language do you both use and what models does this imply?

For all readers
If you have ever accessed health and social care (or another public service), how did
it feel and to what extent were you involved in decisions about your own care or
decisions about services more generally? How easy was it to make your voice heard,
what kinds of decisions did you want to be involved with and what actions took
place as a result?

eight

Support for carers

Overview

This chapter discusses:

- the contribution of carers and the growing recognition of carers' needs;
- key policies to support carers and the limitations of some of these approaches;
- the contested and controversial concept of 'the carer' and associated issues of gender, interdependence and the portrayal of caring as a 'burden';
- notions of citizenship and human rights;
- practice issues such as providing support to those who do not necessarily define themselves as 'carers' and moving beyond health and social care to wider services.

While health and social care in the community has always been based on the support provided by carers (friends, neighbours and families providing support on an unpaid basis), it is only relatively recently that official policies have been developed to support carers in this role. This chapter reviews the emergence of carers (including young carers and older carers) as a policy priority in their own right, the research evidence about the impact of caring, policies to support carers and carers' own priorities for the future. In the process, the chapter summarises current critiques of the notion of 'the carer' and the relative neglect of some types of 'carer' (for example, of people with mental health problems). In particular, it challenges the notion that caring is necessarily a 'burden', while also acknowledging that caring without meaningful choice and without adequate support can most definitely be a negative experience (see **Box 8.1**).

Box 8.1: Carers' stories

John's story

I first met my partner when she was working as a hospital portering assistant and was attracted by her cheerful personality and forthright nature. It was in November 2005 that she first fell ill, quite dramatically. She had a breakdown and ran away to 'live rough' in Brighton, although she was located the next day by the police. When this happened I was left feeling guilty and wondered what I had done wrong.

Now I keep my mobile on at work in case she experiences a crisis and also make several calls throughout the day to make sure she is okay. The only immediate family near us is my partner's sister and her family, who have a young family of their own to tend to and my partner would not be willing to have strangers caring for her. This means I don't have any respite, but when she takes her medication consistently, things calm down and I can take a breather.

The main casualty in our relationship has been trust. My partner often thinks that my concerns, although innocent, are a just way for me to get her into hospital. I often find myself questioning things like 'Has she taken her medication?' or 'Is she about to run away/attempt to take her own life?' There have also been times when members of my family have felt that there is nothing wrong with my partner, that she is only attention seeking. This has been hurtful, maybe even offensive at times.

Obviously my partner is no longer able to work and relies on benefits and I am unable to work extra hours due to my domestic obligations. All this has had a dramatic impact on our finances. In order to cope, I have had to put our unsecured debts onto a debt management plan and to budget the finances very carefully each month in order to meet priority bills.

My health has also suffered due to the pressures of caring; I suffer bouts of depression diagnosed as secondary to my partner's illness, which has caused me to take time off work.

Vicky's story

I became a carer overnight, when my son Paul was born with severe brain damage; I was then just two weeks off my 19th birthday.... When he was just 11 months old I became a single parent/carer as a result of my husband's domestic violence towards me. I needed to protect Paul and devote all my time to his care. In a few short years I had gone from being an office junior to new wife and new mum, to full-time carer. [...]

One of the hardest things I have had to deal with as a carer was hearing my son tell me that he hated his life, himself and that he wanted to die. As a parent I felt completely helpless and the feeling of guilt that I had failed him was enormous.... When ... Paul went to a residential college and all my benefits stopped, I had to try to find full-time employment. I had no paid work experience to put on a CV and despite 25 years of caring found no one was willing to give me a chance, not recognising the transferable skills I had developed as a carer.

Ronnie's story

Ronnie, 61, has cared for his wife Ann for over 15 years. With MS and osteoarthritis in her spine she needs 24-hour care and he had to give up his job 12 years ago to look after her full time. The main worry for Ronnie is the deterioration in Ann's health. She has a progressive form of MS, which has reached the stage where she can only move her head and left hand. Should her left hand no longer work Ronnie will have to feed her. He already sees to most of her everyday needs such as washing, dressing, toileting, lifting her in and out of her wheelchair and cooking. As she cannot move, he also gets up at intervals of four to six hours during the night to change her position and make her more comfortable.

'If Ann was in care it would take three shifts of people working around the clock to look after her.'

[...] Despite the strains of the situation, their relationship has endured. Ronnie says: "You have to accept things as they are. In 37 years we have never had a serious argument." However, Ann's condition makes it difficult for them to plan for the future, as they don't know how her health will change. At an age when many couples would be starting to think of retirement, Ronnie says "We can't plan ahead." When asked what could help he replies:

'There's not enough recognition of what a carer does. When I fill in forms there's no category for full time carer; no one understands what that is.'

Source: Princess Royal Trust for Carers: carers' stories website (www.carers.org/carers-stories)

Policy context

According to the 2001 Census, there are some 5.2 million carers in England and Wales, including over one million people providing more than 50 hours of care per week (National Statistics, 2003a, 2003b; see *Box 8.2* for further data). While caring is often perceived as a negative activity (involving a

Box 8.2: Carers and the 2001 Census

In 2001, the Census included a specific question on caring for the first time. This revealed that:

- there are six million carers throughout the UK (10% of the total population and approximately 12% of the adult population);
- of these, 4.4 million are of working age, over 116,000 are children (aged 5-15) and 1.3 million are over state pension age;
- the number of carers providing support for 20 hours or more every week is increasing, and 1.25 million carers provide over 50 hours per week;
- 58% of carers are women, with the peak age for caring 50-59 (more than one in five carers or around 1.5 million people);
- the proportion of carers reporting poor health increases as weekly hours of care rise (and caring is strongly associated with ill health);
- over three million people combine work with caring (roughly one in eight of all workers in the UK).

Source: Carers UK (2002, 2004a, 2005), Buckner and Yeandle (nd)

considerable physical and emotional burden on the carer), there is clearly scope for caring to be a rewarding and fulfilling relationship – at its best, being a carer *for* someone implies caring *about* them, and many carers speak passionately about the strength of the relationship they form with the person they care for. Many 'carers' also do not conceptualise their role in this way, and simply see themselves as partners, parents, siblings, friends and neighbours rather than as 'carers'. This may be particularly the case for young carers, older people, people from minority ethnic communities and the carers of people with mental health problems (see, for example, SSI, 1997, 1998a, 1998b; Heron, 1998; Rogers, 2000; see below for further discussion).

However, in spite of many often unrecognised positives, there is also considerable evidence to suggest that being a carer (particularly when feeling unsupported and undervalued by health and social care services) can be a difficult and demanding role (see, for example, Finch and Groves, 1983; Ungerson, 1987; Baldwin and Twigg, 1990; Henwood, 1998; DH, 2000b). In response, a series of national policy initiatives have been developed to provide more and better support for carers – both to enable them to continue in their role as carer, and to enable them to live ordinary, fulfilling lives like other citizens (see *Box 8.3*). As a former Prime Minister stated in the country's first carers' strategy (DH, 2000b, p 3):

Box 8.3: Support for carers

In 1986, the Disabled Persons (Services, Consultation and Representation) Act required social services to 'have regard' to carers' ability to provide care.

In 1990, much of the policy and practice guidance accompanying the NHS and Community Care Act 1990 emphasised the importance of meeting the needs of carers (without necessarily providing any additional direct support or rights).

In 1995, the Carers (Recognition and Services) Act (which began as a private member's Bill) required social services to assess the needs of carers (if requested) where they are assessing a potential service user under the NHS and Community Care Act 1990.

In 1999, the National Carers Strategy set out a range of government proposals to support carers as part of a new national strategy.

In 2000, the Carers and Disabled Children Act (another private member's Bill) enabled a number of services to be provided to carers, and gave carers a right to an assessment (even where the 'service user' has refused an assessment of their own needs). Local authorities have the power to provide a wide range of services, including vouchers for short breaks and direct payments.

In 2004, the Carers (Equal Opportunities) Act (another private member's Bill) gave carers a right to information on their rights to an assessment, ensured that social services should consider work, lifelong learning and leisure when assessing carers, and gave local government new powers to enlist the support of other agencies (including the NHS).

The Work and Families Act 2006 gave carers the right to request flexible working.

What is striking about this gradual increase in the rights of carers and the focus placed on their needs is the fact that:

- there is no single definition of a 'carer' and carers have to rely on a number of different pieces of legislation to claim their rights;
- so much carers' legislation began as private members' Bills and were not initially introduced as part of central government policy;
- early legislation in particular focused on a right to an assessment, without conferring any rights to follow-up services or support;

- entitlement has tended to depend on the carer providing or intending to provide a substantial amount of care on a regular basis (although this is not defined in the relevant Acts and has to rely on associated guidance);
- increased responsibilities for social services and other services have rarely been matched with new funds to discharge new duties.

Under the Equality Act 2010, carers now have greater anti-discrimination rights.

Source: Mandelstam (2008), Clements (2011), Carers UK (nd)

When I talk about the importance to Britain of strong communities and of people having responsibilities towards each other, I'm not speaking of abstract ideas, but of real people and real events: the things many people do to make things better for those around them. The extraordinary work that carers do may well be the best example of what I mean. Extraordinary not in ways which make headlines, but in ways which really matter and which really make a difference to those they are caring for. Carers devote large parts of their own lives to the lives of others – not as part of a job, but voluntarily…. For the sick, the frail, the vulnerable and the elderly, carers provide help and support in ways which might otherwise not be available. By their effort, their patience, their knowledge, their understanding, their companionship, their determination and their compassion, carers very often transform the lives of the people they're caring for…. Carers are among the unsung heroes of British life.

This emphasis on the needs of carers has also grown as social changes (for example, increased social mobility and greater female participation in the labour market) have meant that more and more people who use services live (potentially a long way) away from family members (see below for a discussion of the gendered nature of caring). With similar trends also under way in some other developed countries, support for carers often remains limited internationally and this tends to remain a neglected area of policy (see ***Box 8.4***). More recently, the national carers' strategy initially introduced in the later 1990s (DH, 2000b) has since been refreshed and updated on a number of occasions (see HM Government, 2010b, for a recent example), pledging to help carers seek support at an early stage, enable carers to fulfill their educational and employment potential, deliver more personalised support and help carers stay physically and mentally healthy.

Box 8.4: International approaches to support for carers

In Ireland, where there is a strong tradition of family care, carers have no statutory entitlement to an assessment of their needs, with support services all provided by voluntary agencies.

In Germany, support for carers comes through the long-term care insurance of the person being cared for, and can include a cash benefit; respite, holiday or stand-in care; and pension/accident insurance payments for the carer.

In Sweden, women have long been active members of the labour market and there are well-developed formal care services. However, carers' needs are growing in importance as a result of demographic changes, the economic difficulties of the 1990s and the growth of community-based services. As a result, carers can receive a cash benefit and grant funding has been made available to stimulate carers' services.

In the Netherlands, there is little policy interest in carers and few mainstream statutory resources allocated to their support. However, personal budgets can be used to purchase help from family members and there are some rights to paid leave from work.

In Australia, a series of carer resource centres provide support and information for carers, respite care is actively promoted as a service for carers and there are some social security benefits for carers. However, there are no formal legal entitlements to support for carers who are in employment.

Source: Glendinning (2004)

Despite the former Prime Minister's stated commitment to 'caring about carers', there remains substantial evidence to suggest that health and social care services frequently fail to provide sufficient support for carers to enable them to continue in their role and to live a full and satisfying life. At best, carers face financial disadvantage, added stress and exclusion as a result of a lack of support (see, for example, Howard, 2001; Glasby et al, 2010; see also the stories in *Box 8.1*); at worst they face potential damage to their own physical and mental health, the deterioration of their relationship with the person they care for and a complete breakdown of formal and informal support (see *Box 8.5* for examples; see also *Box 8.3* for limitations in the current legal framework). Traditionally, most support for carers has come from the voluntary sector and from self-help groups, and it is no accident that much of the research and evidence cited in the remainder of this chapter derives from leading national carers' charities and organisations (see the 'Further reading/relevant websites' section below for further details). This is particularly the case with regards to seldom heard groups of carers (for example, young carers), where voluntary action has been crucial in identifying previously unmet needs and bringing these to the attention of policy makers (for a summary of the needs of young carers see Chapter Three and 'Further reading/relevant websites' at the end of this chapter).

Box 8.5: Carers' experiences of health and social care

Henwood's (1998) survey of some 3,000 carers found high satisfaction with health services for those who had received them, but also high levels of unmet need, substantial physical and mental health problems among carers themselves, a lack of information about NHS services, a lack of awareness of carers' issues among NHS staff and negative experiences of hospital discharge. When asked to indicate their priorities for the NHS, participants emphasised additional funding, better joint working between health and social care, greater awareness of carers' needs and improving access to primary care for people caring for someone who is frail, confused or immobile.

Research into carers' experience of hospital discharge suggests that many carers feel that they have no choice but to take on a caring role, that a significant proportion are not consulted about discharge, that many carers do not have their needs assessed and that support services available on discharge are insufficient (Hill and Macgregor, 2001; Holzhausen, 2001; see also *Box 4.1*). In the title of one report, carers are *Health's forgotten partners* – crucial to successful discharge but rarely involved in decision making in a meaningful way.

Carers UK (2005) suggests that only around one third of carers receive an assessment of their needs and that those assessments that do take place frequently fail to help carers plan what to do in the event of an emergency.

A study of carers' experiences of providing care to people with long-term conditions found that services for carers are very 'patchy', with many services for carers 'aspirational rather than actual' (Harris et al, 2003, p 63). Carers can have very negative experiences of services and often feel that they are not listened to or valued. Carers also feel that they have to fight for services, and many people receive 'too little too late' (p 64).

As with user involvement in Chapter Seven, support for carers is fundamental for a range of different but interlinked reasons. Previous research into the future reform and cost of adult social care has identified at least three different rationales for supporting cares, some of which may suggest slightly different subsequent policy approaches (Glasby et al, 2010):

- Carers save the state an estimated £87 billion per year (Buckner and Yeandle, 2007). Supporting carers is therefore essential (as the system could not afford to replace the contribution that carers make). Viewed from this angle, supporting carers could be a good way of supporting the person they care for. At the same time, there may also be scope to reduce demands on the NHS by improving the health of carers (see, for example, Carers UK, 2004b).
- Carers are citizens too and more recent policy has recognised their rights to as good a life as anyone else (for example, taking greater account of people's education, employment and leisure needs).
- Viewed more broadly, the evidence suggests that many carers may well be prevented from contributing more fully to the economy and to wider society through having to spend so much of their time caring and because of a lack of support.

Key concepts

Central to any discussion of the role of carers is the deeply unsatisfactory nature of the concept of 'carer' itself. While legislation and services talk about the need to identify and support carers, there is rarely a clear-cut distinction between 'the carer' and 'the person being cared for'. This can be particularly the case for older couples, where identifying a 'carer' and a 'service user' may be especially unhelpful, but is also true of other situations as well. As discussed in Chapter Five, moreover, the concept of dependence can be entirely misleading (as we are all dependent on others to help meet some of our needs), and the notion of interdependence may be much more useful. Rather than seeing themselves as 'carers', therefore, many people see themselves in much more everyday, human terms as friends, neighbours, siblings, children and partners. As Sayce (2000, p 11) observes:

> A further personal dimension was added when I became involved with a partner who has a diagnosis of manic depression. I do not, however, think that this makes me a 'carer', because this is a mutual relationship, not one in which 'care' goes one way, and not one involving 'burden' (an offensive term that should be dropped).

At the same time, the term 'carer' can cause confusion between paid care and people who 'care' as a result of a personal relationship. While the latter is often described in terms of 'informal care', this seems deeply insulting (as it implies that this support is somehow less important than 'proper' or 'formal' care) and tends to be disliked by carers themselves. In addition to this, the term 'carer' can also imply a degree of homogeneity that does not reflect the complexity and diversity of caring relationships. Thus, being a young carer may be very different to being an older couple, while caring for someone with a mental health problem can be very different to caring for someone with a physical impairment. Equally, not all caring needs to involve physical tasks or geographical proximity, and can include people who care at a distance as well as those who live locally and provide more immediate support. Experiences may also be different again for people from minority ethnic communities or same-sex couples.

Also central to much of the literature and debate on the needs of carers is an assumption that caring is always a negative experience and a 'burden' (also highlighted in the Sayce quote above). As the case studies in **Box 8.1** at the start of this chapter suggest, caring can certainly have negative implications (particularly if carers are unsupported), but can also be a positive experience – thus, in **Box 8.1**, Vicky talks briefly about the transferable skills she has learned while Ronnie has never had an argument with his wife in 37 years. At the same time, each of these individuals also speaks powerfully about the negatives of caring and the need for better understanding and additional support. Unfortunately, much of the literature fails to capture some of these positives, and there are many examples of the negative impact that caring can have on carers' health, social opportunities, finances and well-being. Thus, as an illustration, Heron's (1998) helpful guide to *Working with carers* contains two pages on 'the positive side to care' in a 231-page book and an 18-page chapter on 'the impact of caring' (which focuses almost entirely on negative issues). Despite this, an interesting study comes from North America by Greenberg et al (1994), which highlights the contribution made by people with mental health problems in terms of providing family members with companionship, helping with meal preparation and household chores, listening to problems and providing advice, helping with shopping and providing care for others during periods of illness (see also Qureshi and Walker, 1989, ch 6, on exchange and reciprocity).

Above all, however, support for carers seems to be beset by the same tensions as policy and practice around user involvement and around services for people with long-term conditions (see above and Chapters Five and Seven). Should health and social care be supporting carers because this will improve the lives of people who use services (and hence reduce use of services), or should we support carers because they are citizens who deserve as meaningful and satisfying a life as everyone else and can also contribute more generally to the society and the economy if not 'burdened' by caring? At present, different aspects of policy and practice seem to combine these different approaches, and there is certainly some early mileage in arguing that better support for carers has the potential to achieve a number of these aims. In the longer run, however, an approach that tries to support carers in order to reduce the cost to formal services is very different in terms of its underlying value base to a citizenship/human rights agenda, which might be different again to approaches which try to free carers up to play an even greater social/economic role – and there is clearly scope for these to come into conflict (see later for further discussion of human rights).

Policy and practice dilemmas

Chief among practice dilemmas in this area has always been the thorny issue of funding. Despite growing recognition of the needs of carers and in spite of growing legal responsibilities, health and social care were initially expected to provide support for carers from within existing budgets. While specific funding has subsequently materialised, questions remain about the extent to which this is sufficient for local authorities and the NHS to meet their new responsibilities. In one sense, this seems to draw directly on the 'support carers in order to reduce use of formal services' line of thinking set out above, with an implicit assumption that support for carers can improve outcomes for service users and hence be cost-neutral. In addition, a second long-standing dilemma has been the difficulty of providing support (and raising awareness of carers' rights) when so many people in caring roles do not define themselves as 'carers'. This has led to an ongoing debate about the best way forward: on the one hand, a sensible strategy may be to put extra energy and resources into helping people understand that they are 'carers' and that support badged as being for 'carers' is therefore for them. On the other hand, an equally sensible approach seems to be to argue that if the concept of 'carers' does not make sense to carers themselves, then we should abandon this term and find a more helpful concept.

Added to this is the difficulty of embedding an awareness of carers as genuine 'partners in care' (Nolan et al, 2003). In an ideal world, an approach that recognises the distinctive contribution of the service user, the carer and the health and social care practitioner must surely be the most sensible way forward. In practice, however, carers frequently feel that their knowledge and expertise is not valued by services, and that they are sometimes excluded from planning and discussions about what is required.

This has already been highlighted in *Box 8.5* earlier with regard to hospital discharge, but a good example comes from mental health services (where various psychological theories of mental distress usually portray families as being a potential cause of someone's mental distress and hence 'part of the problem' rather than 'part of the solution') (Perring et al, 1990; Arksey et al, 2002; Rethink, 2003; Lester and Glasby, 2010). For Hogman and Pearson (1995), moreover, the carers of people with mental health problems are 'silent partners' in community care: so used to the difficulties associated with caring and with lack of support from formal services that they see this way of life as the norm and do not ask for help. While there are clearly important underlying issues about data protection, many carers also find that their involvement is precluded by workers' insistence on 'confidentiality' – although this may sometimes be a genuine attempt to protect the interests of the 'service user', it can also be used defensively as a means of excluding carers from meaningful participation in decisions about services.

Beyond these initial issues of funding and approach lies a more complex and political issue of gender. While many carers are men (around 42%), some 58% of carers are women, and particular types of caring (for example, providing a large amount of care, caring in middle age for a parent[s], combining paid work, family commitments and care, and providing some forms of physical caring) seem to be disproportionately associated with women (Carers UK, 2005; Buckner and Yeandle, nd). Behind the official statistics, it is hard to avoid the fact that caring can easily be seen as 'women's work' and part of wider assumptions about the role of women in 21st-century society. As Heron (1998, p 28) suggests:

> Traditionally women, with their nurturing child-rearing role, have taken on tasks of caring for other family members ... when this is required. To a large extent the assumptions about this role continue and ... women may internalise these demands so that the expectation to care can become connected with their own sense of identity and self-worth.... Practitioners need to be aware that, because of the mixture of social and personal expectation, women often experience guilt if they are finding difficulties in coping. They may also be reluctant to ask for help, perceiving this as a sign that they have let the person down.

While issues of gender and of discrimination are discussed in greater detail in Chapter Six (with 'Further reading' for those wanting to explore this issue in greater depth), this is clearly part of a much wider debate about the role of women and the way in which different interpretations of this role can become enshrined in health and social care services. Ultimately, while health and social care need to be aware of the gender implications of their work, a solution may have to lie in a more fundamental debate about gender, equality and ways of tackling deeply engrained discrimination and stereotypes. While focusing on the experiences of women, this also has implications for how best to support male carers, who may also be deterred from seeking support by perceptions of caring as a female activity.

As a practical example of the importance of gender, the emphasis on direct payments (see Chapter Five) has provoked a strong debate between feminist and disabled researchers about the extent to which direct payments may lead to worse terms and conditions for personal assistants, and hence exploit a group of people that may well include a large number of low-paid women (perhaps with childcare and family responsibilities) (see Morris, 1997; Ungerson, 1997; Glasby and Littlechild, 2009; see also Ungerson 1999, 2003, 2004, 2006, for further discussion of personalisation and the boundary between care and work). While there are various factual and technical responses to this issue (for example, that many direct payment recipients want to pay their PAs a higher wage and so the answer may lie in higher rates of direct payments), an underlying concern remains that one of the reasons why policy makers have historically been so reluctant to permit direct payment recipients to make payments to family members is not just to guard against exploitation (the official reason given). Instead, it seems more likely that services know that genuinely recompensing carers (and particularly women) for the (currently unpaid) work they do would bankrupt the health and social care system (Glasby and Littlechild, 2009), and that formal services are founded on an unspoken assumption about the (caring) role of women. Given that a high proportion of health and social care workers are women too, this raises a range of issues about gender that current policy and practice seems nowhere near to acknowledging or resolving.

In addition to gender, caring may raise particular issues around ethnicity. As an example, Carers UK (2010) have published research into the experience of England's half a million Black Asian minority ethnic (BAME) carers, who are estimated to save the state some £7.9 billion a year (which is 41% of the local authority spend on social care). As they state (p 3):

> The research shows that BAME carers provide more care proportionately than White British carers, putting them at greater risk of ill-health, loss of paid employment and social exclusion.

Although some minority ethnic communities are younger than the White UK population, there will be growing numbers of older people from minority ethnic communities and a much greater need for more culturally sensitive approaches and services (see also Princess Royal Trust for Carers, 2010).

Also above and beyond health and social care are more recent carers' issues such as employment and social security. While health and social care can undoubtedly do much more to provide meaningful support for carers when and how they need it, changes are also needed in the workplace and in the social security system in order to uphold the rights of carers and to prevent financial exclusion (see, for example, Pickard, 2004a; Buckner and Yeandle, 2006; Yeandle et al, 2007; Glasby et al, 2010; see also the stories in *Box 8.1*). With over three million people combining caring and employment, emerging evidence suggests that employers need to do much more to support carers (for example, by promoting flexible working, raising awareness of carers' issues and developing carers' policies). At a national level, Action for Carers and Employment (ACE) is an initiative designed to improve services and support so that carers can combine work and caring responsibilities. In particular, this suggests that supporting carers can be a 'win–win' situation for employers, with support and understanding able to contribute to increased productivity, reduced absences and direct savings for employers (Howard, 2002; Yeandle et al, 2006). In social security too, there is regular concern that the current benefits are too small, too inflexible and too restrictive, while support available in principle via Jobcentre Plus can suffer from advisers' lack of knowledge about caring and the impact on employment (Arksey et al, 2005).

Finally, as with previous chapters on anti-discriminatory practice and on user involvement, support for carers could ultimately change considerably as a result of the Human Rights Act 1998. While the Act so far seems to have had little impact on health and social care services for carers, there are nevertheless a number of key areas in which the notion of human rights is particularly important (Clements, 2011; Carers UK, nd). Chief among these is the potential that the Act provides for helping practitioners to balance the rights of people using services with the rights of carers (both against each other and against the interests of the wider community). As *Box 8.6* suggests, there are a number of Articles of the Human Rights Act that are directly relevant to the experience of carers. However, research by Carers UK (nd) suggests that formal services rarely consider carers' rights to an adequate extent, and that some services may have no awareness of the Human Rights Act at all. Even those 'rights' that are set out in legislation are rarely real (in the sense of being practical and effective) and resources are inadequate to allow rights to be protected. Despite this, the research is clear that good practice need not be expensive, and the report cites examples of basic but very effective steps that some services have taken to

Box 8.6: Carers and the Human Rights Act 1998

Article 2 gives a right to life, yet Carers UK cites examples of situations where carers have delayed emergency medical treatment (which could have cost them their life) as a result of their caring responsibilities. In other cases, lack of support can put the life of the person being cared for at risk.

Article 3 gives the right to be free from inhuman or degrading treatment, yet carers face significant stresses and threats to their own physical and mental health that may violate this principle.

Article 8 gives a right to respect for private and family life, yet caring can lead to people being unable to continue working, maintain and develop family relationships and pursue outside interests. Older couples who would like to stay together can also be broken up, and all these may infringe the right to a private and family life.

Article 2, Protocol 1 gives a right to an education, yet young carers often have problems missing school.

Source: Carers UK (nd)

tell carers about their rights and support them in their role. As a result, the report makes a series of recommendations for action, calling for:

- legislation to prevent discrimination against people with caring responsibilities;
- guidance for service providers to ensure that they are clear about their responsibilities;
- advice and information on carers' rights;
- action to ensure that services are complying with human rights standards;
- an investigation into whether the Human Rights Act is being correctly applied;
- action to raise awareness of the human rights of older people, disabled people and those who provide support or care.

Summary

Despite the ongoing growth in the emphasis placed on meeting the needs of carers, considerable barriers to further progress remain. From a very low base, support for carers has been gradually creeping up the policy radar – partly in response to social and demographic changes, and partly as a result of the attention drawn to these issues by feminist researchers and campaigners for particular groups (such as young carers). While there is now much more practical support available (together with more legal entitlements than there have been in the past), current policy and practice seem insufficient to meet the needs and aspirations of carers. As the focus broadens beyond traditional health and social care towards wider issues such as employment and social security, significant doubts remain over the underlying motives behind this direction of travel, with potential tension between rights-based approaches, and those that seek to support carers in order to minimise use of formal services. Underlying all this is an unresolved (and largely unacknowledged) debate about the role of women in contemporary society, about family relationships and about citizenship. Despite more and more male carers, many caring tasks remain 'women's work' and the ongoing debate about how best to recognise, reward and support the role of carers continues.

Further reading/relevant websites

For a general introduction to this topic, see the **DH's (2000b)** *Caring about carers* and introductory textbooks such as:

- **Heron's (1998)** *Working with carers*
- **Nolan et al's (2003)** *Partnerships in family care* and **(1996)** *Understanding family care*
- **Qureshi and Walker's (1989)** *The caring relationship*
- **Stalker's (2003)** *Reconceptualising work with 'carers'*

There have since been a number of updates of the national carers' strategy (see, for example, **HM Government, 2010b**). The **Princess Royal Trust for Carers (2009)** and a range of other health and social care partners have also published a guide for health and social care commissioners when buying services to support carers.

Also helpful are **Clements' (2011)** *Carers and their rights – The law relating to carers* and **Carers UK's (nd)** *Whose rights are they anyway? Carers and the Human Rights Act*. A series of studies by the former Audit Commission on support for the carers of older people also provides a useful overview **(Audit Commission, 2004; Glendinning, 2004; Pickard, 2004a, 2004b)**.

A fascinating account of the changing nature of caring relationships is provided by **Townsend's (1957)** study of *The family life of old people*, updated and revisited by **Phillipson et al (2001)**.

In addition, helpful research studies include:

- **Arksey et al's** work on the carers of people with mental health problems **(2002)** and on carers' aspirations around work and retirement **(2005)**
- DH research and policy with regard to family carers and people with learning difficulties **(Ward, 2001)**
- **Henwood's (1998)** *Ignored and invisible? Carers' experiences of the NHS*
- Carers UK's work on carers' experiences of hospital discharge **(Hill and Macgregor, 2001; Holzhausen, 2001)** and a factsheet on older carers **(Buckner and Yeandle, 2005)**
- Research into the experience of BAME community carers **(Carers UK, 2010)**
- Work from Loughborough University on the needs of young carers (see, for example, **Aldridge and Becker, 1993, 2003; Dearden and Becker, 1998, 2004**)
- Work by **Sue Yeandle** and colleagues on employment and caring (see, for example, **Yeandle et al, 2006, 2007**)
- Work by **Clare Ungerson (1999, 2003, 2004, 2006)** on direct payments and the impact on the boundary between care and work

Useful websites include:

www.dh.gov.uk/en/Socialcare/Carers
   Government website with latest Department of Health policies on caring
www.lboro.ac.uk/departments/ss/centres/YCRG
   Young Carers Research Group, Loughborough University

In addition, a number of leading voluntary organisations provide practical support and information, campaign for policy changes and conduct research. Key examples include:

www.carersuk.org
   Carers UK
www.crossroads.org.uk
   Crossroads
www.carers.org
   The Princess Royal Trust for Carers

Particularly powerful are the stories of carers themselves available via www.carersuk.org/get-support/my-life-as-a-carer or www.carers.org/carers-stories

Reflection exercises

For social policy students

From your knowledge of social policy, what sort of barriers might carers face in terms of their employment, finances, health and life chances? Are the policies in place designed to support carers to help users, to recognise that carers are citizens too or to ensure carers are able to make a broader social/economic contribution?

What broader debates about the role of women and the family could colleagues in health and social care benefit from engaging with? How gendered an issue is caring and what impact could the issues in this chapter have around current/future gender inequality?

For health and social care professionals and students

How much time and resources does your profession/agency have to support carers? Do you know when potential service users/patients have caring responsibilities? Where would you signpost carers who wanted more information about their rights? How does your agency help 'carers' to understand that this is a term that applies to them and that support is available?

In interagency settings

Compare and contrast support for carers in both your respective professions/ organisations. Are there interagency differences in the support available and how co-ordinated is this support? What could you both do to develop better support in future, building on the best of both your approaches?

For all readers

Read the stories in **Box 8.1** and access the 'carers' stories' website that they come from. How well are we supporting carers like these and how do these stories make you feel as a private individual? If you have personal experience of caring, how do these stories compare with your own situation?

Postscript:
what happens next?

In the first edition of this book, it was argued that community health and social care remain dominated by institutional forms of provision and by sometimes paternalistic notions of professional power. Despite a series of changes, the first edition identified a number of key issues as policy makers, managers, practitioners and service users try to build a different and better system in future:

- How best to promote more joined-up responses to need in a system that continues to assume that it is possible to distinguish between people who are sick and those who are frail and disabled.
- Whether to support people with long-term conditions because they are citizens with a right to independent living, or simply as a means of reducing reliance on expensive hospital services.
- Whether to focus on challenging discrimination in health and social care or in wider society, and whether to do so via specialist initiatives or via general approaches.
- Whether to involve people with experience of using services because they are 'customers' who can help improve the 'product' or because they are citizens with a right to greater choice and control.
- Whether to support carers because they are currently being exploited by formal services and deserve the same access to a meaningful and stimulating life as everyone else, or whether to focus on the needs of carers as a means of helping the 'service user' and reducing demands on formal services.

In the short term, it was argued, it is probably possible to do a little of each of the 'either-ors' in the bullet points above – to promote partnership in a system that is deeply divided; to tackle discrimination in formal services *and* in wider society; and to support people with long-term conditions, involve service users and support carers for a mixture of (not necessarily compatible) motives. In the long run, however, the jury must remain out on the extent to which the current system can continue to contain these contradictions and tensions.

After what was (with hindsight) a period of plenty, this second edition is appearing in an era of austerity with a different government, massive public spending cuts and an uncertain economic outlook. What will be crucial to watch for is whether this forces us to resolve some of the dilemmas set out above – to really grasp the nettle – or whether the financial challenges we face will not quite be bad enough to make us do something radically new. Depending on your point of view, the future could be so difficult that we do not have the time or space to do anything different. Equally, it could be so challenging that the current system will be unsustainable if we do not do something major. Either way, everyone working in or receiving health and social care – and that is pretty much all of us – perhaps has a duty to engage in these debates and do our best to help resolve them once and for all.

References

6, P., Goodwin, N., Peck, E. and Freeman, T. (2006) *Managing networks of twenty-first century organisations*, Basingstoke: Palgrave.

Abel-Smith, B. (1960) *A history of the nursing profession*, London: Hienemann.

Abel-Smith, B. (1964) *The hospitals: 1800-1948*, London: Heinemann.

Abbott, D. and Howarth, J. (2005) *Secret loves, hidden lives? Exploring issues for people with learning difficulties who are gay, lesbian or bisexual*, Bristol: The Policy Press.

Adams, R. (1996) *The personal social services*, London: Longman.

ADASS (Association of Directors of Adult Social Services) (2010) 'Councils on track to meet 30 per cent target for personal budgets', press release available online via www.adass.org.uk/

ADSS (Association of Directors of Social Services) (2005) *Pressures on learning disability services: The case for review by government of current funding*, London: ADSS.

ADSS/LGA (Local Government Association) (2003) *All our tomorrows: Inverting the triangle of care*, London: ADSS.

Ahmad, W.I.U. and Atkin, K. (1996) *'Race' and community care*, Buckingham: Open University Press.

Alcock, P. (1996) *Social policy: Themes and issues*, Basingstoke: Macmillan.

Alcock, P. (2008) *Social policy in Britain* (3rd edn), Basingstoke: Palgrave.

Alcock, P. (2006) *Understanding poverty* (3rd edn), Basingstoke: Palgrave.

Alcock, P. (2010) 'Building the Big Society: a new policy environment for the third sector in England', *Voluntary Sector Review*, vol 1, no 3, pp 381-91.

Aldridge, J. and Becker, S. (1993) *Children who care: Inside the world of young carers*, Loughborough: Young Carers Research Group, Loughborough University.

Aldridge, J. and Becker, S. (2003) *Children caring for parents with mental illness: Perspectives of young carers, parents and professionals*, Bristol: The Policy Press.

Allen, K. and Glasby, J. (2010) *'The billion dollar question': Embedding prevention in older people's services – 10 high impact changes*, Birmingham: Health Services Management Centre, University of Birmingham.

Anderson-Wallace, M. and Blantern, C. (2005) 'Working with culture', in E. Peck (ed) *Organisational development in healthcare: Approaches, innovations and achievements*, Abingdon: Radcliffe Medical Press.

Appleby, J. (2011) 'How satisfied are we with the NHS?', *British Medical Journal*, 342: d1836 (published 21 March 2011)

Appleby, J., Crawford, R. and Emmerson, C. (2009*) How cold will it be? Prospects for NHS funding: 2011-17*, London: King's Fund/Institute for Fiscal Studies.

Appleby, J et al (2010) *Improving NHS productivity: More with the same not more of the same*, London: King's Fund.

Arber, S. and Ginn, J. (1991) *Gender and later life: A sociological analysis of resources and constraints*, London: Sage Publications.

Arber, S. and Ginn, J. (1995) *Connecting gender and ageing: A sociological approach*, Buckingham: Open University Press.

Arksey, H. et al (2005) *Carers' aspirations and decisions around work and retirement*, London: TSO.

Arksey, H. et al (2002) *Services to support carers of people with mental health problems: Overview report*, York: Social Policy Research Unit, University of York.

Arnstein, S.R. (1969) 'A ladder of citizen participation', *American Institute of Planning Journal*, vol 35, no 4, pp 216-24.

Audit Commission (1998) *A fruitful partnership: Effective partnership working*, London: Audit Commission.

Audit Commission (2004) *Support for carers of older people*, London: Audit Commission.

Audit Commission (2005) *Governing partnerships: Bridging the accountability gap*, London: Audit Commission.

Audit Commission/Healthcare Commission (2008) *Is the treatment working?*, London: Audit Commission/Healthcare Commission.

Baggott, R. (2004) *Health and health care in Britain* (3rd edn), Basingstoke: Palgrave.

Baggott, R., Allsop, J. and Jones, K. (2005) *Speaking for patients and carers: Health consumer groups and the policy process*, Basingstoke: Palgrave.

Bahl, V. (1999) 'Mental illness: a national perspective', in D. Bhugra and V. Bahl (eds) *Ethnicity: An agenda for mental health*, London: Gaskell.

Baker, S. (2000) *Environmentally friendly? Patients' views of conditions on psychiatric wards*, London: Mind.

Baldwin, S. and Twigg, J. (1990) 'Women and community care: reflections on a debate', in M. Maclean and D. Groves (eds) *Women's issues in social policy*, London: Routledge.

Balloch, S. and Taylor, M. (2001) *Partnership working: Policy and practice*, Bristol: The Policy Press.

Banks, S. (2001) 'Social entrepreneurs or sleeping giants? Settlements in Britain today', in R. Gilchrist and T. Jeffs (eds) *Settlements, social change and community action: Good neighbours*, London: Jessica Kingsley.

Barclay, P. (1982) *Social workers: Their role and tasks* (The Barclay Report), London: Bedford Square Press.

Barnes, C. and Mercer, G. (eds) (1997) *Doing disability research*, Leeds: Disability Press.

Barnes, C. and Mercer, G. (2006) *Independent futures: Creating user-led disability services in a disabling society*, Bristol: The Policy Press.

Barnes, D. (1997) *Older people with mental health problems living alone: Anybody's priority?*, London: DH.

Barnes, D., Carpenter, J. and Dickinson, C. (2006) 'The outcomes of partnerships with mental health service users in interprofessional education: a case study', *Health and Social Care in the Community*, vol 14, no 5, pp 426-35.

Barnes, M. (1997) *Care, communities and citizens*, London: Longman.

Barnes, M. and Bennett, G. (1998) 'Frail bodies, courageous voices: older people influencing community care', *Health and Social Care in the Community*, vol 6, no 2, pp 102-11.

Barnes, M. and Bowl, R. (2001) *Taking over the asylum: Empowerment and mental health*, Basingstoke: Palgrave.

Barnes, M. and Walker, A. (1996) 'Consumerism versus empowerment: a principled approach to the involvement of older service users', *Policy & Politics*, vol 24, no 4, pp 375-93.

Barnes, M. and Warren, L. (eds) (1999) *Paths to empowerment*, Bristol: The Policy Press.

Barnes, M., Davis, A. and Tew, J. (2000) 'Valuing experience: users' experiences of compulsion under the Mental Health Act 1983', *Mental Health Review*, vol 5, no 3, pp 11-14.

Barnes, M., Newman, J. and Sullivan, H. (2007) *Power, participation and political renewal: Case studies in public participation*, Bristol: The Policy Press.

Barnes, M. et al (2005) *Health action zones: Partnerships for equity*, London: Routledge.

Barratt, G., Sellman, D. and Thomas, J. (eds) (2005) *Interprofessional working in health and social care*, Basingstoke: Palgrave.

BBC (1999) 'Patients welcome scope of Bristol inquiry', *BBC News* (www.bbc.co.uk), 15 March.

BBC (2000) 'Stolen hearts', *BBC News* (www.bbc.co.uk), 21 February.

BBC (2003) 'NHS still relies on overseas nurses', *BBC News* (www.bbc.co.uk), 5 December.

BBC (2006) 'In depth: the Shipman case', *BBC News* (www.bbc.co.uk).

Beattie, A. et al (2005) '"They don't quite fit the way we organise our services" – results from a UK field study of marginalised groups and dementia care', *Disability and Society*, vol 20, no 1, pp 67-80.

Becker, S. (1997) *Responding to poverty: The politics of cash and care*, Basingstoke: Macmillan.

Becker, S. and MacPherson, S. (eds) (1988) *Public issues, private pain: Poverty, social work and social policy*, London: Insight/Carematters Books.

Begum, N. (2006) *Doing it for themselves: Participation and black and minority ethnic service users*, London: SCIE/Race Equality Unit.

Bell, D. and Bowes, A. (2006) *Financial care models in Scotland and the UK: A review of the introduction of free personal care for older people in Scotland*, York: Joseph Rowntree Foundation.

Beresford, P. (2000) 'What have madness and psychiatric system survivors got to do with disability and disability studies?', *Disability and Society*, vol 15, no 1, pp 167-72.

Beresford, P. (2002) 'Thinking about "mental health": towards a social model', *Journal of Mental Health*, vol 11, no 6, pp 581-4.

Beresford, P. (2003) *It's our lives: A short theory of knowledge, distance and experience*, London: Citizen Press (in association with Shaping Our Lives).

Beresford, P. (2007) 'The role of service user research in generating knowledge-based health and social care: from conflict to contribution', *Evidence and Policy*, vol 3, no 3, pp 329-41.

Beresford, P. and Branfield, F. (2006) 'Developing inclusive partnerships: user-defined outcomes, networking and knowledge – a case study', *Health and Social Care in the Community*, vol 14, no 5, pp 436-44.

Beveridge, W. (1942) *Social insurance and allied services*, London: HMSO.

Billis, D. (1989) *The theory of the voluntary sector: Implications for policy and practice*, London: Centre for Voluntary Organisations, London School of Economics and Political Science.

Black, A. (2006) *The future of acute care*, London: NHS Confederation.

Black, D. (1980) *Inequalities in health: Report of a research working group* (Black Report), London: DHSS.

Blackburn, D.G. (2000) 'Why race is not a biological concept', in B. Lang (ed) *Race and racism in theory and practice*, Oxford: Rowman and Littlefield.

Blakemore, K. and Boneham, M. (1994) *Age, race and ethnicity: A comparative approach*, London: Taylor Francis.

Bochel, H. (ed) (2011) *The Conservative Party and social policy*, Bristol: The Policy Press.

Bosanquet, H. (1914) *Social work in London, 1869-1912: A history of the Charity Organisation Society*, London: John Murray.

Branfield, F. and Beresford, P. with contributions from Andrews, E.J. et al (2006) *Making user involvement work: Supporting service user networking and knowledge*, York: Joseph Rowntree Foundation.

Brindle, D. (2004) 'Private care for learning disabled people is a return to Victorian values', *The Guardian*, 4 August.

Brisenden, S. (1986) 'Independent living and the medical model of disability', *Disability, Handicap and Society*, vol 1, no 2, pp 173-8.

Brodie, D. (2003) 'Partnership working: a service user perspective', in J. Glasby and E. Peck (eds) *Care trusts: Partnership working in action*, Abingdon: Radcliffe Medical Press.

Brody, S. (2006) 'I am living proof there is a future', *Community Care*, 10–16 August, p 14.

Buckner, L. and Yeandle, S. (2005) *Older carers in the UK*, London: Carers UK.

Buckner, L. and Yeandle, S. (2006) *More than a job: Working carers – evidence from the 2001 census*, London: Carers UK.

Buckner, L. and Yeandle, S. (2007) *Valuing carers: Calculating the value of unpaid care*, London: Carers UK.

Buckner, L. and Yeandle, S. (nd) *We care – do you?*, London: Carers UK.

Burgess, P. (1994) 'Welfare rights', in C. Hanvey and T. Philpot (eds) *Practising social work*, London: Routledge.

Bury, M. (2005) *Health and illness*, Cambridge: Polity.

Butt, J. (2006) *Are we there yet? Identifying the characteristics of social care organisations that successfully promote diversity*, London: SCIE.

Byrne, P. (1997) *Social movements in Britain*, London: Routledge.

Bytheway, B. (1995) *Ageism*, Buckingham: Open University Press.

Cabinet Office (2010) *Building the Big Society*, London: Cabinet Office.

Cambridge, P. and Carnaby, S. (eds) (2005) *Person-centred planning and care management with people with learning disabilities*, London: Jessica Kingsley.

Campbell, J. and Oliver, M. (eds) (1996) *Disability politics: Understanding our past, changing our future*, London: Routledge.

Carers UK (2002) *Without us…? Calculating the value of carers' support*, London: Carers UK.

Carers UK (2004a) *Ten facts about caring* (www.carersuk.org/Aboutus/CarersLives/Tenfactsaboutcaring), 29 August.

Carers UK (2004b) *In poor health: The impact of caring on health*, London: Carers UK.

Carers UK (2005) *Facts about carers*, London: Carers UK.

Carers UK (2010) *Half a million voices: Improving support for BAME carers*, London: Carers UK.

Carers UK (nd) *Whose rights are they anyway? Carers and the Human Rights Act*, London: Carers UK.

Carr, S. (2004) *Has service user participation made a difference to social care services?*, London: SCIE.

Carr, S. (2010) *Personalisation: A rough guide* (revised edn), London: Social Care Institute for Excellence.

Centre for Mental Health (2010) *The economic and social costs of mental health problems in 2009/10*, London: Centre for Mental Health.

Challis, D. et al (2002) *Care management in social and primary health care: The Gateshead Community Care Scheme*, Aldershot: Ashgate.

Challis, D. et al (1995) *Care management and health care of older people: The Darlington Community Care Project*, Aldershot: Ashgate.

Chappell, A.L., Goodley, D. and Lawthom, R. (2001) 'Making connections: the relevance of the social model of disability for people with learning difficulties', *British Journal of Learning Disabilities*, vol 29, no 2, pp 45-50.

CHI (Commission for Health Improvement) (2003) *What CHI has found in mental health trusts*, London: CHI.

Clark, H. (2006) 'What's happening? Demography, service patterns and experiences', in N. Raynes, H. Clark and J. Beecham (eds) *Evidence submitted to the Older People's Inquiry into 'That bit of help'*, York: Joseph Rowntree Foundation.

Clark, J. et al (2010) *The UK civil society almanac 2010*, London: National Council for Voluntary Organisations.

Clarke, M. and Stewart, J. (1997) *Handling the wicked issues: A challenge for government*, Birmingham: School of Public Policy, University of Birmingham.

Clements, L. (2011) *Carers and their rights – The law relating to carers* (4th edn), London: Carers UK.

Cohen, P. (1992) 'High risk mix', *Social Work Today*, vol 23, no 31, p 10.

Commission on Funding of Care and Support (2011) *Fairer care funding* (Dilnot Report), London: Commission on Funding of Care and Support.

Community Care (2006a) 'Pensioners risk social care lottery when they choose to retire abroad', *Community Care*, 23 March (www.communitycare.co.uk).

Community Care (2006b) 'Nine years on, the Bournewood gap remains as wide as ever', 15 June (www.communitycare.co.uk).

Connell, J.P. and Kubisch, A.C. (1998) 'Applying a theory of change approach to the evaluation of comprehensive community initiatives: progress, prospects and problems', in K. Fulbright-Anderson, A.C. Kubisch and J.P. Connell (eds) *New approaches to evaluating community initiatives: Volume 2 – Theory, measurement and analysis*, Washington DC: The Aspen Institute.

Conservative Party (2011) 'Prime Minister spells out his vision for a world-class health service', press release, 1 February.

Coote, A. (2010) *Cutting it: the 'Big Society' and the new austerity*, London: New Economics Foundation.

Copperman, J. and Burrows, F. (1992) 'Reducing the risk of assault', *Nursing Times*, vol 88, no 26, pp 64-5.

CQC (Care Quality Commission) (2011) 'CQC publish first of detailed reports into dignity and nutrition for older people', press release, 26 May, London: CQC.

CQC/NMHDU (National Mental Health Development Unit) (2011) *Count me in 2010*, London: CQC/NMHDU.

Crawford, M. (2001) 'Involving users in the development of psychiatric services – no longer an option', *Psychiatric Bulletin*, vol 25, no 3, pp 84-6.

CSCI (Commission for Social Care Inspection) (2004a) *Valuing people – much achieved, more to do*, London: CSCI.

CSCI (2004b) *Leaving hospital – the price of delays*, London: CSCI.

CSCI (2005) *Leaving hospital – revisited*, London: CSCI.

CSCI, Audit Commission and Healthcare Commission (2006) *Living well in later life: A review of progress against the National Service Framework for Older People*, London: Healthcare Commission.

CSCI, General Social Care Council (GSCC) and Social Care Institute for Excellence (SCIE) (nd) *Facing the facts: Social care in England*, London: CSCI/GSCC/SCIE.

Cumming, J. and the Health Reforms 2001 Research Team (2003) *Interim report on Health Reforms 2001 Research Project*, Wellington, New Zealand: Health Services Research Centre, Victoria University of Wellington.

Curry, N. and Ham, C. (2010) *Clinical and service integration: The route to improved outcomes*, London: King's Fund.

Dalrymple, J. and Burke, B. (1995) *Anti-oppressive practice: Social care and the law*, Buckingham: Open University Press.

Darzi, A. (2008) *High quality care for all: NHS next stage review final report* (Darzi Report), London: TSO.

Davis Smith, J., Rochester, C. and Hedley, R. (eds) (1995) *An introduction to the voluntary sector*, London: Routledge.

Dawson, A. and Tylee, A. (2001) *Depression: Social and economic time bomb – strategies for quality care*, London: BMJ Books.

Dearden, C. and Becker, S. (1998) *Young carers in the United Kingdom: A profile*, London: Carers National Association.

Dearden, C. and Becker, S. (2004) *Young carers in the UK*, London: Carers UK.

DH (Department of Health) (1989a) *Working for patients*, London: HMSO.

DH (1989b) *Caring for people*, London: HMSO.

DH (1991) *The patient's charter: Raising the standard*, London: HMSO.

DH (1997) *The new NHS: Modern, dependable*, London: TSO.

DH (1998a) *Modernising mental health services: Safe, sound and supportive*, London: DH.

DH (1998b) *Partnership in action: New opportunities for joint working between health and social services – A discussion document*, London: DH.

DH (1999a) *National Service Framework for mental health: Modern standards and service models*, London: DH.

DH (1999b) *Ex parte Coughlan: Follow up action*, HSC 1999/180, LAC(99)30.

DH (1999c) *Patient and public involvement in the NHS*, London: DH.

DH (2000a) *The NHS Plan: A plan for investment, a plan for reform*, London: TSO.

DH (2000b) *Caring about carers: A national strategy for carers* (2nd edn), London: DH.

DH (2001a) *Shifting the balance of power: Securing delivery*, London: DH.

DH (2001b) *National Service Framework for older people: Modern standards and service models*, London: DH.

DH (2001c) *Valuing people: A new strategy for learning disability for the 21st century*, London: TSO.

DH (2001d) *Continuing care: NHS and local councils' responsibilities*, HSC 2001/015, LAC(2001)18.

DH (2001e) *Guidance on free NHS funded nursing care in nursing homes*, HSC 2001/17, LAC(2001)26.

DH (2001f) *The expert patient: A new approach to chronic disease management for the 21st century*, London: DH.

DH (2002a) *Action for health: Health action plans and health facilitation*, London: DH.

DH (2002b) *Delivering the NHS Plan*, London: TSO.

DH (2002c) *Women's mental health: Into the mainstream*, London: DH.

DH (2003a) *Guidance on NHS funded nursing care*, HSC 2003/006, LAC(2003)7.

DH (2003b) *Delivering race equality: A framework for action – Mental health services – Consultation document*, London: DH.

DH (2003c) *Mainstreaming gender and women's mental health*, London: DH.

DH (2004a) *Chronic disease management: A compendium of information*, London: DH.

DH (2004b) *Commissioning services close to home: Note of clarification for commissioners and regulation and inspection authorities*, London: DH.

DH (2004c) *Research evidence on the usefulness of self care support networks for care of people with minor ailments, acute illness and long-term conditons and those taking initiatives to stay healthy: Full report*, London: DH.

DH (2005a) *Independence, well-being and choice: Our vision for the future of social care for adults in England*, London: TSO.

DH (2005b) *National Service Framework for long-term conditions*, London: DH.

DH (2005c) *Self-care support: A compendium of practical examples across the whole system of health and social care*, London: DH.

DH (2005d) *Examples of self care devices and assistive technologies to support self care*, London: DH.

DH (2005e) *Supporting people with long term conditions: Supporting experienced hospital nurses to move into community matron roles – Executive summary*, London: DH.

DH (2005f) *Supporting people with long term conditions: An NHS and social care model to support local innovation and integration*, London: DH.

DH (2005g) *Case management competences framework for the care of people with long term conditions*, London: DH.

DH (2005h) *Community development workers for black and minority ethnic communities*, London: DH.

DH (2005i) *Delivering race equality in mental health care: An action plan for reform inside and outside services and the government's response to the independent inquiry into the death of David Bennett*, London: DH.

DH (2006a) *Our health, our care, our say: A new direction for community services*, London: TSO.

DH (2006b) *Health reform in England: Update and commissioning framework*, London: DH.

DH (2006c) *National framework for NHS continuing healthcare and NHS-funded nursing care in England: Core values and principles*, London: DH.

DH (2006d) *Supporting people with long term conditions to … self-care: A guide to developing local strategies and good practice*, London: DH.

DH (2006e) *Reward and recognition: The principles and practice of service user payment and reimbursement in health and social care – a guide for service providers, service users and carers*, London: DH.

DH (2008) *Real involvement: Working with people to improve services*, London: DH.

DH (2009) *Living well with dementia: A national dementia strategy*, London: DH.

DH (2010a) *Equity and excellence: Liberating the NHS*, London: TSO.

DH (2010b) *A vision for adult social care: Capable communities and active citizens*, London: DH.

DH (2010c) *Generic long-term conditions model*, London: DH (www.dh.gov. uk/en/Healthcare/Longtermconditions/DH_120915).

DH (2011) 'Andrew Lansley statement on Winterbourne View', Press release, 2 June, www.dh.gov.uk/en/MediaCentre/Statements/DH_127321.

DHSS (Department of Health and Social Security) (1971) *Better services for the mentally handicapped*, London: HMSO.

DHSS (1978) *Report of the Committee of Inquiry into Normansfield Hospital*, London: HMSO.

Dickinson, H. (2008) *Evaluating outcomes in health and social care*, Bristol: The Policy Press.

Dickinson, H. and Glasby, J. (2006) *Free personal care in Scotland*, Discussion paper commissioned by the Wanless Social Care Review, London: King's Fund.

Dickinson, H., Peck, E. and Smith, J. (2006) *Leadership in organisational transition – what can we learn from research evidence? Summary report*, Birmingham: Health Services Management Centre, University of Birmingham.

Dingwall, R., Rafferty, A. and Webster, C. (1988) *An introduction to the social history of nursing*, London: Routledge.

Disabled People's International (1982) *Disabled People's International: Proceedings of the First World Congress*, Singapore: Disabled People's International.

Dominelli, L. (1997) *Sociology for social work*, Basingstoke: Macmillan.

Dominelli, L. (2002) *Anti-oppressive social work theory and practice*, Basingstoke: Palgrave.

Dominelli, L. (2008) *Anti-racist social work* (3rd edn), Basingstoke: Palgrave Macmillan.

Douglas, F. and Evans, S. (2005) 'Occupational therapy', in G. Barratt, D. Sellman and J. Thomas (eds) *Interprofessional working in health and social care: Professional perspectives*, Basingstoke: Palgrave.

Dowling, B., Powell, M. and Glendinning, C. (2004) 'Conceptualising successful partnerships', *Health and Social Care in the Community*, vol 12, no 4, pp 309-17.

Dowling, S. et al (2006) *Person-centred planning in social care: A scoping review*, York: Joseph Rowntree Foundation.

DRC (Disability Rights Commission) (2003) *Policy statement on social care and independent living 2003*, London: DRC (www.drc-gb.org/library/policy/other_issues/drc_policy_statement_on_social.aspx) .

DRC (2004) *You can make a difference: Improving hospital services for disabled people*, Staff leaflet and explanatory notes, London: DH.

DRC (2006) *Equal treatment: Closing the gap*, London: DRC.

Duffy, S. (2003) *Keys to citizenship: A guide to getting good support for people with learning disabilities*, Birkenhead: Paradigm.

DWP (Department for Work and Pensions) (2006) *A new deal for welfare: Empowering people to work*, London: TSO.

Edwards, N. (2010) *The triumph of hope over experience: Lessons from the history of reorganisation*, London: NHS Confederation.

Elliot, L. (2010) 'Spending review cuts hit the poor hardest, says Institute of Fiscal Studies', *The Guardian*, 21 October (www.guardian.co.uk/politics/2010/oct/21/ifs-spending-review-cuts-poor-hit-hardest).

Emerson, E. et al (2005) *Adults with learning disabilities in England 2003/4: Full report*, London: National Statistics/Health and Social Care Information Centre.

Englander, D. (1998) *Poverty and poor law reform in 19th century Britain, 1834-1914: From Chadwick to Booth*, London: Longman.

ENIL (European Network on Independent Living) (1997) *Training on direct payments for personal assistance*, Report from the ENIL Seminar, Berlin, 1-4 May (www.independentliving.org/docs2/enilreport9705.html).

Enthoven, A. (1985) *Reflections on the management of the NHS*, London: Nuffield Provincial Hospitals Trust.

Equality and Human Rights Commission (2011) 'Inquiry reveals failure to protect the rights of older people receiving care at home', press release, 20 June, London: Equality and Human rights Commission.

Esping-Andersen, G. (1990) *Three worlds of welfare capitalism*, Cambridge: Polity Press.

Evans (1993) 'The role of Centres of Independent/Integrated Living and networks of disabled people', in C. Barnes (ed) *Making our own choices: Independent living, personal assistance and disabled people*, Belper: British Council of Disabled People.

Feinmann, J. (1988) 'Corridors of fear', *Nursing Times*, vol 84, no 39, pp 16-17.

Fernando, S. (2010) *Mental health, race and culture* (3rd edn), Basingstoke: Palgrave.

Ferguson, I. (2007) 'Increasing user choice or privatizing risk? The antinomies of personalization', *British Journal of Social Work*, vol 37: 387-403.

Field, J. and Peck, E. (2003) 'Mergers and acquisitions in the private sector: what are the lessons for health and social care?', *Social Policy and Administration*, vol 37, no 7, pp 742-55.

Finch, J. and Groves, D. (eds) (1983) *A labour of love: Women, work and caring*, London: Routledge.

Fine, S. (1998) 'Acute and continuing care for people in Australia', in C. Glendinning (ed) *Rights and realities: Comparing new developments in long-term care for older people*, Bristol: The Policy Press.

Finkelstein, V. (1999a) *Professions allied to the community (PACs)*, Leeds: University of Leeds Disability Archive.

Finkelstein, V. (1999b) *A profession allied to the community: The disabled people's trade union*, Leeds: University of Leeds Disability Archive (also published in E. Stone [ed] [1999] *Disability and development: Learning from action and research on disability in the majority world*, Leeds: The Disability Press).

Fleischman, P. (2000) 'Separating the sexes', *Nursing Standard*, vol 14, no 25, pp 20-1.

Ford, R. et al (1998) 'One day survey by the Mental Health Act Commission of acute adult psychiatric inpatient wards in England and Wales', *British Medical Journal*, vol 317, no 168, pp 1279-83.

Foundation for People with Learning Difficulties (2004) *Green light for mental health: A service improvement toolkit*, London: Foundation for People with Learning Difficulties in association with the South West London NHS Mental Health Trust and St George's Hospital Medical School.

French, S. and Swain, J. (2011) *Working with disabled people in policy and practice: A social model*, Basingstoke: Palgrave Macmillan.

Friedman, M. (1962) *Capitalism and freedom*, Chicago, IL: University of Chicago Press.

Fulop, N. et al (2002) 'Process and impact of mergers of NHS trust: multicentre case study and management cost analysis', *British Medical Journal*, vol 325, pp 246-52.

Fulop, N. et al (2005) 'Changing organisations: a study of the context and processes of mergers of health care providers in England', *Social Science and Medicine*, vol 60, no 1, pp 119-30.

Gilchrist, R. and Jeffs, T. (eds) (2001) *Settlements, social change and community action: Good neighbours*, London: Jessica Kingsley.

Gilliard, J. et al (2005) 'Dementia care in England and the social model of disability', *Dementia*, vol 4, no 4, pp 571-86.

Glasby, A. (2002) 'Meeting the needs of people with learning disabilities in acute care', *British Journal of Nursing*, vol 11, no 21, pp 1389-92.

Glasby, J. (2002) 'The politics of poverty: Settlements and social work practice', in Toynbee Hall (ed) *The Settlement difference*, London: Toynbee Hall.

Glasby, J. (2003) *Hospital discharge: Integrating health and social care*, Abingdon: Radcliffe Medical Press.

Glasby, J. (2004) *Integrated care for older people*, Leeds: Integrated Care Network.

Glasby, J. (2005) 'The integration dilemma: how deep and how broad to go?', *Journal of Integrated Care*, vol 13, no 5, pp 27-30.

Glasby, J. (2011a) 'The Conservatives and community care', in H. Bochel (ed) *The Conservatives and social policy*, Bristol: The Policy Press.

Glasby, J. (ed) (2011b) *Evidence, policy and practice: critical perspectives in health and social care*, Bristol: The Policy Press.

Glasby, J. and Beresford, P. (2006) 'Who knows best? Evidence-based practice and the service user contribution', *Critical Social Policy*, vol 26, no 1, pp 268-84.

Glasby, J. and Dickinson, H. (eds) (2009) *International perspectives on health and social care: Partnership working in action*, Oxford: Blackwell-Wiley.

Glasby, J. and Hasler, F. (2004) *A healthy option? Direct payments and the implications for health care*, Birmingham/London: Health Services Management Centre, University of Birmingham/National Centre for Independent Living.

Glasby, J. and Henwood, M. (2007) 'Part of the problem or part of the solution? The role of care homes in tackling delayed hospital discharges', *British Journal of Social Work*, vol 37, 299-312.

Glasby, J. and Littlechild, R. (2009) *Direct payments and personal budgets: putting personalisation into practice* (2nd edn), Bristol: The Policy Press.

Glasby, J. and Littlechild, R. (2004) *The health and social care divide: The experiences of older people* (2nd edn), Bristol: The Policy Press.

Glasby, J. and Peck, E. (eds) (2003) *Care trusts: Partnership working in action*, Abingdon: Radcliffe Medical Press.

Glasby, J., Dickinson, H. and Miller, R. (2011) *All in this together? Making best use of health and social care resources in an era of austerity*, Birmingham: Health Services Management Centre, University of Birmingham (policy paper no. 9).

Glasby, J., Dickinson, H. and Peck, E. (2006a) Partnership working in health and social care, Special edition of *Health and Social Care in the Community*, vol 14, no 5.

Glasby, J., Smith, J. and Dickinson, H. (2006b) *Creating 'NHS local': A new relationship between PCTs and local government*, Birmingham: Health Services Management Centre, University of Birmingham.

Glasby, J. et al (2003) *Cases for change in mental health*, Colchester: National Institute for Mental Health.

Glasby, J. et al (2010) *The case for social care reform – the wider economic and social benefits* (for the Department of Health/Downing Street), Birmingham: Health Services Management Centre, University of Birmingham/ Institute of Applied Social Studies.

Glendinning, C. (ed) (1998) *Rights and realities: Comparing new developments in long-term care for older people*, Bristol: The Policy Press.

Glendinning, C. (2004) *Support for carers of older people – some international and national comparisons: A review of the literature*, London: Audit Commission.

Glendinning, C. and Kemp, P.A. (eds) (2006) *Cash and care: Policy challenges in the welfare state*, Bristol: The Policy Press.

Glendinning, C. et al (2002a) *National evaluation of notifications for the use of the Section 31 partnership flexibilities in the Health Act 1999: Final project report*, Leeds/Manchester: Nuffield Institute for Health/National Primary Care Research and Development Centre.

Glendinning, C., Powell, M. and Rummery, K. (eds) (2002b) *Partnerships, New Labour and the governance of welfare*, Bristol: The Policy Press.

Godfrey, M. et al (2008) *Reimbursement in practice: The last piece of the jigsaw? A comparative study of delayed hospital discharge in England and Scotland*, Stirling, Leeds and London: University of Stirling, University of Leeds, King's College London.

Goodinge, S. (2000) *A jigsaw of services: Inspection of services to support disabled adults in their parenting role*, London: SSI/DH.

Greenberg, J.S., Greenley, J.R. and Benedict, P. (1994) 'Contributions of persons with serious mental illness to their families', *Hospital and Community Psychiatry*, vol 45, no 5, pp 475-9.

Greener, I. (2009) *Healthcare in the UK: Understanding continuity and change*, Bristol: The Policy Press.

Greenhalgh, T., Humphrey, C. and Woodard, F. (eds) (2010) *User involvement in health care*, London: Wiley Blackwell.

Griffiths, R. (1983) *NHS management inquiry* (Griffiths Report), London: DHSS.

Griffiths, R. (1988) *Community care: Agenda for action* (Griffiths Report), London: HMSO.

Griffiths, R. (1992) 'Seven years of progress – general management in the NHS', *Health Economics*, vol 1, no 1, pp 61-70.

GSCC (General Social Care Council) (2010) *Code of practice for social care workers and code of practice for employers of social care workers*, London: GSCC.

Halloran, J. (eds) (1998) *Towards a people's Europe: A report on the development of direct payments in 10 member states of the European Union*, Vienna: European Social Network.

Ham, C. (2005) 'Lost in translation? Health systems in the US and the UK', *Social Policy and Administration*, vol 39, no 2, pp 192-209.

Ham, C. (2006) *Developing integrated care in the NHS: Adapting lessons from Kaiser*, Birmingham: Health Services Management Centre, University of Birmingham.

Ham, C. (2009) *Health policy in Britain* (6th edn), Basingstoke: Palgrave.

Ham, C. and Coulter, A. (2001) 'Explicit and implicit rationing: taking responsibility and avoiding blame for health care choices', *Journal of Health Services Research and Policy*, vol 6, no 3, pp 163-9.

Ham, C. and Smith, J. (2010) *Removing the policy barriers to integrated care in England*, London: Nuffield Trust.

Hardill, I. et al (2005) 'Severe health and social care issues among British migrants who retire to Spain,' *Ageing & Society*, vol 25, no 5, pp 769-83.

Harris, J., Piper, S. and Morgan, H. (2003) *Experiences of providing care to people with long-term conditions: Full report,* York: Social Policy Research Unit.

Hasler, F. (2003) *Users at the heart: User participation in the governance and operations of social care regulatory bodies,* London: SCIE.

Hawes, D. and Rees, D. (2005) 'Physiotherapy', in G. Barratt, D. Sellman and J. Thomas (eds) *Interprofessional working in health and social care: Professional perspectives,* Basingstoke: Palgrave.

Hayek, F. (1944) *The road to serfdom,* London: Routledge and Kegan Paul.

Healthcare Commission (2007) *Investigation into the service for people with learning disabilities provided by Sutton and Merton Primary Care Trust,* London: Healthcare Commission.

Healthcare Commission (2008) *The path to recovery: A review of NHS acute inpatient mental health services,* London: Healthcare Commission.

Healthcare Commission/CQC (Care Quality Commission) (2006) *Joint investigation into the provision of services for people with a learning disability at Cornwall Partnership NHS Trust,* London, Healthcare Commission/CQC.

Health Foundation (2011) *Helping people help themselves: A review of the evidence considering whether it is worthwhile to support self-management,* London: Health Foundation.

Health Service Journal (2006) 'Government launches media offensive amid £500m deficit', 8 June, p 5.

Health Service Ombudsman (2003) *NHS funding for long term care,* London: TSO.

Hennessy, P. (2011) 'Half a million "sick" are fit to work', *Daily Telegraph,* 2nd April (www.telegraph.co.uk/news/politics/8423775/Half-a-million-sick-are-fit-to-work.html#).

Henwood, M. (ed) (1994) *Hospital discharge workbook: A manual on hospital discharge practice,* London: DH.

Henwood, M. (1998) *Ignored and invisible? Carers' experience of the NHS,* London: Carers National Association.

Henwood, M. (2004a) *Reimbursement and delayed discharges,* Leeds: Integrated Care Network.

Henwood, M. (2004b) *Continuing health care: Review, revision and restitution,* Heathencote: Melanie Henwood Associates.

Henwood, M. (2006) 'Effective partnership working: a case study of hospital discharge', *Health and Social Care in the Community,* vol 14, no 5, pp 400-7.

Henwood, M. and Waddington, E. (2005) *Charging for the privilege of being ill? Problems and opportunities with long term care,* London: Royal College of Nursing.

Heron, C. (1998) *Working with carers*, London: Jessica Kingsley.

Hill, M. (eds) (2000) *Local authority social services: An introduction*, London: Blackwell.

Hill, M. and Macgregor, G. (2001) *Health's forgotten partners? How carers are supported through hospital discharge*, London: Carers UK.

Hirschman, A. (1970) *Exit, voice or loyalty*, Cambridge, MA: Harvard University Press.

HM Government (2005) *The Kerr/Haslam inquiry*, London: TSO.

HM Government (2007) *Putting people first: A shared vision and commitment to the transformation of adult social care*, London: HM Government.

HM Government (2008) *The case for change: Why England needs a new care and support system*, London: DH.

HM Government (2009a) *Shaping the future of care together*. London: TSO.

HM Government (2009b) *Valuing people now: A new three-year strategy for people with learning disabilities*, London: DH.

HM Government (2010a) *Building the national care service*, London: TSO.

HM Government (2010b) *Recognised, valued and supported: Next steps for the carers strategy*, London: DH.

HM Government (2011a) *No health without mental health*, London: DH.

HM Government (2011b) *Opening doors, breaking barriers: A strategy for social mobility*, London: HM Government.

HM Treasury (2003) *Every child matters*, London: TSO.

HM Treasury (2010) *Spending review*, London: TSO.

Hoggett, P. (1992) 'The politics of empowerment', *Going Local*, vol 19, pp 18-19.

Hogman, G. and Pearson, G. (1995) *The silent partners: The needs and experiences of people who provide informal care to people with a severe mental illness*, Kingston upon Thames: National Schizophrenia Fellowship (now Rethink).

Holzhausen, E. (2001) *'You can take him home now': Carers' experiences of hospital discharge*, London: Carers National Association.

House of Commons Health Committee (2002) *Delayed discharges* (Third Report of Session 2001-02, HC 617-1), London: TSO.

House of Commons Health Committee (2005) *NHS continuing care* (Sixth Report of Session 2004-05, HC 3991-1), London: TSO.

House of Lords/House of Commons Joint Committee on Human Rights (2008) *A life like any other? Human rights of adults with learning disabilities*, London: TSO.

Howard, M. (2001) *Paying the price: Carers, poverty and social exclusion*, London: Carers UK/Child Poverty Action Group.

Howard, M. (2002) *Redressing the balance: Inclusion, competitiveness and choice – A report on barriers and bridges for carers in employment*, London: Carers UK.

Hudson, B. (2003) 'Care trusts: a sceptical view', in J. Glasby and E. Peck (eds) *Care trusts: Partnership working in action*, Abingdon: Radcliffe Medical Press.

Hudson, B. (2005) 'Pick up the pieces', *Community Care*, 22 September (www.communitycare.co.uk).

Hudson, B. and Henwood, M. (2002) 'The NHS and social care: the final countdown?', *Policy & Politics*, vol 30, no 2, pp 153-66.

Hudson, B. et al (1997) *Inter-agency collaboration: Final report*, Leeds: Nuffield Institute for Health.

Hunter, M. (2006) 'Flip side of private provision', *Community Care*, 3-9 August, pp 26-7.

Hutchings, D. (1998) *Monyhull 1908-1998: A history of caring*, Studley: Brewin Books.

Hyde, C. (2011) *Local justice: Family-focused reinvestment*, Sheffield/Birmingham: Centre for Welfare Reform/Health Services Management Centre, University of Birmingham.

In Control (2006) *Individual budgets: A guide for local authorities on creating a local system of self-directed support* (www.in-control.org.uk) 28/07/2006.

Independent Commission on Social Services in Wales (2010) *From vision to action*, Independent Commission on Social Services in Wales.

Johri, M., Béland, F. and Bergman, H. (2003) 'International experiments in integrated care for the elderly: a synthesis of the evidence', *International Journal of Geriatric Psychiatry*, vol 18, pp 222-5.

Jones, L. (1994) *The social context of health and health work*, Basingstoke: Palgrave.

Jupp, B. (2000) *Working together: Creating a better environment for cross-sector partnerships*, London: Demos.

Kelly, A. and Symonds, A. (2003) *The social construction of community nursing*, Basingstoke: Palgrave.

Kemshall, H. and Littlechild, R. (eds) (2000) *User involvement and participation in social care*, London: Jessica Kingsley.

Kendall, J. and Knapp, M. (1996) *The voluntary sector in the UK*, Manchester: Manchester University Press.

King's Fund (2011) *Improving the quality of care in general practice*, London: King's Fund.

Klein, R. (1995) *The new politics of the NHS* (3rd edn), London: Longman.

Kodner, D. (2003) 'Consumer-directed services: lessons and implications for integrated systems of care', *International Journal of Integrated Care*, 17 June (www.ijic.org).

Kodner, D. (2006) 'Whole system approaches to health and social care partnerships for the frail elderly: an exploration of North American models and lessons', *Health and Social Care in the Community*, vol 14, no 5, pp 384-90.

Kodner, D. and Kay Kyriacou, C. (2000) 'Fully integrated care for frail elderly: two American models', *International Journal of Integrated Care*, vol 1, November (www.ijic.org).

Laming, H. (2009) *The protection of children in England: A progress report*, London: TSO.

Langan, M. and Day, L. (eds) (1992) *Women, oppression and social work: Issues in anti-discriminatory practice*, London: Routledge.

Laurance, J. (2003) *Pure madness: How fear drives the mental health system*, London: Routledge.

Law Commission (2010) *Adult social care: A consultation paper*, London: Law Commission.

Law Commission (2011) *Adult social care*, London: TSO.

Leese, J. and Bornat, J. (eds) (2006) *Developments in direct payments*, Bristol: The Policy Press.

Le Grand, J. (2007) *The other invisible hand: Delivering public services through choice and competition*, Princeton, NJ: Princeton University Press.

Le Grand, J., Mays, N. and Mulligan, J. (eds) (1998) *Learning from the NHS internal market*, London: King's Fund.

Lester, H. and Glasby, J. (2040) *Mental health policy and practice* (2nd edn), Basingstoke: Palgrave.

Leutz, W. (1999) 'Five laws for integrating medical and social services: lessons from the United States and the United Kingdom', *Milbank Memorial Fund Quarterly*, vol 77, pp 77-110.

Levin, E. (2004) *Involving service users and carers in social work education*, London: SCIE.

Lewis, J. (1995) *The voluntary sector, the state and social work in Britain*, Aldershot: Edgar Arnold.

Lewis, J. and Glennerster, H. (1996) *Implementing the new community care*, Buckingham: Open University Press.

Lindow, V. (1999) 'Power, lies and injustice: the exclusion of service users' voices', in M. Parker (eds) *Ethics and community in the health care professions*, London: Routledge.

Lundsgaard, J. (2005) *Consumer direction and choice in long-term care for older persons, including payments for informal carers: How can it help improve care outcomes, employment and fiscal sustainability?*, Paris: OECD.

Lunt, N., Hardey, M. and Mannion, R. (2010) 'Nip, tuck and click: medical tourism and the emergence of web-based health information', *Open Medical Informatics Journal*, vol 4, pp 1-11.

Lymberry, M. (2005) *Social work with older people: Context, policy and practice*, London: Sage Publications.

Lyons, M. (2006) *National prosperity, local choice and civic engagement: A new partnership between central and local government for the 21st century* (Lyons Inquiry into Local Government), London: Lyons Inquiry/TSO.

Mannion, R. (2011) 'General practitioner-led commissioning in the NHS: progress, prospects and pitfalls', *British Medical Bulletin*, pp 1-9.

Marmot, M. (2010) *Fair societies, healthy lives* (the Marmot Review), London: Marmot Review, Department for Epidemiology and Public Health, University College London.

McCoy, D. et al (2007) 'Carrot and sticks? The Community Care Act (2003) and the effect of financial incentives on delays in discharge from hospitals in England', *Journal of Public Health*, vol 29, pp 281-287.

McDonald, A. (2006) *Understanding community care: A guide for social workers*, Basingstoke: Palgrave.

McKay, S. and Rowlingson, K. (1999) *Social security in Britain*, Basingstoke: Macmillan.

McKenzie, K. and Bhui, K. (2007) 'Institutional racism in mental health care', *British Medical Journal*, vol 334, pp 649-650.

Mackintosh, N. (2006) *Guide to fully funded NHS care*, London: Royal College of Nursing.

Mandelstam, M. (2008) *Community care practice and the law* (4th edn), London: Jessica Kingsley.

Manthorpe, J. (2002) 'Settlements and social work education: absorption and accommodation', *Social Work Education*, vol 21, no 4, pp 409-19.

Marshall, T.H. (1950) *Citizenship and social class and other essays*, Cambridge: Cambridge University Press.

Martin, G. (2001) 'Social movements, welfare and social policy: a critical analysis', *Critical Social Policy*, vol 21, no 3, pp 361-83.

Martin, J.P. (1984) *Hospitals in trouble*, Oxford: Basil Blackwell.

Maynard, A. and Bloor, K. (1996) 'Introducing a market to the United Kingdom's National Health Service', *New England Journal of Medicine*, vol 334, pp 604-8.

Meads, G. et al (2005) *The case for interprofessional collaboration in health and social care*, Oxford: Blackwell.

Means, R. and Smith, R. (1998a) *From Poor Law to community care*, Basingstoke: Macmillan.

Means, R. and Smith, R. (1998b) *Community care: Policy and practice* (2nd edn), Basingstoke: Macmillan.

Means, R., Morbey, H. and Smith, R. (2002) *From community care to market care? The development of welfare services for older people*, Bristol: The Policy Press.

Means, R., Richards, S. and Smith, R. (2008) *Community care: Policy and practice* (4th edn), Basingstoke: Palgrave.

Mencap (2004) *Treat me right: Better healthcare for people with a learning disability*, London: Mencap.

Mencap (2007) *Death by indifference*, London: Mencap.

Meyerson, D. and Martin, J. (1987) 'Cultural change: an integration of three different views', *Journal of Management Studies*, vol 24, no 6, pp 623-43.

Michael, J. (2008) *Healthcare for all: Report of an independent inquiry into access to healthcare for people with learning disabilities*, London: DH.

Millar, R., Snelling, I. and Brown, H. (2011) *Liberating the NHS: Orders of change*, Birmingham: Health Services Management Centre, University of Birmingham.

Miller, R., Dickson, H. and Glasby, J. (2011) *The vanguard of integration or a lost tribe? Care trusts ten years on*, Birmingham: Health Services Management Centre, University of Birmingham.

Mind (2004) *Ward watch*, London: Mind.

Mitchell, D. (2002) 'A contribution to the history of learning disability nursing', *Nursing Times Research*, vol 7, no 3, pp 201-10.

Moller, C. (2002) 'Comment: mad, bad and dangerous law', *The Guardian*, 27 June.

Morris, J. (1991) *Pride against prejudice*, London: Women's Press.

Morris, J. (1997) 'Care or empowerment? A disability rights perspective', *Social Policy and Administration*, vol 31, no 1, pp 54-60.

Morris, J. (2003) *The right support: Report of the task force on supporting disabled adults in their parenting role*, York: Joseph Rowntree Foundation.

Morris, J. (2004) *'One town for my body, another for my mind': Services for people with physical impairments and mental health support needs*, York: Joseph Rowntree Foundation.

Morris, J. and Wates, M. (2006) *Supporting disabled parents and parents with additional support needs*, London: SCIE.

Morris, J. and Wates, M. (2007) *Working together to support disabled parents*, London: SCIE.

Munday, B. and Ely, P. (eds) (1996) *Social care in Europe*, Hemel Hempstead: Prentice Hall.

Murray, C. (1990) *The emerging British underclass*, London: IEA Health and Welfare Unit.

Murray, C. (1994) *Underclass: The crisis deepens*, London: IEA Health and Welfare Unit.

National Schizophrenia Fellowship (2000) *No change?*, London: National Schizophrenia Fellowship.

National Statistics (2003a) *Census 2001: Carers* (www.statistics.gov.uk/cci/nuget.asp?id=347) (accessed 25.07.2006).

National Statistics (2003b) *Census 2001: Informal care*, 13 February, London: ONS.

Needham, C. (2010) *Commissioning for personalisation: From the fringes to the mainstream*, London: Public Management and Policy Association.

Needham, C. (2011) *Personalising public services: Understanding the personalisation narrative*, Bristol: The Policy Press.

Neill, J. and Williams, J. (1992) *Leaving hospital: Older people and their discharge to community care*, London: HMSO.

Newman, J. and Vidler, E. (2006) 'Discriminating customers, responsible patients, empowered users: consumerism and the modernisation of health care,' *Journal of Social Policy*, vol 35, no 2, pp 193–209.

Newnes, C., Long, N. and MacLachlan, A. (2001) 'Recruits you, sir', *OpenMind*, vol 108, p 12.

NHS Confederation (2006) *Why we need fewer hospital beds*, London: NHS Confederation.

NHS Confederation (2010) *The NHS handbook, 2010-11*, London: NHS Confederation.

NHS Executive (1992) *Local voices: The views of local people in purchasing for health*, Leeds: NHS Executive.

NHS Executive (1994) *Developing NHS purchasing and GP fundholding*, EL 1994/79, Leeds: NHS Executive.

NHS Executive (1996) *Patient partnership: Building a collaborative strategy*, Leeds: NHS Executive.

Nichols, A. (2006) *Assessing the mental health needs of older people*, London: SCIE.

NIMHE (National Institute for Mental Health in England) (2003a) *Engaging and changing: Developing effective policy for the care and treatment of black and minority ethnic detained patients*, Leeds: NIMHE.

NIMHE (2003b) *Inside outside: Improving mental health services for black and minority ethnic communities in England*, Leeds: NIMHE.

NIMHE (2004) *Celebrating our cultures: Guidelines for mental health promotion with black and minority ethnic communities*, Leeds: NIMHE.

NMC (Nursing and Midwifery Council) (2004) *The NMC code of professional conduct: Standards for conduct, performance and ethics*, London: NMC.

Nolan, M., Grant, G. and Keady, J. (1996) *Understanding family care: A multidimensional model of care and coping*, Buckingham: Open University Press.

Nolan, M. et al (eds) (2003) *Partnerships in family care: Understanding the caregiving career*, Maidenhead: Open University Press.

Norfolk, Suffolk and Cambridgeshire SHA (Strategic Health Authority) (2003) *Independent inquiry into the death of David Bennett*, Cambridge: Norfolk, Suffolk and Cambridgeshire SHA.

Norman, A. (1985) *Triple jeopardy: Growing old in a second homeland*, London: Centre for Policy on Ageing.

NPSA (National Patient Safety Agency) (2004) *Understanding the patient safety issues for people with learning disabilities*, London: NPSA.

NPSA (2006) *With safety in mind: Mental health services and patient safety*, London: NPSA.

O'Brien, J. and Duffy, S. (2009) 'Self-directed support as a framework for partnership working', in J. Glasby and H. Dickinson (eds) (2009) *International perspectives on health and social care: Partnership working in action*, Oxford: Blackwell-Wiley.

ODPM (Office of the Deputy Prime Minister) (2004) *Mental health and social exclusion* (Social Exclusion Unit Report), London: ODPM.

ODPM (2006) *Reaching out: An action plan for social inclusion*, London: ODPM.

Oldman, C. and Beresford, P. (2000) *Making homes fit for children: Working together to meet the housing needs of disabled children*, Bristol: The Policy Press.

Oliver, M. (1990) *The politics of disablement*, Basingstoke: Macmillan.

Oliver, M. (2009) *Understanding disability: from theory to practice* (2nd edn), Basingstoke: Palgrave Macmillan.

Oliver, M. and Barnes, C. (1998) *Disabled people and social policy: From exclusion to inclusion*, Harlow: Longman.

Oliver, M. and Sapey, B. (1999) *Social work with disabled people* (2nd edn), Basingstoke: Macmillan.

Oliver, M. and Sapey, B. (2006) *Social work with disabled people* (3rd edn), Basingstoke: Palgrave.

ONS (Office for National Statistics) (2008) *Public sector productivity*, London: ONS.

Ouchi, W. and Johnson, A. (1978) 'Types of organisational control and their relationship to organisational well-being', *Administrative Science Quarterly*, vol 23, pp 292-317.

Parker, H. (2009) *Evidence for transforming community services: Services for long-term conditions*, Birmingham: Health Services Management Centre, University of Birmingham (on behalf of the DH).

Parker, M. (2000) *Organisational culture and identity*, London: Sage Publications.

Parliamentary and Health Service Ombudsman (2011) *Care and compassion? Report of the Health Service Ombudsman on ten investigations into NHS care of older people*, London: Parliamentary and Health Service Ombudsman.

Parliamentary and Health Service Ombudsman/Local Government Ombudsman (2009) *Six lives: the provision of public services to people with learning disabilities*, London: Parliamentary and Health Service Ombudsman/Local Government Ombudsman.

Patel, B. and Kelley, N. (2006) *The social care needs of refugees and asylum seekers*, London: SCIE.

Pawson, R. and Tilley, N. (1997) *Realistic evaluation*, London: Sage Publications.

Payne, G. (ed) (2000) *Social divisions*, Basingstoke: Macmillan.

Payne, G. (ed) (2006) *Social divisions* (2nd edn), Basingstoke: Palgrave.

Payne, M. (2000) *Teamwork in multiprofessional care*, Basingstoke: Macmillan.

Payne, M. (2005a) *The origins of social work: Continuity and change*, Basingstoke: Palgrave.

Payne, M. (2005b) *Modern social work theory*, Basingstoke: Palgrave.

Payne, M. (2006) *What is professional social work?* (2nd edn), Bristol: The Policy Press.

Payne, S. (1998) '"Hit and miss": the success and failure of psychiatric services for women', in L. Doyal (ed) *Women and health services*, Buckingham: Open University Press.

Payne, S. (2006) *The health of men and women*, Cambridge: Polity.

Peck, E. (2002) 'Integrating health and social care', *Managing Community Care*, vol 10, no 3, pp 16–19.

Peck, E. (ed) (2005) *Organisational development in healthcare: Approaches, innovations and achievements*, Abingdon: Radcliffe Medical Press.

Peck, E. and Crawford, A. (2004) *'Culture' in partnerships: What do we mean by it and what can we do about it?*, Leeds: Integrated Care Network.

Peck, E. and Freeman, T. (2005) *Reconfiguring PCTs: Influences and options*, Briefing paper prepared for the NHS Alliance, Birmingham: Health Services Management Centre, University of Birmingham.

Peck, E., Gulliver, P. and Towell, D. (2002) *Modernising partnerships: An evaluation of Somerset's innovations in the commissioning and organisation of mental health services – Final report*, London: Institute of Applied Health and Social Policy, King's College.

Peckham, S. and Exworthy, M. (2003) *Primary care in the UK: Policy, organisation and management*, Basingstoke: Palgrave.

Perkins, N. et al (2010) 'What counts is what works'? New Labour and partnerships in public health', *Policy & Politics*, vol 38, pp 101–17.

Perring, C., Twigg, J. and Atkin, K. (1990) *Families caring for people diagnosed as mentally ill: The literature re-examined*, London: HMSO.

Phillipson, C. et al (2001) *The family and community life of older people*, London: Routledge.

Philpot, T. (2006) 'Prison's ageing population', *Community Care*, 7–13 September, pp 30-1.

Picht, W. (1914) *Toynbee Hall and the English Settlement movement* (revised edn, translated from German by L.A. Cowell), London: G. Bell and Sons.

Pickard, L. (2004a) *Caring for older people and employment: A review of the literature*, London: Audit Commission.

Pickard, L. (2004b) *The effectiveness and cost-effectiveness of support and services to informal carers of older people: A review of the literature*, London: Audit Commission.

Pierre, S. (1999) 'The experiences of African and Afro-Caribbean people in acute psychiatric hospital: a qualitative study', *Mental Health Care*, vol 3, no 2, pp 52-6.

Poll, C. et al (2006) *A report on In Control's first phase, 2003-2005*, London: In Control Publications.

Pollard, K., Thomas, J. and Miers, M. (eds) (2010) *Understanding interprofessional working in health and social care*, Basingstoke: Palgrave Macmillan.

Porter, R. (1997) *The greatest benefit to mankind*, London: HarperCollins.

Powell, E. (1961) Speech to the Annual Conference of the National Association of Mental Health (now Mind).

Powell, M. (ed) (1999) *New Labour, new welfare state?*, Bristol: The Policy Press.

Powell, M. (ed) (2002) *Evaluating New Labour's welfare reforms*, Bristol: The Policy Press.

Powell, M. (ed) (2008) *Modernising the welfare state: The Blair legacy*, Bristol: The Policy Press.

Powell Davies, G., Dennis, C. and Walker, C. (2009) Self-management with others: The role of partnerships in supporting self-management for people with long-term conditions, in J. Glasby and H. Dickinson (eds) *International perspectives on health and social care*, Oxford: Blackwell-Wiley.

Prime Minister's Strategy Unit (2005) *Improving the life chances of disabled people*, London: Prime Minister's Strategy Unit.

Princess Royal Trust for Carers et al (2009) *Commissioning for carers*, London: Princess Royal Trust for Carers et al.

Princess Royal Trust for Carers (2010) *Caring for all carers: A survey of services for BME and seldom heard carers…*, London: Princess Royal Trust for Carers.

Pring, J. (2004) 'The frequency and potential consequences of the failure to visit learning disabled adults in out of area placements', *Learning Disability Review*, vol 9, no 2, pp 35-42.

Qureshi, H. and Walker, A. (1989) *The caring relationship: Elderly people and their families*, Basingstoke: Macmillan.

RCN (Royal College of Nursing)/CSIP(Care Services Improvement Partnership)/(NIMHE) National Institute for Mental Health in England (2008) *Informed gender practice: Mental health acute care that works for women*, London: CSIP/DH.

Race, D., Boxall, K. and Carson, I. (2005) 'Towards a dialogue for practice: reconciling Social Role Valorization and the social model of disability', *Disability and Society*, vol 20, no 5, pp 507-21.

Reason, W. (ed) (1898) *University and social Settlements*, London: Methuen and Co.

Rethink (2003) *Who cares? The experiences of mental health carers accessing services and information*, London: Rethink.

Rittel, H. and Webber, M. (1973) 'Dilemmas in a general theory of planning', *Policy Sciences*, vol 4, pp 155-69.

Robinson, R. and Le Grand, J. (eds) (1994) *Evaluating the NHS reforms*, London: King's Fund.

Robbins, D. (2006) *Choice, control and individual budgets: Emerging themes*, London: SCIE.

Rogers, A. and Pilgrim, D. (2001) *Mental health policy in Britain* (2nd edn), Basingstoke: Palgrave.

Rogers, A. and Pilgrim, D. (2003) *Mental health and inequalities*, Basingstoke: Palgrave.

Rogers, A. and Pilgrim, D. (2010) *A sociology of mental health and illness* (4th edn), Maidenhead: Open University Press.

Rogers, H. (2000) 'Breaking the ice: developing strategies for collaborative working with carers of older people with mental health problems', in H. Kemshall and R. Littlechild (eds) *User involvement and participation in social care: Research informing practice*, London: Jessica Kingsley.

Rooff, M. (1972) *One hundred years of family social work: A study of the Family Welfare Association, 1869-1969*, London: Michael Joseph.

Rose, D. (2001) *Users' voices: The perspectives of mental health service users on community and hospital care*, London: Sainsbury Centre for Mental Health.

Rose, D. et al (2002) *User and carer involvement in change management in a mental health context: Review of the literature*, London: Service User Research Enterprise, Institute of Psychiatry.

Rose, M.E. (1988) *The relief of poverty, 1834-1914* (2nd edn), Basingstoke: Macmillan.

Royal Commission on Long-term Care (1999) *With respect to old age: Long term care – rights and responsibilities*, London: TSO.

Rummery, K. (ed) (2006a) 'Partnerships, governance and citizenship', special edition of *Social Policy and Society*, vol 5, no 2, pp 223-326.

Rummery, K. (2006b) 'Disabled citizens and social exclusion: the role of direct payments', *Policy and Politics*, vol 34, no 4: 633-650.

Sainsbury Centre for Mental Health (2002) *Breaking the circles of fear*, London: Sainsbury Centre for Mental Health.

Samuel, M. (2006) 'Department of Health's record on race "probably Whitehall's worst"', *Community Care*, 31 August-6 September, p 12.

Sanderson, H. (2000) *Person-centred planning: Key features and approaches*, York: Joseph Rowntree Foundation.

Sayce, L. (2000) *From psychiatric patient to citizen: Overcoming discrimination and social exclusion*, Basingstoke: Palgrave.

SCIE (Social Care Institute for Excellence) (2005) *Direct payments: Answering frequently asked questions*, London: SCIE.

SCIE (2009) *Think child, think parent, think family: A guide to parental mental health and child welfare*, London: SCIE.

Scott, J. et al (2001) *Organisational culture and performance in the NHS: A review of the theory, instruments and evidence*, York: Centre for Health Economics.

Seebohm, F. (1968) *Report of the Committee on Local Authority and Allied Personal Social Services* (The Seebohm Report), London: HMSO.

Seebohm, P. and Grove, B. (2006) *Leading by example: Making the NHS an exemplar employer of people with mental health problems*, London: Sainsbury Centre for Mental Health.

Shaw, M. et al (1999) *The widening gap: Health inequalities and policy in Britain*, Bristol: The Policy Press.

Singh, D. and Ham, C. (2006) *Improving care for people with long-term conditions: A review of UK and international frameworks*, Birmingham: Health Services Management Centre, University of Birmingham (for the NHS Institute for Innovation and Improvement).

Skills for Care (2010) *The state of the adult social care workforce in England, 2010*, London: Skills for Care.

Smith, J. and Goodwin, N. (2006) *Towards managed primary care: The role and experience of primary care organizations*, Aldershot: Ashgate.

Smith, J. et al (2004) *A review of the effectiveness of primary care-led commissioning and its place in the NHS*, London: The Health Foundation.

Smith, M.J. (1956) *Professional education for social work in Britain: An historical account*, London: George Allen and Unwin.

Spandler, H. (2004) 'Friend or foe? Towards a critical assessment of direct payments', *Critical Social Policy*, vol 24, no 2: 187–209.

SSI (Social Services Inspectorate) (1997) *Young carers: Something to think about*, London: DH.

SSI (1998a) *Young carers: Making a start*, London: DH.

SSI (1998b) *A matter of chance for carers? Inspection of local authority support for carers*, London: DH.

SSI/Audit Commission (2004) *Old virtues, new virtues: An overview of the changes in social care services over the seven years of Joint Reviews in England, 1996-2003*, London: SSI/Audit Commission.

Stalker, K. (ed) (2003) *Reconceptualising work with 'carers': New directions for policy and practice*, London: Jessica Kingsley.

Stanley, N. and Manthorpe, J. (eds) (2004) *The age of the inquiry: Learning and blaming in health and social care*, London: Routledge.

Starfield, B. (1998) *Primary care: Balancing health needs, services and technology*, Oxford: Oxford University Press.

Swain, J. et al (eds) (2004) *Disabling barriers – Enabling environments* (2nd edn), London: Sage Publications.

Sullivan, H. and Skelcher, C. (2002) *Working across boundaries: Collaboration in public services*, Basingstoke: Palgrave.

Tanner, D. (2010) *Managing the ageing experience: Learning from older people*, Bristol: The Policy Press.

Taylor, I. and Le Riche, P. (2006) 'What do we know about partnership with service users and carers in social work education and how robust is the evidence base?', *Health and Social Care in the Community*, vol 14, no 5, pp 418-25.

Taylor, P.J. and Gunn, J. (1999) 'Homicides by people with mental illness: myth and reality', *British Journal of Psychiatry*, vol 174, pp 9-14.

Tew, J. (ed) (2005) *Social perspectives in mental health: Developing social models to understand and work with mental distress*, London: Jessica Kingsley.

Thompson, G. et al (1991) *Markets, hierarchies and networks: The coordination of social life*, London: Sage Publications in association with the Open University.

Thompson, N. (1998) 'Beyond orthodoxy', *Care: the Journal of Practice and Development*, vol 7, no 1, pp 5-13.

Thompson, N. (2005) *Understanding social work: Preparing for practice* (2nd edn), Basingstoke: Palgrave.

Thompson, N. (2006) *Anti-discriminatory practice* (4th edn), Basingstoke: Palgrave.

Thompson, N. (2011) *Promoting equality: Working with diversity and difference* (3rd edn), Basingstoke: Palgrave Macmillan.

Thorlby, R., Rosen, R. and Smith, J. (2011) *GP commissioning: Insights from medical groups in the United States*, London: Nuffield Trust.

Thornicroft, G. (2006) *Shunned: Discrimination against people with mental illness*, Oxford: Oxford University Press.

Timmins, N. (2001) *The five giants: A biography of the welfare state* (2nd edn), London: HarperCollins.

Tinker, A. (1996) *Older people in modern society* (4th edn), Harlow: Longman.

Townsend, P. (1957) *The family life of old people*, London: Routledge and Kegan Paul.

Townsley, R. et al (2002) *Committed to change? Promoting the involvement of people with learning difficulties in staff recruitment*, Bristol/York: The Policy Press/Joseph Rowntree Foundation.

TSO (The Stationery Office) (2006) *Explanatory notes to Equality Act 2006*, London: TSO.

Tudor Hart, J. (1971) 'The inverse care law', *The Lancet*, 27 February, pp 405–12.

Turner, M. and Beresford, P. (2005a) *User controlled research: Its meanings and potential*, Eastleigh: INVOLVE (in association with Shaping Our Lives and the Centre for Citizen Participation).

Turner, M. and Beresford, P. (2005b) *Contributing on equal terms: Service user involvement and the benefits system*, London: SCIE.

Turning Point (2003) *A hospital is not a home: Time to move on – why is it taking so long to move people with a learning disability out of long-stay hospitals?*, London: Turning Point.

Ungerson, C. (1987) *Policy is personal: Sex, gender and informal care*, London: Tavistock.

Ungerson, C. (1997) 'Give them the money: is cash a route to empowerment?', *Social Policy and Administration*, vol 31, no 1, pp 45–53.

Ungerson, C. (1999) 'Personal assistants and disabled people: An examination of a hybrid form of work and care', *Work, Employment and Society*, vol 13, no 4, PP 583–600.

Ungerson, C. (2003) 'Commodified care work in European labour markets', *European Societies*, vol 5, no 4, pp 377–96.

Ungerson, C. (2004) 'Whose empowerment and independence? A cross-national perspective on 'cash for care' schemes', *Ageing and Society*, vol 24, pp 189–212.

Ungerson, C. (2006) 'Direct payments and the employment relationship: Some insight from cross-national research', in J. Leece and J. Bornat (eds) *Developments in direct payments*, Bristol: The Policy Press.

Unison (2002) *What's good about the NHS and why it matters who provides the service*, London: Unison.

UPIAS (Union of the Physically Impaired Against Segregation) (1976) *Fundamental principles of disability*, London: UPIAS.

Victor, C. (2010) *Ageing, health and care*, Bristol: The Policy Press.

Walshe, K. and Smith, J. (2001a) 'Drowning not waving', *Health Service Journal*, 16 August, pp 12–13.

Walshe, K. and Smith, J. (2001b) 'Cause and effect', *Health Service Journal*, 11 October, pp 20–3.

Walshe, K. and Smith, J. (eds) (2011) *Healthcare management* (2nd edn), Maidenhead: Open University Press.

Wanless, D. (2002) *Securing our future health: Taking a long-term view – final report*, London: HM Treasury.

Wanless, D. (2003) *The review of health and social care in Wales*, Cardiff: Welsh Assembly.

Wanless, D. (2006) *Securing good care for older people: Taking a long-term view*, London: King's Fund.

Wanless, D. et al (2007) *Our future health secured?*, London: King's Fund.

Ward, C. (2001) *Family matters: Counting families in*, London: DH.

Warner, L. and Ford, R. (1998) 'Conditions for women in in-patient psychiatric units: the Mental Health Act Commission 1996 national visit', *Mental Health Care*, vol 1, no 7, pp 225-8.

Warrington, C. (2006) 'You only have to ask', *Community Care*, 14-20 September, pp 38-9.

Wates, M. (2002) *Supporting disabled adults in their parenting role*, York: Joseph Rowntree Foundation.

Watson, A. (2001) *Detained: Inspection of compulsory mental health admissions*, London: DH.

Whitehead, M. (1987) *The health divide*, London: Health Education Council.

WHO (World Health Organisation) (1978) *Declaration of Alma Ata*, International Conference on Primary Health Care, Alma Ata, USSR, 6-12 September, Geneva: WHO.

WHO (1980) *International classification of impairments, disabilities and handicaps*, Geneva: WHO.

WHO (1999) *The world health report: Making a difference*, Geneva: WHO.

Wilding, P. (1982) *Professional power and social welfare*, London: Routledge and Kegan Paul.

Williams, I. (2006) *Offender health and social care: Literature review*, Birmingham: Health Services Management Centre, University of Birmingham.

Williams, V. and Heslop, P. (2005) 'Mental health support needs for people with a learning difficulty: a medical or a social model?', *Disability and Society*, vol 20, no 3, pp 231-45.

Williams, V. (2012) *Learning disability and inclusion: Policy and practice*, Basingstoke: Palgrave Macmillan (forthcoming).

Wilson, M. and Francis, J. (1997) *Raised voices: African-Caribbean and African users' views and experiences of mental health services in England and Wales*, London: Mind Publications.

Wilton, T. (2000) *Sexualities in health and social care*, Maidenhead: Open University Press.

Wistow, G. and Fuller, S. (1982) *Joint planning in perspective*, Birmingham: Centre for Research in Social Policy and National Association of Health Authorities.

Woodroofe, K. (1962) *From charity to social work in England and the United States*, London: Routledge and Kegan Paul.

Yeandle, S. et al (2006) *Who cares wins: The social and business benefits of supporting working carers*, London: Carers UK.

Yeandle, S. et al (2007) *Managing caring and employment*, London/Leeds: Carers UK/University of Leeds.

Yeates, N. et al (eds) (2011) *In defence of welfare: The impacts of the Comprehensive Spending Review*, Social Policy Association (available via www.social-policy.org.uk).

Young, A. and Ashton, E. (1956) *British social work in the nineteenth century*, London: Routledge and Kegan Paul.

Younghusband, E. (1947) *Report on the employment and training of social workers*, Dunfermline: Carnegie United Kingdom Trust.

Younghusband, E. (1951) *Social work in Britain*, Dunfermline: Carnegie United Kingdom Trust.

Younghusband, E. (1959) *Report of the working party on social workers in the local authority health and welfare services*, London: HMSO.

Younghusband, E. (1978) *Social work in Britain, 1950-1975: A follow-up study – Volume 2*, London: George Allen & Unwin.

Index